D1571250

THE BOOK OF
HERB LORE

JOHN PARKINSON

(From the statue erected by Mr. H. Thompson at Sefton Park, Liverpool)

THE BOOK OF
HERB LORE

(FORMERLY TITLED: THE BOOK OF HERBS)

Lady Rosalind Northcote

DOVER PUBLICATIONS, INC.

NEW YORK

This Dover edition, first published in 1971, is an unabridged republication of the second edition as published by John Lane: The Bodley Head in 1912 under the title *The Book of Herbs*.

International Standard Book Number: 0-486-22694-8
Library of Congress Catalog Card Number: 75-143676

Manufactured in the United States of America
Dover Publications, Inc.
180 Varick Street
New York, N. Y. 10014

CONTENTS

CONTENTS

LIST OF ILLUSTRATIONS

HISTORY OF THE CRIES OF LONDON

Here's fine rosemary, sage and thyme.
Come, buy my ground ivy.
Here's featherfew, gilliflowers and rue.
Come, buy my knotted marjoram, ho !
Come, buy my mint, my fine green mint.
Here's fine lavender for your cloaths,
Here's parseley and winter savory,
And heartsease which all do choose.
Here's balm and hyssop and cinquefoil,
All fine herbs it is well known.
Let none despise the merry, merry cries
Of famous London Town.

Here's penny royal and marygolds.
Come, buy my nettle-tops.
Here's water-cresses and scurvy grass,
Come buy my sage of virtue, ho !
Come, buy my wormwood and mugworts.
Here's all fine herbs of every sort.
Here's southernwood that's very good.
Dandelion and houseleek.
Here's dragon's tongue and wood sorrel,
With bear's-foot and horehound.
Let none despise the merry, merry cries
Of famous London Town.

Roxburghe Ballads.

THE BOOK OF HERBS

INTRODUCTION

WHAT is a Herb ? I have heard many definitions, but
never one that satisfied the questioner, and shall,
therefore, take warning by the failures of others
and make no attempt to define the word here. It is,
however, fairly safe to say generally that a herb is a
plant, green, and aromatic and fit to eat, but it is impossible to deny that there are several undoubted herbs that
are not aromatic, a few more grey than green, and one or
two unpalatable, if not unwholesome. So no more space
shall be devoted to discussing their " nature," but I will
endeavour to present individual ones to the reader as
clearly as possible, in order that from their collective
properties he may form his own idea of a herb. The
objection may be raised that several plants included in
this book are outside the subject. To answer this, I
would point out that the boundaries of a herb-garden
are indefinite, and that the old writers' views of them
were liberal. Besides this, every garden must have an
outside hedge or wall, and if this imaginary herb-garden
has a row of elder bushes on the East, barberry trees on
the West, some bay trees on the South, and a stray willow
or so on the North, who can say that they are inap-
propriately placed ? The bay and barberry hold an
undisputable position, and the other trees have each an

interesting history in folk-lore, magic and medicine. Herbs have been used in all countries and from the earliest times, but I have confined myself, as a rule, to those spoken of by British authors, and used in the British Isles, though not scrupling to quote foreign beliefs or customs where they give weight or completeness to our own or our forefathers' practices, or are themselves of much interest. We have forgotten much that would be profitable to us.

Mr Dillon, writing in the *Nineteenth Century*, April, 1894, on " A Neglected Sense "—the sense of smell— describes a Japanese game, the object of which was that while one of the players burned certain kinds of incense or fragrant woods, singly or in combination, the others ventured opinions from the odours arising, and recorded their conjectures by means of specially marked counters on a board. The delicate equipment for it included a silver, open-worked brazier; a spatula, on which the incense was taken up, also of silver, sometimes delicately inlaid with enamel; and silver-framed mica plates (about one inch square), on which the incense had been heated, were set to cool on " a number of medallions, mother-of-pearl, each in the shape of a chrysanthemum flower or of a maple leaf."

Both Mr Dillon and Miss Lambert (*Nineteenth Century*, May 1880) attribute the importance early attached to odours to religious reasons. He says that it was believed that the gods, being spirits, neither required nor desired solid offerings, but that the ethereal nature of the ascending fragrance was gratifying and sustaining to them. Miss Lambert quotes an account of the tribes of Florida " setting on the tops of the trees, as offerings to the sun, skins of deer filled with the best fruits of the country, crowned with flowers and sweet herbs. Among the Aztecs of Mexico the festival of the goddess of flowers, Coatlicue, was kept by Xochenanqui, or traders in flowers. Offerings of "curiously woven garlands" were made, and it was "forbidden to everyone to smell the flowers of which they were composed before their dedication to the goddess." The Tahitians had the idea that "the scent was the spirit of the offering and corresponded to the spirit of man," and therefore they laid sweet-scented offerings before their dead till burial, believing that the spirit still hovered near. These instances show clearly the high regard in which delicate odours were once held.

Herbs and flowers were early used in rites and ceremonies of the Church. Miss Lambert quotes from a poem of Fortunatus, Bishop of Poitiers. "When winter binds the earth with ice, all the glory of the field perishes with its flowers. But in the spring-time when the Lord overcame Hell, bright grass shoots up and buds come forth. . . . Gather these first-fruits and you bear them to the churches and wreath the altars with them till they glow with colour. The golden crocus is mingled with the purple violet, dazzling scarlet is relieved by gleaming white, deep blue blends with green. . . . One triumphs in its radiant beauty, another conquers by its sweet perfume; gems and incense bow before them." In England, the flowers for the Church were grown under the special care of the Sacristan, and as early as the ninth century there was a "gardina sacristæ" at Winchester.[1] Miss Amherst gives a most careful description of the several gardens into which the whole monastery enclosures were often divided, and herbs were specially grown in the kitchen-garden and in the Infirmarian's garden, the latter, of course, being devoted to herbs for healing. Many herbs were introduced by the Romans, among them Coriander, Chervil, Cumin, Featherfew, Fennel, Lovage, Mallow, Mint, Parsley, Rue and Mustard. Some of these are sup-

[1] "History of Gardening in England."

posed to have died out after the Romans withdrew from
England and have been re-introduced, but it is certain
that they have been for a very long time cultivated in
England.   I cannot refrain from referring to a miracle,
an account of which is quoted by Miss Amherst from
Dugdale's "Monasticon" (vol. i. p. 473, new ed.), which
was wrought at the tomb of St Etheldreda :—

A "servant to a certain priest was gathering herbs in
the garden on the Lord's Day, when the wood in her
hand, and with which she desired to pluck the herbs
unlawfully, so firmly adhered (to her hand) that no man
could pluck it out for the space of five years." At the
end of this time she was miraculously healed at the
tomb, which was much revered by the people.

Banks and benches of mould, fronted with stone or
brick, and planted on the top with sweet-smelling herbs,
were made in all fifteenth-century gardens.   Later,
again, Bacon recommends alleys to be planted with
" those which perfume the air most delightfully being
trodden upon and crushed . . . to have the pleasure
when you walk or tread."   In his " Pastime of Pleasure "
(1554) Stephen Hawes speaks of :—

> In divers knottes of marveylous greatnes
> Rampande lyons, stode by wonderfully
> Made all of herbes, with dulset sweetnes
> With many dragons, of marveylous likenes
> Of divers floures, made full craftely.

More modern still is the delightful notion of a sun-dial
made of herbs and flowers, that will mark the time of
day by the opening and closing of their blossoms.
Linnæus had such a dial, with each plant so placed
that at each successive hour a flower should open or
fold up.   Ingram[1] gives an appropriate list for this
purpose, beginning with Goats' Beard, which he says
opens at 3 A.M. and shuts at 9 A.M., and ending with

[1] " Flora Symbolica."

Chickweed whose stars are not disclosed till 9.15 A.M., when they display themselves for exactly twelve hours. Andrew Marvell wrote these pretty lines on this device :—

> How well the skilful gardener drew
> Of flow'rs and herbs this dial new ;
> Where, from above the milder sun,
> Does through a fragrant zodiack run,
> And, as it works, th' industrious bee
> Computes its time as well as we !
> How could such sweet and wholesome hours
> Be reckon'd but with herbs and flow'rs !
>
> *The Garden.*

The *Quarterly* for June 1842 quotes this charming description of a garden in which herbs were not disregarded. "Quaint devices of all kinds are found here. Here is a sun-dial of flowers arranged according to the time of day at which they open and close. Here are peacocks and lions in livery of Lincoln green. Here are berceaux and harbours, and covered alley and enclosures containing the primest of the carnations and cloves in set order, and miniature canals that carry down a stream of pure water to the fish ponds below. . . . From thence (the shrubbery) winds a path, the deliciæ of the garden, planted with such herbs as yield their perfume when trodden upon and crushed. . . . It were tedious to follow up the long shady path not broad enough for more than two—the 'lovers' walk." The reviewer himself continues in a less sentimental strain, and his observations make a very proper introduction to a book on Herbs.

"The olitory or herb-garden is a part of our horticulture now comparatively neglected, and yet once the culture and culling of simples was as much a part of female education as the preserving and tying down of 'rasps and apricocks.' There was not a Lady Bountiful in the kingdom but made her dill-tea and diet-drink from herbs of her own planting ; and there is a neatness and prettiness about our thyme, and sage, and mint and marjoram, that might yet, we think, transfer them from the patronage of the blue serge to that of the white muslin apron. Lavender and rosemary, and rue, the feathery fennel, and the bright blue borage, are all pretty bushes in their way, and might have a due place assigned to them by the hand of beauty and taste. A strip for a little herbary half-way between the flower and vegetable garden would form a very appropriate transition stratum and might be the means, by being more under the eye of the mistress, of re-covering to our soups and salads some of the compara-tively neglected herbs of tarragon, and French sorrel, and purslane, and chervil, and dill, and clary, and others whose place is now nowhere to be found but in the pages of the old herbalists. This little plot should be laid out, of course, in a simple, geometric pattern ; and having tried the experiment, we can boldly pronounce on its success. We recommend the idea to the con-sideration of our lady-gardeners."

CHAPTER I

OF THE CHIEF HERBS USED IN THE PRESENT TIME

> J'ai des bouquets pour tous les goûts ;
> Venez choisir dans ma corbeille :
> De plusieurs les parfums sont doux,
> De tous, la vertu sans pareille.
>
> J'ai des *soucis* pour les galoux ;
> La *rose* pour l'amant fidèle ;
> De *l'éllebore* pour les tous
> Et pour l'amitié l'immortelle.
> > *La petite Corbeille de fleurs.*

> Herbs, too, she knew, and well of each could speak
> That in her garden sip'd the silv'ry dew ;
> Where no vain flow'r disclos'd a gaudy streak ;
> But herbs for use, and physic, not a few,
> Of grey renown within those borders grew ;
> The tufted basil, pun-provoking thyme,
> Fresh baum, and mary-gold of cheerful hue ;
> The lowly gill,[1] that never dares to climb ;
> And more I fain would sing, disdaining here to rhyme.

> Yet euphrasy [2] may not be left unsung,
> That gives dim eyes to wander leagues around ;
> And pungent radish, biting infant's tongue ;
> And plantain ribb'd, that heals the reaper's wound ;
> And marj'ram sweet, in shepherd's posie found ;
> And lavender, whose spikes of azure bloom
> Shall be, ere-while, in arid bundles bound
> To lurk amidst the labours of her loom,
> And crown her kerchiefs clean with mickle rare perfume.
> > *The Schoolmistress.*—SHENSTONE.

JOHN EVELYN once wrote an essay called " Acetaria : a Discourse of Sallets," and dedicated it to Lord Somers, the President of the Royal Society. The Dedication is

Ground-ivy.   [2] Eye-bright.

highly laudatory and somewhat grandiloquent, comparing the Royal Society to King Solomon's Temple, and declaring it established for the acquirement of " solid and useful knowledge by the *Investigation* of *Causes, Principles, Energies, Powers* and *Effects* of Bodies and *Things visible*; and to improve them for the Good and Benefit of Mankind. . . . And now, *My Lord*, I expect some will wonder what my Meaning is, to usher in a *Trifle* with so much magnificence, and end at last in a fine *Receipt* for the *dressing* of a *Sallet* with an handful of Pot-herbs! But yet, my Lord, this Subject as low and despicable as it appears challenges a Part of *Natural History;* and the Greatest Princes have thought it no disgrace, not only to make it their *Diversion*, but their *Care*, and to promote and encourage it in the midst of their weightiest Affairs." This disquisition casts an unlooked-for air of dignity over the Salad-bowl! The discourse itself is very practical, and begins with the *Furniture* and *Materials* of which a Salad may be composed. Eighty-two items are mentioned, but all cannot be called strictly in order, as Oranges, Turnips, Rosemary, and Judas Tree flowers, and Mushrooms are amongst them!

In the table at the end of this list Evelyn, "by the assistance of Mr *London*, His Majesty's Principal Gardener, reduced them to a competent number, not exceeding thirty-five," though he suggests that this may be " vary'd and enlarg'd by selections from the foregoing list."

The essay finishes with philosophical reasoning on the subject of vegetarianism. History is called upon to furnish examples of sages, of all times, favourably inclined to it, but Noah is allowed to differ on account of the " humidity of the atmosphere " after the Deluge, which must have necessitated a generous diet. Most people would think thirty-five different kinds a liberal allowance for salad herbs alone, but Abercrombie, writing in 1822, gives forty-four, and it is worthy of notice, that within the last eighty years, ox-eye daisy, yarrow, lady's-smock, primrose and plantain were counted among them.

In this chapter, the herbs mentioned are those chiefly used nowadays; in the next chapter, these that were favourites *au temps jadis*. It is a difficult line to draw, for the popularity of many of them is, like themselves, evergreen, but I have tried to put in the second chapter those that have passed the zenith of their fame, though they may still ride high in public estimation.

ANISE (*Pimpinella Anisum*).

His chimney side
Could boast no gammon, salted well and dried
And hook'd behind him; but sufficient store
Of bundled anise and a cheese it bore.
The Salad. Trans. from "Virgil."—COWPER.

In Virgil's time Anise evidently must have been used as a spice. It is a graceful, umbelliferous plant, a native of Egypt, but the seeds will ripen in August in England if it is planted in a warm and favourable situation. Abercrombie [1] says "its chief use is to flavour soups, but Loudon [2] includes it among confectionery herbs."

BALM (*Melissa officinalis*).

The several chairs of order look you scour
With juice of Balm and every precious flower.
Merry Wives of Windsor, V. v. 65.

Then Balm and Mint helps to make up
My chaplet.
The Muses Elysium.—DRAYTON.

My garden grew Self-heal and Balm,
And Speedwell that's blue for an hour,
Then blossoms again, O, grievous my pain,
I'm plundered of each flower.
Devonshire Song.

---

[1] "Every Man his own Gardener."
[2] "Encyclopædia of Gardening," 1822.

The lemon-scent of Balm makes it almost the most delicious of all herbs, and it is for its fragrance that Shakespeare and Drayton have alluded to it in these passages. In the song it is mentioned for another reason, for the flowers here are used as emblems. The first verse describes a garden of fair blossoms stolen, alas! from their owner. This verse of the song shows she has planted flowers whose nature is to console—Self-heal, Balm and the Speedwell, which, after every shock, hasten to bloom again, but she is again bereft of her treasures, and finally despairs and tells us that she grows naught but weeds and the symbols of desolation. There was once a "restorative cordial" called Carmelite water, which enjoyed a great reputation, and which was composed of the spirit of Balm, Angelica root, lemon-peel and nutmeg. In the early part of the last century, Balm wine was made, and was described as being "light and agreeable," but now Balm is seldom used, except when claret-cup is improved by its flavour. A most curious legend is told by Aubrey[1] of the Wandering Jew, the scene being on the Staffordshire moors. "One Whitsun evening, overcome with thirst, he knocked at the door of a Staffordshire cottager, and craved of him a cup of small beer. The cottager, who was wasted with a lingering consumption, asked him in, and gave him the desired refreshment. After finishing the beer, Ahasuerus asked his host the nature of the disease he was suffering from, and being told that the doctors had given him up, said, 'Friend, I will tell thee what thou shalt do.' He then told him to go into the garden the next morning on rising, and gather three Balm leaves, and to put them into a cup of small beer. He was to drink as often as he needed, and refill the cup when it was empty, and put in fresh Balm leaves every fourth day, and, 'before twelve days shall be past, thy disease

[1] "Miscellanies."

shall be cured and thy body altered.' So saying, and declining to eat, he departed and was never seen again. But the cottager gathered his Balm-leaves, followed the prescription of the Wandering Jew, and before twelve days were passed was a new man."

SWEET BASIL (*Ocymum basilium*) AND BUSH BASIL (*O. minimum*).

> Madonna, wherefore hast thou sent to me
> Sweet basil and mignonette?
> Embleming love and health which never yet
> In the same wreath might be.
> *To Emilia Viviani.*—SHELLEY.

Basil is beloved of the poets, and the story of Isabella and the Basil-pot keeps the plant in memory, where it is itself never, or very rarely, seen. The opening lines of Drayton's pretty poem beginning with Claia's speech :—

> Here damask roses, white and red,
> Out of my lap first take I—

are well known, and it is a pity that the whole of it is not oftener quoted. Two maidens make rival chaplets, and then examine the store of simples just gathered by a hermit. Claia chooses her flowers for beauty, Lelipa hers for scent, and Clarinax, the hermit, plucks his for their " virtue " in medicine. Lelipa says :—

> A chaplet, me, of herbs I'll make,
> Than which, though yours be braver,
> Yet this of mine, I'll undertake,
> Shall not be short in favour.
> With Basil then I will begin,
> Whose scent is wondrous pleasing.

and a goodly number of sweet-herbs follows.

Parkinson[1] says of it, " The ordinary Basill is in a manner wholly spent to make sweete, or washing waters, among other sweet herbes, yet sometimes it is put into nosegays. The Physicall properties are

[1] " Earthly Paradise," 1629

to procure a cheerfull and merry hearte, whereunto the seede is chiefly used in powder." With such "physicall properties" Basil is too much neglected nowadays. He also refers to the extraordinary but very general idea that it bred scorpions. "Let me, before I leave, relate unto you a pleasant passage between Francisius Marchio, as Advocate of the State of *Genoa* sent in embassage to the Duke of Milan, and the said Duke, who, refusing to heare his message or to agree unto the conditions proposed, brought an handfull of Basill and offered it to him, who, demanding of him what he meant thereby, answered him, that the properties of that hearbe was, that being gently handled, it gave a pleasant smell, but being hardly wrung and bruised, would breed scorpions, with which witty answer the Duke was so pleased that he confirmed the conditions, and sent him honourably home. It is also observed that scorpions doe much rest and abide under these pots and vessells wherein Basill is planted." Culpepper,[1] too, had suspicions about it. "This is the herb which all authors are together by the ears about and rail at one another (like lawyers). Galen and Dioscorides hold it not fitting to be taken inwardly, and Chrysippus rails at it with downright Billingsgate rhetoric; Pliny and the Arabians defend it. Something is the matter, this herb and rue will not grow together, no, nor near one another, and we know rue is as great an enemy to poison as any that grows." Tusser[2] puts both Basils in his list of "strewing herbs," and also says :—

> Fine basil desireth it may be her lot,
> To grow as the gilliflower, trim in a pot;
> That ladies and gentles, to whom ye do serve,
> May help her, as needeth, poor life to preserve.
>
> *May's Husbandry.*

To which (in Mavor's edition, 1812) is appended this

[1] English Physitian, popularly known as Culpepper's Herbal, 1652.
[2] "Five Hundred Points of Good Husbandry."

prim note, " Garden basil, if stroked, leaves a grateful smell on the hand, and the author insinuates that it receives fresh life from being touched by a fair lady." Both basils are annuals, though Bush Basil may occasionally live through the winter. They are small plants with oval leaves and white, labiate flowers. A modern gardener writes that sweet basil has the flavour of cloves, that it is always demanded by French cooks, and that it is much used to flavour soups, and occasionally salads. M. de la Quintinye,[1] director of the gardens to Louis XIV., shows that over two hundred years ago French cooks were of the same mind about basil as they are to-day; besides mentioning it for the uses just named, he adds, " It is likewise used in ragouts, especially dry ones, for which reason we take care to keep some for winter." An Italian name for it is *Bacia-Nicola*.

BORAGE (*Borago officinalis*).

> Here is sweet water, and borage for blending,
> Comfort and courage to drink to your fill.
> N. HOPPER.

This reference to Borage touches a long-lived belief—

> I, borage,
> Give courage—

briefly states one reason of its popularity, which has lasted ever since Pliny praised the plant; besides this, it was supposed to exhilarate the spirits and drive away melancholy. De Gubernatis[2] only found one charge against it, amid universal praise, and this is in a Tuscan *ninnerella*, a cradle song, where it is accused of frightening a baby! But this evidence is absolutely unsupported by any tradition, and he considers it worthless. Borage

---

[1] The Complete Gardener. Trans. by T. Evelyn, 1693.
[2] *La Mythologie des Plantes.*

was sometimes called Bugloss by the old writers.[1]   In
1810 Dr Thornton calls it "one of the four grand
cardiac plants," but shows a lamentable lack of faith
himself.   Dr Fernie [2] finds that Borage has a " cucumber-
like odour," and that its reputed powers of "refreshing"
and " invigorating" are not all due to the imagination ;
" The fresh juice," he says, "affords thirty per cent. of
nitrate of potash.   Thornton had already commented on the
nitre it contains, and to prove this he advises that the
dried plant be thrown on the fire, when it emits a sort
of coruscation, with a slight detonation."   Personal
experience teaches that this is easier to observe if the
plant is set on fire and burned by itself.   Borage might
be grown for the sake of its lovely blue flowers alone,
and Parkinson gives it a place in his " Earthly Paradise,"
because, though it is " wholly in a manner spent for
Physicall properties or for the Pot, yet the flowers have
alwaies been interposed among the flowers of women's
needle-work "—a practice which would add to the beauty
of modern embroidery.   He adds that the flowers "of
gentlewomen are candid for comfits," showing that they
did not allow sentiment to soar uncontrolled !   Bees love
borage, and it yields excellent honey, yet another reason
for growing it.   In the early part of the nineteenth
century the young tops were still sometimes boiled for
a pot-herb, but in the present day, if used at all, it is
put into claret-cup.   Till quite lately it was an ingredient
in " cool tankards " of wine or cider.

BUGLOSS (*Anchusa officinalis*).

So did the maidens with their various flowers
Deck up their windows, and make neat their bowers ;
Using such cunning as they did dispose
The ruddy piny (peony) with the lighter rose,

---

[1] *Family Herbal*, 1810.   [2] *Herbal Simples*, 1895

The monkshood with the bugloss, and entwine
The white, the blue, the flesh-like columbine
With pinks, sweet williams.
Britannia's Pastorals, Book II.—W. BROWNE.

A spiny stem of bugloss flowers,
Deep blue upon the outer towers.
Winchester Castle—N. HOPPER.

Gerarde put Bugloss in one chapter, and Alkanet or Wild Bugloss in another, but nowadays Bugloss or Alkanet are names for the same plant, *Anchusa officinalis*. The drawings of his Bugloss resemble our Alkanet much more closely than they do any other plant called Bugloss, such as *Lycopsis arvensis*, small Bugloss, or *Echium vulgare*, Viper's Bugloss. The old herbalists, however, were most confusing on the subject. They apply the name Bugloss alternately to *Borago officinalis* and to different varieties of *Anchusa*, and then speak of *Buglossum* as if it were a different species! Evelyn describes it as being "in nature much like Borage but something more astringent," and recommends the flowers of both as a conserve, for they are "greatly restorative." As Hogg says that *Anchusa officinalis* had formerly "a great reputation as a cordial," Evelyn's description applies to this plant; we may take it that this is the Bugloss he was thinking of. It is a good plant for a "wild garden," but has a great tendency to spread. I have found it growing wild in Cornwall. Gerarde tells us that the roots of *Anchusa Tinctoria* were used to colour waters, syrups, and jellies, and then follows a line of scandal— "The gentlewomen of France doe paint their faces with these roots, as it is said." Rouge is still made from Alkanet.

BURNET (*Poterium Sanguisorba*).

The even mead, that erst brought sweetly forth
The freckled Cowslip, Burnet and green Clover.
Henry V., V. ii. 48.

Burnet has "two little leives like unto the winges
of birdes, standing out as the bird setteth her winges
out when she intendeth to flye. . . . Yᵉ Duchmen call
it Hergottes berdlen, that is God's little berde, because
of the colour that it hath in the toppe." This is Turner's[1]
information. He has a pleasant style, and tells us out-
of-the-way facts or customs in a charming manner.
Burnet is the first of the three plants that Sir Francis
Bacon desired to be set in alleys, "to perfume the air
most delightfully, being trodden upon and crushed."
The others were wild thyme and water-mint. It was a
Salad-herb, and has (like Borage) a flavour of cucumber,
but it has, most undeservedly, gone out of fashion.
The taste is "somewhat warm, and the leaves should
be cut young, or else they are apt to be tough. Culpepper and Parkinson advise that a few leaves should
be added to a cup of claret wine because" it is "a
helpe to make the heart merrie." Canon Ellacombe[2]
says it was "and still is valued as a forage plant that
will grow and keep fresh all the winter in dry, barren
pastures, thus giving food for sheep when other food
was scarce. It has occasionally been cultivated, but
the result has not been very satisfactory, except on very
poor land, though, according to the Woburn experiments, as reported by Sinclair, it contains a larger
amount of nutritive matter in the spring than most of
the grasses. It has brown flowers from which it is
supposed to derive its name (Brunetto)."

CARAWAY (*Carum carvi*).

Shallow. Now, you shall see my orchard, where, in an arbour
we will eat a last year's Pippin of my own grafting, with a dish of
Caraways, and so forth. *II. Henry IV.* v. 3.

In Elizabethan days, Caraway Seeds were appreciated

[1] Turner's Herbal is beautifully illustrated; five initial letters from
it are here reproduced.
"Plant-lore and Garden-Craft of Shakespeare."

INITIAL LETTERS FROM TURNER'S "HERBAL"

at dessert, and Canon Ellacombe says that the custom
of serving roast apples with a little saucerful of Caraway
Seed is still kept up at some of the London livery
dinners. It was the practice to put them among baked
fruits or into bread-cakes, and they were also " made
into comfits." In cakes and comfits they are used to-day,
and in Germany I have seen them served with potatoes
fried in slices. The roots were boiled and "eaten as
carrots," and made a " very welcome and delightful
dish to a great many," though some found them rather
strong flavoured. " The [1] Duchemen call it Mat kumell or
Wishenkumel and the Freses, Hofcumine. It groweth in
great plentye in Freseland in the meadows there betweene
Marienhoffe and Werden, hard by the sea banke."

CELERY (*Apium graveolens*).

This is quite without romance. The older herbalists did
not know it and Evelyn says : " Sellery . . . was formerly
a stranger with us (nor very long since in *Italy* itself).
. . . Nor is it a distinct *species* of *smallage* or Macedonian
Parsley, tho' somewhat more hot and generous, by its
frequent transplanting, and thereby render'd sweeter
scented." For its "high and grateful taste, it is ever
plac'd in the middle of the *grand sallet*, at our great
men's tables, and Proctor's Feasts, as the grace of the
whole board." But though Parkinson did not know
the plant under this name, he did see some of the
first introduced into England, and gives an interesting
account of this introduction to " sweete Parsley or sweet
Smallage. . . . This resembles sweete Fennell. . . .
The first that ever I saw was in a Venetian Ambassador's
garden in the spittle yard, near Bishop's Gate Streete.
The first year it is planted with us it is sweete and
pleasant, especially while it is young, but after it has
grown high and large hath a stronger taste of smallage,

[1] "Turner's Herbal," 1538.

and so likewise much more the following yeare. The
Venetians used to prepare it for meate many waies, both
the herbe and roote eaten rawe, or boyled or fryed to be
eaten with meate, or the dry'd herb poudered and
strewn upon meate; but most usually either whited
and so eaten raw with pepper and oyle as a dainty
sallet of itselfe, or a little boyled or stewed . . . the
taste of the herbe being a little warming, but the seede
much more."

CHERVIL (*Scandix Cerefolium*).

Chibolles and Chervelles and ripe chiries manye.
Piers Plowman.

Chervil was much used by the French and Dutch
" boyled or stewed in a pipkin.   De la Quintinye recommends it to give a ' perfuming rellish' to the salad, and
Evelyn says the ' *Sweete* (and as the *French* call it *Musque*)
Spanish Chervile,' is the best and ought ' never to be
wanting in our sallets,' for it is ' exceeding wholesome
and charming to the spirits.' . . . This (as likewise
Spinach) is used in tarts and serves alone for divers
sauces."

CIBOULES, CHIBOULES OR CHIBBALS (*Allium Ascalonium*).

Acorns, plump as Chibbals.
The Gipsies Metamorphosed.—BEN JONSON.

Ciboules are a small kind of onion; De la Quintinye
says, "Onions degenerated."   From the reference
to them in *Piers Plowman*, they were evidently in
common use here in the time of Langlande.   The French
gardener adds that they are " propagated only by seeds
of the bignes of a corn of ordinary gun-powder," and
Mr Britten identifies them with Scallions or Shallot
(*A. ascalonium*).

CIVES, OR CHIVES, OR SEIVES (*Allium Schænoprasum*).

> Straightways follow'd in
> A case of small musicians, with a din
> Of little Hautbois, whereon each one strives
> To show his skill; they all were made of seives,
> Excepting one, which puff'd the player's face,
> And was a Chibole, serving for the bass.
> *Britannia's Pastorals*, Book III.

Cives and Ciboules are often mentioned together, as in this account of King Oberon's feast. The leaves are green and hollow and look like rushes *en miniature,* and would serve admirably for elfin Hautbois. Miss Amherst[1] says that they are mentioned in a list of herbs (Sloane MS., 1201) found "at the beginning of a book of cookery recipes, fifteenth century." She also tells us that when Kalm came to England (May 1748) he noticed them among the vegetables most grown in the nursery-gardens round London. They were "esteemed milder than onions," and of a "quick rellish," but their fame has declined in the last hundred years. Loudon says that the leaves are occasionally used to flavour soup salads and omelettes—unlike ciboules, the bulb is not used—but the chief purpose for which I have heard them required is to mix with the food for young guinea-fowls and chickens.

CORIANDER (*Coriandrum sativum*).

> And Coriander last to these succeeds
> That hangs on slightest threads her trembling seeds.
> *The Salad.*—COWPER.

The chief interest attached to Coriander is that in the Book of Numbers, xi. 7, Manna is compared to the seed. It was originally introduced from the East, but is now naturalised in Essex and other places, where it has long been cultivated for druggists and confectioners. The

[1] "History of Gardening in England."

seeds are quite round, like tiny balls, and Hogg remarks
that they become fragrant by drying, and the longer they
are kept the more fragrant they become. "If taken
oute of measure it doth trouble a manne's witt, with
great jeopardye of madnes." [1] Nowadays one comes across
them oftenest in little round pink and white comfits
for children.

CUMIN (*Cuminum cyminum*).

Cummin good for eyes,
The roses reigning the pride of May,
Sharp isope good for greene woundes remedies. [2]

Cumin is also mentioned in the Bible by Isaiah ; and also
in the New Testament, as one of the plants that were
tithed. It is very seldom met with, but the seeds have the
same properties as caraway seeds. Gerarde says it has
"little jagged leaves, very finely cut into small parcels,"
and "spoky tufts" of red or purplish flowers. "The
root is slender, which perisheth when it hath ripened
his seed," and it delights in a hot soil. He recommends
it to be boyled together with wine and barley meale
"to the forme of a pultis" for a variety of ailments.
In Germany the seeds are put into bread and they figure
in folklore. De Gubernatis says it gave rise to a
saying among the Greeks : "Le cumin symbolisait, chez
le Grecs, ce qui est petit. Des avares, ils disaient,
qu'ils auraient même partagé le cumin."

CRESSES.

Darting fish that on a summer morn
Adown the crystal dykes of Camelot,
Come slipping o'er their shadows on the sand. . . .
Betwixt the cressy islets, white in flower.
Geraint and Enid.

To purl o'er matted cress and ribbed sand,
Or dimple in the dark of rushy coves.
Ode to Memory.—TENNYSON.

[1] Turner. [2] *Muiopotmos.*—Spenser.

> Valley lilies, whiter still
> Than Leda's love and cresses from the rill.
> *Endymion.*

> Cresses that grow where no man may them see.
> *Ibid.*

> I linger round my shingly bars,
> I loiter round my cresses.
> *The Brook.*—TENNYSON.

Cresses have great powers of fascination for the poets, and "the cress of the Herbalist is a noun of multitude," says Dr Fernie. Of these now cultivated, St Barbara's Cress (*Barbarea vulgaris*) has the most picturesque name, and is the least known. It was once grown for a winter salad, but American Cress (*Erysimum præcox*) is more recommended for winter and early spring. Indian Cress (*Tropæolum majus*), usually known as nasturtium, is seldom counted a herb, although it is included in some old gardening lists, for the sake of the pickle into which its unripe fruits were made. Abercrombie adds that the flowers and young leaves are used in salads, but this must be most rare in England; though, when once in Brittany, I remember that the *bonne* used to ornament the salad on Sundays with an artistic decoration of scarlet and striped nasturtium flowers. Garden Cress (*Lepidium sativum*), the tiny kind, associated in one's mind since nursery days with "mustard," used to be known as *Passerage*, as it was believed to drive away madness. Dr Fernie continues, that the Greeks loved cress, and had a proverb, "Eat Cresses and get wit." They were much prized by our poor people, when pepper was a luxury. "The Dutchmen[1] and others used to eate Cresses familiarly with their butter and breade, as also stewed or boyled, either alone or with other herbs, whereof they make a Hotch-Potch. We doe eate it mixed

---

[1] Parkinson

with Lettuce and Purslane, or sometimes with Tarragon or
Rocket with oyle, vinegar, and a little salt, and in that
manner it is very savoury."

Water-Cress (*Nasturtium officinale*) is rich in mineral
salts and is valuable as food. The leaves remain
"green when grown in the shade, but become of a
purple brown because of their iron, when exposed to
the sun," says Dr Fernie. "It forms the chief
ingredient of the *Sirop Antiscorbutique*, given so success-
fully by the French faculty." "Water-Cress pottage"
is a good remedy "to help head aches. Those that
would live in health may use it if they please, if they
will not I cannot help it." This is Culpepper's advice,
but he relents even to those too weak-minded to avail
themselves of a cure, salutary but unpalatable. "If
they fancy not pottage they may eat the herb as a
sallet.

DANDELION (*Leontodon taraxacum*).

Dandelion, with globe and down,
The schoolboy's clock in every town,
Which the truant puffs amain,
To conjure lost hours back again.

WILLIAM HOWITT.

Dandelion leaves used to be boiled with lentils, and one
recipe bids one have them "chopped as pot-herbes, with
a few Allisanders boyled in their broth." But generally
they were regarded as a medicinal, rather than a salad
plant. Evelyn, however, includes them in his list, and
says they should be "macerated in several waters, to extract the Bitterness. It was with this Homely Fare the
Good Wife Hecate entertain'd *Theseus*." A better way of
"extracting the Bitterness" is to blanch the leaves, and
it has been advised to dig up plants from the road-sides
in winter when salad is scarce, and force them in pots
like succory. He continues that of late years "they have
been sold in most *Herb Shops* about *London* for being a

SWEET CICELY AND OTHER HERBS

wonderful Purifier of the Blood." Culpepper, whose fiery frankness it is impossible to resist quoting, manages on this subject to get his knife into the doctors, as, to do him justice, he seldom loses an opportunity of doing. "You see what virtues this common herb hath, and this is the reason the French and Dutch so often eate them in the spring, and now, if you look a little further, you may see plainly, without a pair of spectacles, that foreign physicians are not so selfish as ours are, but more communicative of the virtues of plants to people." The Irish used to call it Heart-Fever-Grass. The root, when roasted and ground, has been substituted for coffee, and gave satisfaction to some of those who drank it. Hogg relates a tale of woe from the island of Minorca, how that once locusts devoured the harvest there, and the inhabitants were forced to, and did subsist on this root, but does not mention for what length of time.

DILL (*Anethum graveolens*).

The nightshade strews to work him ill,
Therewith her vervain and her dill.
Nymphidia.—DRAYTON.

Here holy vervayne and here dill,
'Gainst witchcraft much availing,
The Muses Elysium.

The wonder-working dill he gets not far from these.
Polyolbion. Song xiii.

Dill is supposed to have been derived from a Norse word to "dull," because the seeds were given to babies to make them sleep. Beyond this innocent employment it was a factor in working spells of the blackest magic! Dill is a graceful, umbelliferous plant—not at all suggestive of Dr Jekyll and Mr Hyde—and the seeds resemble caraway seeds in flavour, but are smaller, flatter and lighter. There is *something* mysterious about it, because, besides being employed in spells by witches and wizards, it was used by other people to resist spells cast by traffickers in magic, and was equally powerful to do this! Dill is very like fennel, but the leaves are shorter, smaller, and of a " stronger and quicker taste. The leaves are used with Fish, though too strong for every-one's taste, and if added to ' pickled Cowcumbers' it ' gives the cold fruit a pretty, spicie taste.' Evelyn also praises ' *Gerckens muriated* ' with the seeds of *Dill*," and Addison writes : " I am always pleased with that par ticular time of the year which is proper for the pickling of dill and cucumbers, but, alas ! his cry, like the song of the nightingale, is not heard above two months." [1]

ENDIVE (*Cichorium Endivia*).

The Daisy, Butter-flow'r and Endive blue.
Pastorals.—GAY.

There at no cost, on onions rank and red,
Or the curl'd endive's bitter leaf, he fed.
The Salad.—COWPER.

Endive is a plant of whose virtues our prosaic days have robbed us. Once upon a time it could break all bonds and render the owner invisible, and if a lover carried it about him, he could make the lady of his choice believe that he possessed all the qualities she specially admired! Folkard quotes three legends of it from Germany, one each from Austria and Roumania, and an unmistakably Slav story—all of them of a romantic character—and *we* regard it as a salad herb! " There are three sorts : Green-curled leaved ; principal sort for main crops, white-curled leaved, and broad Batavian " (Loudon). The green-curled leaved is the hardiest and fittest for winter use. The Batavian is not good for salads, but is specially in demand for stews and soups.

[1] *Spectator,* XXV. I.

All kinds must, of course, be carefully blanched. Mrs Roundell[1] reminds one that endive is a troublesome vegetable to cook, as it is apt to be crowded with insects. The leaves should be all detached from the stem and carefully washed in two or three salted waters. She also gives receipts for endive, dressed as spinach, made into a purée or cooked alone. Parkinson said : " Endive whited is much used in winter, as a sallet herbe with great delighte."

Succory, Chicory, or Wild Endive may be mentioned as making an excellent salad when forced and blanched, and it is popular in France, where it is called *Barbe de Capucin.* Its great advantage is, as Loudon says, that " when lettuce or garden-endive are scarce, chicory can always be commanded by those who possess any of the most ordinary means of forcing." He adds that it has been much used as fodder for cattle, and that the roots, dried and ground, are well known—only too well known, " partly along with, and partly as a substitute for coffee."

FENNEL (*Fæniculum vulgare*).

Ophelia. There's fennel for you and columbines.
Hamlet, iv. 5.

Fenel is for flatterers,
An evil thing it is sure,
But I have alwaies meant truely
With constant heart most pure.
A Handfull of Pleasant Delightes.—C. ROBINSON.

Christopher. No, my good lord.
Count. Your *good lord!* Oh! how this smells of fennel!
The Case Altered, ii. 2.—BEN JONSON.

"Hast thou ought in thy purse?" quod he.
"Any hote spices?"
"I have peper, pionies," quod she, "and a pound garlike
A ferdyng worth of fenel-seed for fastyng dayes."
Piers Plowman.

---

[1] "Practical Cookery Book."

> Oh ! faded flowers of fennel, that will not bloom again
> For any south wind's calling, for any magic rain.
>
> *The Faun to his Shadow.*—N. HOPPER.

> " Sow Fennel, sow Sorrow."—*Proverb.*

Few realise from how high an estate fennel has fallen. In Shakespeare's time we have the plainest evidence that it was the recognised emblem of flattery. Ben Jonson's allusion is almost as pointed as Robinson's. It is said that Ophelia's flowers were all chosen for their significance, so, perhaps, it was not by accident that she offers fennel to her brother, in whose ears the cry must have been still ringing,

> " Choose we ; Laertes shall be king ! "

with the echo :—

> " Caps, hand, and tongues, applaud it to the clouds,
> ' Laertes shall be king, Laertes king ! ' "

Nor was it only in our own land that Fennel had this significance, for Canon Ellacombe quotes an Italian saying : " Dare Finocchio " (to give fennel), meaning " to flatter." As to the reason that fennel should be connected with sorrow, the clue is lost, but the proverb is said still to live in New England. The conversation which takes place in " Piers Plowman," between a priest and a poor woman, illustrates a use to which fennel was put in earlier days. The poor got it, Miss Amherst says, " to relieve the pangs of hunger on fasting days." But it was by no means despised by the rich, for " As much as eight and a half pounds of Fennel seed was bought for the King's Household (Edward I., 1281) for one month's supply." She quotes from the Wardrobe Accounts. Our use either of Common Fennel, or Sweet Fennel, or Finocchio is so limited that the practice of Parkinson's contemporaries shall be quoted. " Fenell is of great use to trim up and strowe upon fish, as also to boyle or put among fish of divers sorts, Cowcumbers

pickled and other fruits, etc. The rootes are used with
Parsley rootes to be boyled in broths. The seed is
much used to put in Pippin pies and divers others such
baked fruits, as also into bread, to give it the better
relish. The Sweet Cardus Fenell being sent by Sir
Henry Wotton to John Tradescante had likewise a large
direction with it how to dress it, for they used to white
it after it hath been transplanted for their uses, which
by reason of sweetnesse by nature, and the tendernesse
by art, causeth it to be more delightfull to the taste."
" Cardus Fenell" must have been Finocchio.

Goat's Beard (*Tragopogon pratensis*).

And goodly now the noon-tide hour,
When from his high meridian tower,
The sun looks down in majesty,
What time about the grassy lea
The Goat's Beard, prompt his rise to hail
With broad expanded disk, in veil
Close mantling wraps his yellow head,
And goes, as peasants say, to bed.

Bp. Mant.

The habits of Goat's Beard, or as it is often called,
John-go-to-bed-at-noon, are indicated by the latter
name. It is less known as Joseph's Flower, which Mr
Friend [1] says " seems to owe its origin to pictures in
which the husband of Mary is represented as a long-
bearded old man," but Gerarde gives the Low-Dutch
name of his time, " Josephe's Bloemen," and says " when
these flowers be come to their full maturity and ripeness,
they grow into a downy blow-ball, like those of the
Dandelion, which is carried away by the winde." Evelyn
praises it, and is indignant with the cunning of the seed-
sellers. " Of late they have Italianiz'd the name, and
now generally call it *Salsifex* ... to disguise it, being a very
common field herb, growing in most parts of *England*,

[1] " Flowers and Flower-lore."

would have it thought (with many others) an Exotick."
He does not give the full Latin name, so one cannot tell
whether it is our Salsify (*Tragopogon porrifolius*) that he
means, or *T. pratensis*, the variety once more generally
cultivated. The latter seems the likeliest, as its yellow
flowers are far more common than the purple ones of
salsify. *T. porrifolius* is extremely rare in a wild state,
but *T. pratensis* grows in "medows and fertil pastures
in most parts of England." *T. pratensis* is never cultivated
now, and "Salsify" applies exclusively to Purple Goat's
Beard (*T. porrifolium*). The old herbalists praised it very
highly.

Horse-Radish (*Cochlearia Armoracia*).

Dr Fernie translates its botanical name, *Cochlearia*, from
the shape of the leaves, which resemble, he says, an old-
fashioned spoon; *ar*, near; *mor*, the sea, from its
favourite locality. "For the most part it is planted
in gardens . . . yet have I found it wilde in Sundrie
places . . . in the field next unto a farme house leading
to King's land, where my very good friend Master
Bredwell, practitioner in Phisick, a learned and diligent
searcher of Samples, and Master *William Martin*, one
of the fellowship of Barbers and Chirugians, my deere
and loving friend, in company with him found it and
gave me knowledge of the plant, where it flourisheth
to this day. . . . Divers think that this Horse-Radish
is an enemie to Vines, and that the hatred between
them is so greate, that if the roots hereof be planted
neare to the Vine, it bendeth backward from it, as not
willing to have fellowship with it. . . . Old writers
ascribe this enmitie to the vine and Brassica, our Cole-
wortes." Both he and Parkinson think, that in trans-
ferring the "enmitie" from the cabbage to the horse-
radish, the "Ancients" have been mistranslated. The
Dutch called it Merretich; the French, Grand Raifort;

the English, locally, Red Cole. Evelyn calls it an
"excellent, universal Condiment," and says that first
steeped in water, then grated and tempered with vinegar,
in which a little sugar has been dissolved, it supplies
"Mustard to the Sallet, and serving likewise for any
Dish besides."

HYSSOP (*Hyssopus officinalis*).

Hyssop, as an herb most prime,
Here is my wreath bestowing.
Muses Elysium.—DRAYTON.

Iago. "Our bodies are our gardeners; so that if we will plant nettles,
or sow lettuce, set hyssop and weed up thyme . . . why the power
and corrigible authority of this lies in our wills." *Othello*, i. 3.

Parkinson opens his "Theatre of Plants" with the
words: "From a Paradise of pleasant Flowers, I am
fallen (*Adam* like) to a world of Profitable Herbs and
Plants . . . and first of the Hisopes. . . . Among other
uses, the golden hyssop was of so pleasant a colour,
that it provoked every gentlewoman to wear them in
their heads and on their arms with as much delight as
many fine flowers can give." It is a hardy, evergreen
shrub, with a strong aromatic odour. The flowers are
blue, and appear more or less from June till October.
The *Ussopos* of Dioscorides was named from *azob*, a
holy herb, because it was used for cleansing sacred
places, and this is interesting when one thinks of Scrip-
tural allusions to the plant, although the hyssop of the
Bible is most probably not our hyssop. The identity of
that plant has occasioned much divergence of opinion, and
a decision, beyond reach of criticism, has not yet been
reached. Mazes were sometimes planted with "Marjoram
and such like, or Isope and Time. It may eyther be sette
with Isope and Time or with Winter Savory and Time,
for these endure all the Winter thorowe greene."[1]

[1] "Art of Gardening," Hill, 1563.

It was more often used for " Broths and Decoctions"
than for salads, but the tops and flowers were sometimes
powdered and strewn on the top of one. It is not much
used nowadays, but I once saw an excitable Welsh cook
seize on a huge bunch of " dear Hyssop" with exclamations of joy. In the East, " some plants diverted fascination by their smell,"[1] and hyssop was one of these, and
as a protection against the Evil Eye, was hung up in
houses.

Lamb's Lettuce or Corn Salad (*Valeriana Locusta*).

Lamb's Lettuce is variously known as *mâche, doucette,
salade de chanoine, poule-grasse,* and was formerly called
" Salade de Prêter, for their being generally eaten in
Lent." It is a small plant, with " whitish-greene, long
or narrow round-pointed leaves . . . and tufts of small
bleake blue flowers." In corn-fields it grows wild, but
Gerarde says, " since it hath growne in use among the
French and Dutch strangers in England, it hath been
sowen in gardens as a salad herbe," and adds that among
winter and early spring salads " it is none of the worst."
The fact of its being " recognised" at a comparatively late
date, by the English, and even then through the practices
of the French, perhaps accounts for the lack of English
" pet" names, conspicuous beside the number bestowed
on it on the other side of the Channel. De la Quintinye is
not in accord with his countrymen on the subject, for he
calls it a " wild and rusticall Salad, because, indeed, it is
seldom brought before any Noble Company." Despite
this disparaging remark, it is still a favourite in France,
and it is surprising that a salad plant that stands cold so
well should not be more cultivated in this country. Lettuce
is so much more recognised as a vegetable than a herb
that it will not be mentioned here.

[1] Friend.

MARJORAM (*Origanum*).

Lafeu. 'Twas a good lady, 'twas a good lady. We may pick a thousand
salads ere we light on such another herb.
Clown. Indeed, Sir, she was the Sweet Marjoram of the Salad, or rather
the herb of grace.

All's Well that Ends Well, iv. 5.

Not all the ointments brought from Delos' Isle,
Nor that of quinces, nor of marjoram,
That ever from the Isle of Coös came,
Nor these, nor any else, though ne'er so rare,
Could with this place for sweetest smells compare.

Britannia's Pastorals.

O, bind them posies of pleasant flowers,
Of marjoram, mint and rue.

Devonshire Song.

The scent of marjoram used to be very highly prized,
and in some countries the plant is the symbol of honour.
Dr Fernie says *Origanum* means in Greek the "joy of
the mountains," so charming a name one wishes it could
be more often used. Among[1] the Greeks, if it grew
on the grave it augured the happiness of the departed;
" May many flowers grow on this newly-built tomb " (is
the prayer once offered); " not the dried-up Bramble,
or the red flower loved by goats; but Violets and
Marjoram, and the Narcissus growing in water, and
around thee may all Roses grow."

Parkinson writes it was " put in nosegays, and in the
windows of houses, as also in sweete pouders, sweete bags,
and sweete washing waters. . . . Our daintiest women
doe put it to still among their sweet herbes." Pusser
mentions it among his " herbs for strewing," and in some
recipes for *pot pourri* it is still included. *Origanum vulgare*
grows wild, and the dry leaves are made into a tea
" which is extremely grateful." The different kinds of
marjoram are now chiefly used for soups and stuffings.
Isaac Walton gives instructions for dressing a pike, and

[1] Friend.

directs that among the accessories should be sweet marjoram, thyme, a little winter savoury and some pickled
oysters!

MINT (*Mentha*).

The neighb'ring nymphs each in her turn . . .
Some running through the meadows with them bring
Cowslips and mint.

Britannia's Pastorals, book i.

In strewing of these herbs . . . with bounteous hands and free,
The healthful balm and mint from their full laps do fly.

Polyolbion, Song xv.

Sunflowers and marigolds and mint beset us,
Moths white as stitchwort that had left its stem,
. . . Loyal as sunflowers we will not swerve us,
We'll make the mints remembered spices serve us
For autumn as in spring.

N. HOPPER.

" Mint," says De la Quintinye, " is called in French
Balm," which sounds rather confusing; but Evelyn says
it is the " Curled Mint, *M. Sativa Crispa*," that goes
by this name.   Mint was also called " Menthe de Notre
Dame," and in Italy, " Erba Santa Maria," and in Germany, " Frauen Münze," though this name is also
applied to costmary.   This herb used to be strewn
in churches.   All the various kinds of it were thought
to be good against the biting of serpents, sea-scorpions,
and mad dogs, but violently antagonistic to the healing
processes of wounds.   " They are extreme bad for
wounded people, and they say a wounded man that
eats Mints, his wound will never be cured, and that is
a long day!   But they are good to be put into Baths." [1]
The " gentler tops of Orange Mint " (*Mentha citrata* ?) are
recommended " mixed with a Salad or eaten alone, with
the juyce of Orange and a little Sugar."
The mint we commonly use is *Mentha Viridis* or Spear

[1] Culpepper.

POT MARJORAM

Mint. "Divers have held for true, that Cheeses will not corrupt, if they be either rubbed over withe the juyce or a decoction of Mints, or they laid among them." It has been said, too, that an infusion of mint will prevent the rapid curdling of milk. Being dried, mint was much used to put with pennyroyal into puddings, and also among "pease that are boyled for pottage." The last is one of the few uses that survives. Parkinson complains of all sorts of mints, that once planted in a garden they are difficult to get rid of!

Cat Mint, or *Nep* (*Nepeta Cataria*) is eaten in Tansies. "According to Hoffman the root of the Cat Mint, if chewed, will make the most gentle person fierce and quarrelsome."[1]

Pepper Mint is still retained, as is Spear Mint, in the British Pharmacopœia. "The leaves have an intensely pungent aromatic taste resembling that of pepper, and accompanied with a peculiar sensation of coldness" (Thornton).

MUSTARD (*Sinapis*).

Bottom. Your name, I beseech you, sir?
Mustardseed. Mustardseed.
Bottom. Good Master Mustardseed, I know your patience well: that same cowardly, giant-like ox-beef hath devoured many a gentleman of your house: I promise you your kindred hath made my eyes water ere now. I desire your more acquaintance, good Master Mustardseed.
Midsummer-Night's Dream, iii. 1.

In 1664 Evelyn wrote that mustard is of "incomparable effect to quicken and revive the Spirits, strengthening the Memory and expelling Heaviness. . . . In *Italy*, in making *Mustard*, they mingle *Lemon* and *Orange* Peels with the seeds." In England the best mustard came from Tewkesbury. It is a curious instance of the instability of fashion that only twenty-four years before Evelyn made

[1] Folkard.

these remarks, Parkinson wrote: " Our ancient forefathers, even the better sort, in the most simple, and
as I may say the more healthful age of the world, were
not sparing in the use thereof . . . but nowadayes it
is seldom used by the successors, being accounted the
clownes sauce, and therefore not fit for their tables ;
but is transferred either to the meyny or meaner sort,
who therefore reap the benefit thereof." He adds it
is " of good use, being fresh for Epilepticke persons . . .
if it be applyed both inwardly and outwardly." There
were some drawbacks to being sick or sorry in the
" good old days." It was customary in Italy to keep
the mustard in balls till it was wanted, and these
balls were made up with honey or vinegar and a
little cinnamon added. When the mustard was required, the ball was " relented " with a little more vinegar. Canon Ellacombe says : " Balls were the form
in which Mustard was usually sold, till Mrs Clements
of Durham, in the last century, invented the method
of dressing mustard flour like wheat flour and made her
fortune with Durham Mustard ! " We cultivate *Sinapis
nigra* for its seed and *Sinapis alba* as a small salad herb.

PARSLEY (*Petroselinum sativum*).

The tender tops of Parsley next he culls,
Then the old rue bush shudders as he pulls.
The Salad.

Quinces and Peris ciryppe (syrup) with parcely rotes,
Right so begyn your mele.
RUSSELL's *Boke of Nature.*

Fat colworts and comforting perseline,
Cold lettuce and refreshing rosmarine.
Muiopotmos.—SPENSER.

Parsley has the " curious botanic history that no one
can tell what is its native country. Probably the plant has
been so altered by cultivation as to have lost all likeness

to its original self." [1] Superstitions connected with it
are myriad, and Folkard gives two Greek sayings that
are interesting. It was the custom among them to
border the garden with parsley and rue, and from this
arose an idiom, when any undertaking was talked of,
but not begun, " Oh! we are only at the Parsley and
Rue." Parsley was used, too, to strew on graves, and
hence came a saying " to be in need of parsley," signifying to be at death's door. Mr Friend quotes an English
adage that " Fried parsley will bring a man to his saddle
and a woman to her grave," but says that he has heard
no reason given for this strange and apparently pointless
dictum. Plutarch tells of a panic created in a Greek
force, marching against the enemy, by their suddenly
meeting some mules laden with parsley, which the
soldiers looked upon as an evil omen; and W. Jones,
in his " Crowns and Coronations," says, " Timoleon
nearly caused a mutiny in his army because he chose his
crown to be of parsley, when his soldiers wished it to
be of the pine or pitch tree." In many parts of England
it is considered unlucky, and I quote from a paper read
before the Devon and Exeter Gardeners' Association in
1897. " It is one of the longest seeds to lie in the
ground before germinating; it has been said to go to
the Devil and back again nine times before it comes up.
And many people have a great objection to planting parsley, saying if you do there will sure to be a death in the
Family within twelve months." It is only fair to add
that this delightful lapse into folk-lore comes in the
midst of most excellent and practical advice for its cultivation. " Quite recently (in 1883) a gentleman, living
near Southampton, told his gardener to sow some Parsley
seed. The man, however, refused, saying that it would
be a bad day's work to him if ever he brought Parsley
seed into the house. He said that he would not mind

[1] Plant Lore and Garden Craft of Shakespeare.

bringing a plant or two and throwing them down, that his master might pick them up if he chose, but he would not bring them to him for anything." [1]

The "earliest known, really original work on gardening, written in English," is, Miss Amherst says, "a treatise in verse," by Mayster Ion Gardener. It consists of a prologue and eight divisions, and one of these is devoted to "Perselye" alone. The manuscript in the Library of Trinity College, Cambridge, that she quotes from, was written about 1440, but it is thought that the poem is older. Parsley was "much used in all sortes of meates, both boyled, roasted and fryed, stewed, etc., and being green it serveth to lay upon sundry meates. It is also shred and stopped into powdered beefe. . . . The roots are put into broth, or boyled or stewed with a legge of Mutton . . . and are of a very good rellish, but the roots must be young and of the first year's growth." [2]

The seeds of parsley were sometimes put into cheese to flavour it, and Timbs ("Things not generally Known") tells this anecdote : "Charlemagne once ate cheese mixed with parsley seeds at a bishop's palace, and liked it so much that ever after he had two cases of such cheese sent yearly to Aix-la-Chapelle."

In the edition of Tusser's "Five Hundred Points of Good Husbandry," edited by Mavor, it is noted, "Skim-milk cheese, however, might be advantageously mixed with seeds, as is the practice in Holland." Though not strictly relevant, these lines taken by Mrs Milne-Home ("Stray Leaves from a Border-Garden") from the family records of the Earls of Marchmont, must find place. They were written by a boy of eight or nine, on the occasion of his elder brother's birthday.

This day from parsley-bed, I'm sure,
Was dug my elder brother, Moore,

[1] Friend.   [2] Parkinson.

Had Papa dug me up before him,
So many now would not adore him,
But hang it! he's but onely one
And if he trips off, I'm Sr John.

Horse-radish was treated here as a seasoning, but *radish* is counted among vegetables proper.

SAGE (*Salvia officinalis*).

Sage is for sustenance
  That should man's life sustaine,
For I do stil lie languishing
  Continually in paine,
And shall doe still until I die,
  Except thou favour show,
My paine and all my grievous smart,
  Ful wel you do it know.
      Handful of Pleasant Delights.

And then againe he turneth to his playe,
To spoyle the pleasures of the Paradise,
The wholesome saulge and lavender still gray.
      Muiopotmos.—SPENSER.

Sage is one of those sympathetic plants that feel the fortunes of their owners; and Mr Friend says that a Buckinghamshire farmer told him his recent personal experience. "At one time he was doing badly, and the Sage began to wither, but, as soon as the tide turned, the plant began to thrive again." Most of the Continental names of the plant are like the botanical one of *Salvia*, from "*Salvo*," to save or heal, and its high reputation in medicine lasted for ages. The Arabians valued it, and the medical school of Salerno summed up its surpassing merits in the line, *Cur morietur homo cui Salvia crescit in horto?* (How can a man die who grows sage in his garden?) Perhaps this originated the English saying:—

He that would live for aye
Must eat Sage in May.

Parkinson mentions that it is " Much used of many in the month of May fasting," with butter and parsley, and

is "held of most" to conduce to health.   "It healeth
the pricking of the fishe called in Latine *pastinaca marina*,
whych is like unto a flath, with venomous prickes, about
his tayle.   It maketh hayre blacke; it is good for
woundis."[1] The "Grete Herball" contains a remedy for
Lethargy or Forgetfulness, which consists of making a
decoction "of tutsan, of smalage and of sauge," and
bathing the back of the head with it.

Pepys notes that in a little churchyard between
Gosport and Southampton the custom prevailed of
sowing the graves with sage.   This is rather curious,
as it has never been one of the plants specially connected
with death.

Evelyn sums up its "Noble Properties" thus: "In
short 'tis a Plant endu'd with so many and wonderful
Properties, as that the assiduous use of it is said to
render Men *Immortal*.   We cannot therefore but allow
the tender *Summities* of the young Leaves, but princi-
pally the Flowers in our *Sallet*; yet so as not to
domineer. . . . 'Tis credibly affirmed, that the *Dutch*
for some time drove a very lucrative Trade with the
dry'd Leves of what is called *Sage of Vertue* and *Guernsey
Sage*. . . . Both the Chineses and Japaneses are great
admirers of that sort of Sage, and so far prefer it to
their own Tea . . . that for what *Sage* they purchase of
the *Dutch*, they give triple the quantity of the choicest
Tea in exchange."

"Frytures" (fritters) of Sage are described as having
place at banquets in the Middle Ages (Russell's "Boke
of Nurture").   Besides these other uses the seeds of sage
like parsley seeds were used to flavour cheese.   Gay
refers to this :—

> Marbled with Sage,
> The hardening cheese she pressed,

and to "Sage cheese," too, and Timbs says, "The

[1] Turner.

practice of mixing sage and other herbs with cheese
was common among the Romans."

SAVORY (*Satureia*).

> Some Camomile doth not amiss,
> With Savoury and some tansy.
>
> *Muses Elysium.*

> Here's flowers for you,
> Hot Lavender, Mints, Savory, Marjoram.
>
> *Winter's Tale*, iv. 4.

> Sound savorie, and bazil, hartie-hale,
> Fat Colwortes and comforting Perseline.
> Cold Lettuce and refreshing Rosmarine.
>
> *Muiopotmos.*

Savory, satureia, was once supposed to belong to the
satyrs. "Mercury claims the dominion over this herb.
Keep it dry by you all the year, if you love yourself
and your ease, and it is a hundred pounds to a penny
if you do not." Culpepper follows this advice with a
long list of ailments, for all of which this herb is an
excellent remedy. Summer savory (*S. hortensis*) and
winter savory (*S. Montana*) are the only kinds considered in England as a rule, though Gerarde further
mentions "a stranger," which, "because it groweth
plentifully upon the rough cliffs of the Tyrrhenian Sea
in Italie, called Saint Julian rocke," is named after the
saint, *Satureia Sancti Juliani.* In other countries summer
savory used to be strewn upon the dishes as we strew
parsley, and served with peas or beans ; rice, wheat
and sometimes the dried herb was "boyled among
pease to make pottage." Winter savory used to be
dried and powdered and mixed with grated bread,
"to breade their meate, be it fish or flesh, to give it a
quicker rellish." Here Parkinson breaks off to deliver
a severe reproof to "this delicate age of ours, which is
not pleased with anything almost that is not pleasant

to the palate," and therefore neglects many viands which would be of great benefit.   Both savories are occasionally used more or less in the way he suggests, winter savory being the favourite.   In Cotton's sequel to the "Complete Angler," a "handful of sliced horse-radish-root, with a handsome little faggot of rosemary, thyme and winter savoury" is recommended in the directions for "dressing a trout."   One of the virtues attributed to both savories by the old herbalists is still agreed to by some gardeners : "A shoot of it rubbed on wasp or bee stings instantly gives relief."

SORREL (*Rumex*).

Simplest growth of Meadow-sweet or Sorrel
Such as the summer-sleepy Dryads weave.

Swinburne.

Cresses that grow where no man may them see,
And sorrel, untorn by the dew-claw'd stag ;
Pipes will I fashion of the syrinx flag.

Endymion.

There flourish'd starwort and the branching beet
The sorrel acid and the mallow sweet

The Salad.

Here curling sorrel that again
We use in hot diseases
The medicinable mallow here . . .

Muses Elysium.

Sorrel and mallow seem to have been associates anciently, perhaps because it was thought that the virtues of the one would counterbalance those of the other.   "From May to August the meadows are often ruddy with the sorrel, the red leaves of which point out the graves of the Irish rebels who fell at Tara Hill in the 'Ninety-eight,' the local tradition asserting that the plants sprang from the patriots' blood."[1]   The Spaniards used to call sorrel, Agrelles

[1] Folkard.

THE LAVENDER WALK AT STRATHFIELDSAYE.

and Azeda, and the French Aigrette and Surelle. In England it used to be "eaten in manner of a Spinach tart or eaten as meate," and the French and Dutch still do, I believe, and at anyrate did quite lately, use it as spinach. Sorrel was often added by them to herb-patience when that was used as a pot-herb, and was said to give it an excellent flavour. The same recipe has been tried and approved in England as well as (a little) sorrel cooked with turnip-tops or spinach ; the former of these dishes is said to be good and the second certainly is. Evelyn thought that sorrel imparted " so grateful a quickeness to the salad that it should never be left out," and De la Quintinye says that in France besides being mixed in salads it is generally used in Bouillons or thin Broths. Of the two kinds, Garden Sorrel, *Rumex Acetosa*, and French Sorrel, *R. Scutatus*, either may be used indifferently in cooking, though some people decidedly prefer the French kind. Mrs Roundell says that sorrel carefully prepared can be cooked in any of the ways recommended for spinach, but that it should be cooked as soon as it is picked, and if this is impossible must be revived in water before being cooked.

TARRAGON (*Artemisia Dracunculus*).

" Tarragon is cherished in gardens. . . . Ruellius and such others have reported many strange tales hereof scarce worth the noting, saying that the seede of flaxe put into a radish roote or sea onion, and so set, doth bring forth this herbe Tarragon." This idea was apparently still current though discredited by the less superstitious in Gerarde's time. Parkinson mentions a great dispute between ancient herbalists as to the identity of the flower called Chysocoma by Dioscorides. After quoting various opinions and depreciating some of them he approves the decision of Molinaus that Tarragon was the plant. He describes it "in leaves . . . like unto the ordinary long-leafed Hisope . . . of the colour of *Cyperus*, of a taste not unpleasant which is somewhat austere with the sweetnesse." It is a native of Siberia, but has long been cultivated in France, and the name is a corruption of the French *Esdragon* and means "Little Dragon." Though no reason for this war-like title is obvious, the name is practically the same in several other countries. The leaves were good pickled, and it is altogether a fine aromatic herb for soups and salads. Vinegars for salads and sauce used often in earlier days to be "aromatized" by steeping in them rosemary, gilliflowers, barberries and so forth, but the only herb used for this purpose at the present time is tarragon. Tarragon vinegar can still be easily obtained. "The volatile essential oil of tarragon is chemically identical with that of anise" (Fernie).

THYME (*Thymus vulgaris*).

The bees on the bells of thyme
. . . .
Were as silent as ever old Timolus was
Listening to my sweet pipings.

Pan's Music—SHELLEY.

In my garden grew plenty of thyme,
It would flourish by night and by day,
O'er the wall came a lad, he took all that I had,
And stole my thyme away.

O! And I was a damsel so fair,
But fairer I wished to appear,
So I washed me in milk, and I dressed me in silk,
And put the sweet thyme in my hair.

Devonshire Songs.

Beneath your feet,
Thyme that for all your bruising smells more sweet.

N. HOPPER.

Some from the fen bring reeds, wild thyme from downs,
Some from a grove, the bay that poets crowns.

Br. Pastorals, book ii.

> Here, dancing feet fall still,
> Here, where wild thyme and sea-pinks brave wild weather.
> N. Hopper

> O ! Cupid was that saucy boy,
> Who furrows deeply drew.
> He broke soil, destroyed the soil
> Of wild thyme wet with dew.
> Before his feet, the field was sweet
> With flowers and grasses green,
> Behind, turn'd down, and bare and brown
> By Cupid's coulter keen.
> *Devonshire Songs.*

"Among the Greeks, thyme denoted graceful elegance of the Attic style," and was besides an emblem of activity. " 'To smell of Thyme' was therefore an expression of praise, applied to those whose style was admirable" (Folkard). In the days of chivalry, when activity was a virtue very highly rated, ladies used "to embroider their knightly lovers' scarves with the figure of a bee hovering about a sprig of thyme." [1] In the south of France wild thyme or *Ferigoule* is a symbol of advanced Republicanism, and tufts of it were sent with the summons to a meeting to members of a society holding those views. Gerarde, in his writings, plainly shows that he and his contemporaries did *not* indiscriminately call all plants " herbs," but distinguished them with thought and care. "*Ælianus* seemeth to number wild time among the floures. *Dionysius Junior* (saith he) comming into the city Locris in Italy, possessed most of the houses of the city, and did strew them with roses, wild time and other such kinds of floures. Yet Virgil, in the Second Eclogue of his Bucolicks doth most manifestly testifie that wilde Time is an herbe." Here he translates :—

> Thestilis, for mower's tyr'd with parching heate,
> Garlike, wild Time, strong smelling herbs doth beate.

Modern opinion confirms the view that *Thymus capitatus*

[1] " Flora Symbolica." *Ingram.*

was the thyme of the ancients. The affection of bees for thyme has often been noticed, and the " fine flavour to the honey of Mount Hymettus "[1] is said to be due to this plant. Evelyn speaks of it as having " a most agreeable *odor*," and a " considerable quantity being frequently, by the Hollanders, brought from *Maltha*, and other places in the *Streights*, who sell it at home, and in *Flanders* for strewing amongst the *Sallets* and Ragouts ; and call it *All-Sauce*." Gerarde divides the garden thyme (*T. vulgaris*) and Wild Thyme or Mother of Thyme (*T. serpyllum*) into two chapters, but Parkinson takes them together and describes eleven kinds, including Lemmon Thyme, which has the " sent of a Pomecitron or Lemmon "; and " Guilded or embrodered Tyme," whose leaves have " a variable mixture of green and yellow." Abercrombie's information is always given in a concentrated form. " An ever-green, sweet-scented, fine-flavoured, aromatic, under-shrub, young tops used for various kitchen purposes."

Viper's Grass or Scorzonera (*Scorzonera Hispanica*).

The virtues of this herb were known, but not much regarded, before " Monardus,[2] a famous physician in *Sivell*," published a book in which was " set downe that a Moore, a bond-slave, did help those that were bitten of that venomous beast or Viper . . . which they of Catalonia, where they breed in abundance, call in their language *Escuersos* (from whence *Scorsonera* is derived), with the juice of the herb, and the root given them to eate," and states that this would effect a cure when other well-authorised remedies failed. " The rootes hereof, being preserved with sugar, as I have done often, doe eate almost as delicate as the Eringus roote." Evelyn is loud in its praise. It is " a very sweete and pleasant *Sallet*,

[1] Hogg, " The Vegetable Kingdom and its Products."   [2] Parkinson.

being laid to soak out the Bitterness, then peel'd may be eaten raw or *condited*; but, best of all, stew'd with *Marrow, Spice, Wine*. . . . They likewise may bake, fry or boil them; a more excellent Root there is hardly growing." As "Spanish Salsify" it is much recommended by other writers.

WOOD-SORREL (*Oxalis Acetosella*).

Who from the tumps with bright green masses clad,
Plucks the Wood-Sorrel with its light green leaves,
Heart shaped and triply folded; and its root
Creeping like beaded coral.

CHARLOTTE SMITH.

The Wood-Sorrel has many pretty names: Alleluia, Hearts, *Pain de Coucou, Oseille de Bûcheron*; in Italy, *Juliola*. Wood-Sorrel is a plant of considerable interest. It has put forward strong claims to be identified with St Patrick's shamrock, and it has been painted, Mr Friend says, "in the foreground of pictures by the old Italian painters, notably Fra Angelico." For the explanation of the names: "It is called by the Apothecaries in their shoppes *Alleluia* and *Lugula*, the one because about that time it is in flower, when *Alleluja* in antient times was wont to be sung in the Churches; the other came corruptly from *Juliola*, as they of Calabria in Naples doe call it." By the "Alleluja sung in the churches," Parkinson means the Psalms, from Psalm cxiii. to Psalm cxvii. (and including these two), for they end with "Hallelujah," and were specially appointed to be sung between Easter and Whitsuntide.

"It is called Cuckowbreade, either because the Cuckowes delight to feed thereon, or that it beginneth to flower when the Cuckow beginneth to utter her voyce." Another name was Stubwort, from its habit of growing over old "stubs" or stumps of trees, and in Wales it was called Fairy Bells, because people thought that the music which called the elves to "moonlight dance and revelry" came from the swinging of the tiny bells. The Latin name is a reminder that oxalic acid is obtained from this plant.

As Evelyn includes it amongst his salad herbs, I mention it here, though feeling bound to add that anyone must be a monster who could regard the graceful leaves and trembling, delicately-veined bells of this plant, full of poetry, with any other sentiment than that of passive admiration!

CHAPTER II

The wyfe of Bath was so wery, she had no wyl to walk ;
She toke the Priores by the honde, " Madam, wol ye stalk
Pryvely into the garden to se the herbis growe ? "
. . . And forth on they wend
Passing forth softly into the herbery.

Prologue to Beryn—URRY's Edition

ALEXANDERS (*Smyrnum Olusatrium*).

Alexanders, Allisanders, the black Pot-herb or Wild
Horse-Parsley, as it is variously called, grows naturally
near the sea, and has often been seen growing wild near
old buildings. The Italians call it *Herba Alexandrina*,
according to some writers, because it was supposed
originally to have come from Alexandria; according to
others, because its[1] old name was *Petroselinum Alex-
andrinum*, or *Alexandrina*, " so-called of *Alexander*, the
finder thereof." The leaves are " cut into many parcells
like those of Smallage," but are larger; the seeds have
an " aromaticall and spicy smell " ; the root is like a little
radish and good to be eaten, and if broken or cut
" there issueth a juice that quickly waxeth thicke, having
in it a sharpe bitterness, like in taste unto Myrrh."
The upper parts of the roots (being the tenderest) and
leaves were used in broth; the young tops make an
" excellent Vernal Pottage," and may be eaten as salad, by
themselves or " in composition in the Spring, or, if they
be blanched, in the Winter." They were chiefly recom-

---

[1] Britten, "Dictionary of English Plant-Names."

mended for the time of Lent, in a day when Lent was
more strictly kept than it is now, because they are
supposed to go well with fish.   Alexanders resemble
celery, by which it has been almost entirely sup-
planted, and if desired as food should be sown every
year, for though it continues to grow, it produces
nothing fit for the table after the second year.   Pliny
says it should be " digged or delved over once or twice,
yea, and at any time from the blowing of the western
wind Favonius in Februarie, until the later Equinox in
September be past."   The reference to Favonius reminds one of those lines of exquisite freshness translated
from Leonidas.

> 'Tis time to sail—the swallow's note is heard!
> Who chattering down the soft west wind is come.
> The fields are all a-flower, the waves are dumb,
> Which ersts the winnowing blast of winter stirred.
>
> Loose cable, friend, and bid your anchor rise,
> Crowd all your canvas at Priapus' hest,
> Who tells you from your harbours, " Now, 'twere best,
> Sailor, to sail upon your merchandise."

ANGELICA (*Archangelica officinalis*).

> Contagious aire, ingendring pestilence,
> Infects not those that in their mouths have ta'en,
> Angelica that happy Counterbane,
> Sent down from heav'n by some celestial scout,
> As well the name and nature both avow't.
> *Du Bartas*—SYLVESTER'S TRANSLATION, 1641.
>
> And Master-wort, whose name Dominion wears,
> With her, who an Angelick Title bears.
> *Of Plants*, book ii.—COWLEY.

As these lines declare, Angelica was believed to have
sprung from a heavenly origin, and greatly were its
powers revered.   Parkinson says, " All Christian nations
likewise in their appellations hereof follow the Latine
name as near as their Dialect will permit, onely in Sussex

ANGELICA

they call the wilde Kinde Kex, and the weavers wind their yarne on the dead stalkes." The Laplanders crowned their poets with it, believing that the odour inspired them, and they also thought that the use of it "strengthens life." The roots hung round the neck " are available against witchcraft and inchantments," so Gerarde says, and thereby makes a concession to popular superstition, which he very rarely does. A piece of the root held in the mouth drives away infection of pestilence, and is good against all poisons, mad dogs or venomous beasts ! Parkinson puts it first and foremost in a list of specially excellent medicinal herbs that he makes " for the profit and use of Country Gentlewomen and others," and writes : " The whole plante, both leafe, roote, and seede is of an excellent comfortable sent, savour and taste." No wonder with such powers that it gained its name. Angelica comes into a remedy for a wound from an *arque-busade* or arquebuse, called *Eau d'Arquebusade*, which was first mentioned by Phillippe de Comines in his account of the battle of Morat, 1476. " The French still prepare it very carefully from a great number of aromatic herbs. In England, where it is the *Aqua Vulneria* of the Pharmacopœias, the formula is : Dried mint, angelica tops and wormwood, angelica seeds, oil of juniper and spirit of rosemary distilled with rectified spirit and water (Timbs)." It must be borne in mind that Timbs wrote some time ago, and that the knowledge of modern French scientists, like that of our own, has increased since then.

Although it is of no value in medicine (it is next to none when cultivated) our garden angelica also grows wild, and can be safely eaten. Gerarde is amusing on this point. He says it grows in an " Island in the North called Island (Iceland ?). It is eaten of the inhabitants, the barke being pilled off, as we understand by some that have travelled into Island, who were sometimes compelled to eate hereof for want of other food ; and they report that it hath a good and pleasant taste *to them that are hungry*." The last words are significant! Formerly, the leaf-stalks were blanched, and eaten as celery is, but now they are chiefly used, candied, for dessert. The art of candying seems to have been brought closer to perfection abroad than at home in Turner's time, for he says: " The rootes are now condited in Danske, for a friend of mine in London, called Maister Aleyne, a merchant man, who hath ventured over to Danske, sent me a little vessel of these, well condited with honey, very excellent good. Wherefore they that would have anye Angelica maye speake to the Marchauntes of Danske, who can provide them enough." The fruit is used to flavour *Chartreuse* and other " cordials."

BLITES (*Blitum*).

Dr Prior confirms Evelyn, in calling *Bonus Henricus* Blites, but the older herbalists seem to have given this name to another plant of the same tribe, the *Chenopodiaceæ*, because they treat of *Blites* and *Bonus Henricus* in separate chapters. Parkinson is very uncomplimentary to them. " Blitum are of the species Amaranthum, Flower Gentle. They are used as arrach, eyther boyled of itself or stewed, which they call Loblolly. . . . It is altogether insipid and without taste. The unsavouriness whereof hath in many countries grown into a proverb, or by-word, to call dull, slow or lazy persons by that name." The context points to the nickname coming from " Blites," but no such term of reproach now exists, though the contemptuous *sobriquet* " Loblolly-boy " is sometimes seen in old-fashioned nautical novels. Blites were said to be hurtful to the eyes, a belief that draws a scathing remark from Gerarde, " I have heard many old wives say to their servants, ' Gather no Blites to put in my pottage, for they are not good for the eyesight'; whence they had those words I know not, it may be of some doctor that never went to school." Culpepper mentions that wild blites " the fishes are delighted with, and it is a good and usual bait, for fishes will bite fast enough at them if you have but wit enough to catch when they bite." Altogether this insipid vegetable gives scope for a good many sharp things to be said.

Blitum capitatum, usually known as strawberry-spinach, is sometimes grown in flower gardens.

BLOODWORT (*Lapathum Sanguineum*).

The modern Latin name for this dock is *Rumex Sanguineus*, but Gesner had a more imposing title, *Sanguis draconis herba* (Dragon's blood plant). These names are, of course, derived from the crimson colour of its veins, and are the finest thing about it. The little notice it does get is not unmixed praise. "Among the sorts of pot-herbes, Blood-worte hath always been accounted a principall one, although I *doe not see any great reason therein.*" This is Parkinson's opinion, but the italics are mine.

BUCK'S-HORNE (*Senebiera Coronopus*).

As true as steel,
As Plantage to the moon.
Troilus and Cressida, iii. 2.

And plantain ribb'd that heals the reaper's wound,
And marg'ram sweet, in shepherds' posies found.
The School-Mistress.—SHENSTONE.

Buck's-horne is distinct from Buckshorn Plantain (*Plantago Coronopus*), but it is the latter which is chiefly interesting, and which is meant here. In Evelyn's day the Latin name was *Cornu Cervinum*, and other names are *Herba Stella*, Herb Ivy and *Corne de Cerf.* Some kinds of plantain were considered good for wounds, but the saying that "plantage" is true to the moon is hard to solve. Buck's-horne is a plant that has gone altogether out of fashion. In 1577 Hill wrote, "What care and skil is required in the sowing and ordering of the Buck's-horne, Strawberries and Mustardseede,"—and how odd it looks now to see it coupled with the two other names, as a cherished object to spend pains upon! Le Quintinye says that the leaves, when tender, were used in "Sallad Furnitures . . . and the little Birds are very greedy of them." It used to be held profitable for agues if "the rootes, with the rest of the herb," were hung about the necke, "as nine to men and seven to women and children, but this as many other are idle amulets of no worth or value . . . yet, since, it hath been reported to me for a certaintie that the leaves of Buck'shorne Plantane laid to their sides that have an ague, will suddenly ease the fit, as if it had been done by witcherie; the leaves and rootes also beaten with some bay salt and applied to the wrestes, worketh the same effects, which I hold to be more reasonable and proper." Parkinson is very ready to lay down the law as to the limits of empiricism. He is very severe about a superstition connected with Mugwort, but though the same tradition exists of plantain, and (under Mugwort) he quotes Mizaldus as mentioning it, he says nothing about this folly here. Aubrey, however, gives an account of it in his " Miscellanies." "The last summer, on the day of St John Baptist, I accidently was walking in the pasture behind Montague House; it was twelve o'clock. I saw there about two or three and twenty young women, most of them well habited, on their knees, very busie, as if they had been weeding. I could not presently learn what the matter was; at last a young man told me that they were looking for a coal under the root of a plantain, to put under their heads that night, and they should dream who would be their husbands. It was to be found that day and hour." This miraculous "coal" also preserved the wearer from all sorts of diseases.

CAMOMILE (*Anthemis nobilis*).

Diana !
Have I (to make thee crowns) been gathering still,
Fair-cheek'd Eteria's yellow camomile?

Br. Pastorals.

Flowers of the field and windflowers springing glad
—In airs Sicilian, and the golden bough
Of sacred Plato, shining in its worth.
. . . With phlox of Phœdimas and chamomile,
The crinkled ox-eye of Antagoras.

Trans. from Meleager.

The healthful balm and mint from their full laps do fly,
The scentful camomile.

Polyolbion, Song xv.

Falstaff. Though the Camomile the more it is trodden on the faster it grows, yet youth the more it is wasted the sooner it wears.—1 *Henry IV*. ii. 4.

The camomile is dedicated to St Anne, mother of the Virgin Mary, and Mr Friend thinks that the Latin name of wild camomile, *Matricaria*, comes from a "fanciful derivation" of this word, from *mater* and *cara*, or "Beloved Mother." The name camomile itself is derived from a Greek word meaning "earth-apples," and its pleasant, refreshing smell is rather like that of ripe apples. The Spaniards call it *Manzanilla*, "a little apple." It was grown "both for pleasure and profit, both inward and outward diseases, both for the sicke and the sound," and was "planted of the rootes in alleys, in walks, and on banks to sit on, for that the more it is trodden upon and pressed down in dry weather, the closer it groweth and the better it will thrive." This was a common belief in earlier days, as Falstaff's remark shows.

Culpepper is as trenchant as usual on the subject.

" Nichersor, saith the Egyptians, dedicated it to the sun, because it cured agues, and they were like enough to do it, for they were the arrantest apes in their religion I have ever read of." Why his indignation is so much excited is not clear, but probably it is because Agues (being watery diseases) were under the moon, and therefore they should have dedicated a herb that cured agues to the Moon. However, he holds to the view that camomile is good for all agues, although it is an herb of the sun —who has nothing to do with such diseases, as a rule. Turner criticises Amatus Lusitanus with some shrewdness. This writer, who had apparently taken upon him to teach " Spanyardes, Italians, Frenchmen and Germans the name of Herbes in their tongues, writeth that Camomile is commonlye knowne," and with this bald statement contented himself. " Wherefore it is lykely he knoweth nether of both [kinds of Camomile]. Wherefore he had done better to have sayde, ' I do knowe nether of both, then thus shortly to passe by them.' Camomile is still officinal, and is used for fomentations. ' If taken internally it should be infused with cold water, as heat dissipates the oil.' "

Feverfew is so nearly related to camomile that it may be mentioned here. Indeed some writers call it " a Wild Camomile," and give it *Matricaria Parthenum* for a Latin name. Most botanists, however, place it " in the genus *Pyrethrum*." Mr Britten calls it *Pyrethrum Parthenium*. " Feverfew " comes from " febrifuge," for it was supposed to have wonderful power to drive away fevers and agues ; and it is still a favourite remedy with village people. Nora Hopper brings it in among the fairies :—

> There's many feet on the moor to-night,
> And they fall so light as they turn and pass,
> So light and true, that they shake no dew,
> From the featherfew and the Hungry-Grass.
>
> *The Fairy Music.*

Cardoons (*Cynara Cardunculus*).

This plant is also called Spanish Cardoon or Cardoon of Tours. It is a kind of artichoke "which becomes a truly gigantic herbaceous vegetable. The tender stalks of the inner leaves are sometimes blanched and stewed, or used in soups and salads"; but it is much less used in England than on the Continent. Cardoons are said to yield a good yellow dye.

Clary (*Salvia Sclarea*).

Percely, clarey and eke sage,
And all other herbage.
                                    John Gardener.

"Clary, or more properly Clear-eyes," which indicates one of its supposed chief virtues plainly enough. Wild Clary was called *Oculus Christi*, and was even more valued than the garden kind. Clary was once "used for making wine, which resembles Frontignac, and is remarkable for its narcotic qualities."[1] It was also added to "Ale and Beere in these Northern regions (I think the Netherlands are meant here) to make it the more heady." The young plant itself was eaten, and an approved way of dressing it was to put it in an omelette "made up with cream, fried in sweet butter" and eaten with sugar and the juice of oranges or lemons. It is now sometimes used to season soups, and Hogg tells us that it was used "in Austria as a perfume; in confectionery, and to the jellies of fruits, it communicates the flavour of pine-apple." The herbalists speak of a plant called Yellow Clary or "Jupiter's Distaff," and Mr Britten suggests that this was *Phlomus fruticosa*.

[1] Timbs.

Dittander (*Lepidium Latifolium*).

Dittander or Pepperwort grows wild in a few places in England, but was once cultivated. It was sometimes used as " a sauce or sallet to meate, but is too hot, bitter and strong for everyone's taste." These qualities have gained it the names of Poor Man's Pepper, and from Tusser, Garden Ginger. Culpepper's opinion is briefly expressed: " Here is another martial herb for you, make much of it." It is so " hot and fiery sharpe" that it is said to raise a blister on the hand of anyone who holds it for a while, and *therefore* (on homœopathic principles) it was recommended " to take away marks, scarres . . . and the marks of burning with fire or Iron."

Elecampane (*Inula Helenium*).

Elecampane, the beauteous Helen's flower,
Mingles among the rest her silver store.

RAPIN.

" Some think it took the name from the teares of *Helen*, from whence it sprang, which is a fable ; others that she had her hands full of this herbe when *Paris* carried her away ; others say it was so called because *Helen* first found it available against the bitings and stingings of venomous beasts; and others thinke that it tooke the name from the Island Helena, where the best was found to grow." Parkinson gives a wide choice for opinions on the origin of Elecampane, the two first "fables" are very picturesque. The radiant gold of the flowers would be gorgeous but beautiful, in a loose bunch, in a meadow, though in-doors they would be apt to look big and glaring. Gerarde speaks of them being "in their braverie in June and July," and adds that the root "is marvellous good for many things." Since the days of Helen the fairies have laid hold of the plant, and another

name for it (in Denmark) is Elf-Dock. Elecampane
has had a great reputation since the days of Pliny, and
was considered specially good for coughs, asthma and
shortness of breath. Elecampane lozenges were much
recommended, and the root was candied and eaten as a
sweetmeat till comparatively lately. It is said to have
antiseptic qualities, and according to Dr Fernie has been
used in Spain as a surgical dressing.

FENUGREEK (*Trigonella fœnum græcum*).

Fenugreek " hath many leaves, but three alwayes set
together on a foot-stalke, almost round at the ends, a
little dented about the sides, greene above and grayish
underneath ; from the joynts with the leaves come forth
white flowers, and after them, crooked, flattish long
hornes, small pointed, with yellowish cornered seedes
within them." This description is very exact, and,
indeed, the conspicuous horn-like pods, singularly large
for the size of the plant, are its most marked charac-
teristic. Turner says : " This herbe is called in Greek
Keratitis, y^t is horned, aigō keros y^t is gotes horne, and
ŏ onkeros, that is cows horne." Fenugreek was a
Favourite of the " antients," and Folkard gives an
account of a festival held by Antiochus Epiphanus, the
Syrian king, of which one feature was a procession,
where boys carried golden dishes containing frankincense, myrrh and saffron, and two hundred women,
out of golden watering-pots, sprinkled perfume on the
assembled guests. All who went to watch the games
in the gymnasium were anointed with some perfume
from fifteen gold dishes, which held saffron, amaracus,
lilies, cinnamon, spikenard, fenugreek, etc. In England it was used for more prosaic purposes, " Galen and
others say that they were eaten as Lupines, and the
Egyptians and others eate the seedes yet to this day as

Pulse or meate." The herb, he continues, he has never heard of as being used in England, because it was very little grown, but the seed was used in medicine. Gerarde gives us one of its pleasantest preparations as a drug. In old diseases of the chest, without a fever, fat dates are to be boiled with it, with a great quantitie of honey. In 1868 Rhind[1] writes that the seeds are no longer given in medicine, and but rarely used in "fomentations and cataplasms." Since that date, I should imagine, it is even more rarely used. Fenugreek was at one time prescribed by veterinary surgeons for horses.

GOOD KING HENRY (*Chenopodium Bonus Henricus*).

This plant is otherwise known as Fat Hen, Shoe-maker's Heels, English Mercury, or as Evelyn says, Blite. He begins with praise: "The Tops may be eaten as Sparagus or sodden in Pottage, and as a very salubrious Esculent. There is both a white and red, much us'd in Spain and Italy"; but he finishes lamely for all his praise: "'tis insipid enough." Gerarde says: "It is called of the Germans *Guter Heinrick*, of a certaine good qualitie it hath," and its name is much the most interesting thing about it. Various writers have tried to attach it to our successive kings of that name, with a want of ingenuousness and ingenuity equally deplorable. Grimm[2] traces it back till he finds that this was one of the many plants appropriated to Heinz or Heinrich—the "household goblin," who plays tricks on the maids or helps them with their work, and asks no more than a bowl of cream set over-night for his reward—who, in fact, holds much the same place as our Robin Good-fellow holds here.

[1] "History of the Vegetable Kingdom."
[2] Teutonic Mythology.

HERB-PATIENCE (*Rumex Patienta*).

Sequestered leafy glades,
That through the dimness of their twilight show
Large dock-leaves, spiral fox-gloves, or the glow
Of the wild cat's-eyes, or the silvery stems
Of delicate birch trees, in long grass which hems
A little brook.

Calidore—KEATS.

La *tulipe* est pour la fierté,
Pour le malheur la *patience*.

La Petite Corbeille.

The Herb-Patience does not grow in every man's garden.
Proverb.

Herb-Patience was also called Patience-Dock or
Monk's Rhubarb. The French call Water-Dock,
Patience d'eau and *Parelle des Marais*, so the name of
the quality that is, in nursery rhyme, a "virtue," and
a "grace," clings to this dock! Parkinson compares it
unfavourably with Bastard Rhubarb, though he says
the root is often used in "diet beere"; but Gerarde
calls it an "excellent, wholesome pot-herbe," and relates
a tale, in which responsibilities are treated with such
delightful airiness that it must be repeated here. He
begins by saying that he himself is "no graduate, but a
country scholler," but hopes his "good meaning will be
well taken, considering I doe my best, not doubting but
some of greater learning will perfect that which I have
begun, according to my small skill, especially the ice
being broken unto him and the wood rough-hewed to
his hands." Nevertheless, he (who dictates on these
matters, to a great extent, through his Herbal) thinks
that the learned may gain occasionally from his knowledge. "One *John Bennet*, a chirurgion, of Maidstone in
Kent, a man as slenderly learned as myselfe," undertook
to cure a butcher's boy of an ague. "He promised him
a medicine, and for want of one for the present (he him-

selfe confessed unto me) he tooke out of his garden three
or four leaves of this plant" and administered them in
ale, with entire success. "Whose blunt attempt may
set an edge upon some sharper wit and greater judgment
in the faculties of plants." Any anticipation that his
experiment might lead to disaster does not seem to have
troubled him! The root of Patience-Dock "boiled in
the water of *Carduus Benedictus*" was also given at a
venture for an ague, and this experiment was tried by
"a worshipfull gentlewoman, mistresse Anne Wylbraham,
upon divers of her poore Neighbours, with good success."
Mistress Anne Wylbraham must have been a woman of
temerity!

Garden-patience used to be a good deal cultivated as
spinach, but is now very much ignored, partly because few
people know how to cook it. The leaves should be
used early in the spring while they are still tender, and
the flavour will be very much improved if about a
fourth part of common sorrel is added to them. This
way of dressing patience-dock was very popular in
Sweden, and is described as "forming an excellent
spinach dish." Patience is sometimes spoken of as
"passions," but this name properly belongs to *Polygonum
Bistorta*, the leaves of which were the principal
ingredient in a herb-pudding, formerly eaten on Good
Friday in the North of England. Parkinson also speaks
in this chapter of the "true rhubarb of Rhapontick,"
which has "leaves of sad or dark-greene colour . . . of
a fine tart or sourish taste, much more pleasant than the
garden or wood sorrell." Dr Thornton, however, says
that Parkinson was mistaken, and that the first seeds of
true rhubarb were sent "by the great Boerhaave to our
famous gardener, Miller, in 1759 "—more than a hundred
years later. Very soon after Miller had it, rhubarb was
cultivated in many parts of England and in certain
localities in Scotland.

A FIELD OF ENGLISH RHUBARB

HOREHOUND (*Marrubium vulgare*).

Here hore-hound 'gainst the mad dog's ill
By biting, never failing.
Muses Elysium.

Pale hore-hound, which he holds of most especiall use.
Polyolbion, Song xiii.

Folkard says that horehound is one of the five plants
stated by the Mishna to be the " bitter herbs," which
the Jews were ordered to take for the Feast of the
Passover, the other four being coriander, horse-radish,
lettuce and nettle.   The name *Marrubium* is supposed
to come from the Hebrew *Marrob*, a bitter juice.   De
Gubernatis writes that horehound was once regarded
as a " contre-poison magique," but very little is said
about it on the whole, and it is an uninteresting
plant to look at, and much like many others of the
labiate tribe.   Long ago the Apothecaries sold " sirop
of horehound " for " old coughs " and kindred disorders,
and horehound tea and candied horehound are still made
to relieve the same troubles.   Candied horehound is
made by boiling down the fresh leaves and adding
sugar to the juice thus extracted, and then again boiling
the juice till it has become thick enough to pour into
little cases made of paper.

LADY'S-SMOCK (*Cardamine pratensis*).

Then comes Daffodil beside
Our ladye's smock at our Ladye-tide.
An Early Calendar of English Flowers.

When daisies pied and violets blue
And lady-smocks all silver white
And cuckoo-buds of yellow hue
Do paint the meadows with delight.
Love's Labour Lost, v. 2.

And some to grace the show,
Of lady-smocks do rob the neighbouring mead.
Wherewith their looser locks most curiously they braid.
Polyolbion, Song xx.

And now and then among, of eglantine a spray,
By which again a course of lady-smocks they lay.

Song xv.

The honeysuckle round the porch has wov'n its wavy bowers,
And by the meadow-trenches blow the faint, sweet cuckoo flowers,
And the wild march-marigold shines like fire on swamps and hollows
gray.

The May Queen.—TENNYSON.

"Cuckoo-flower" is a name laid claim to by many
flowers, and authorities differ as to which one Shakespeare meant by it. Certainly not the plant under
discussion, which is the one we most generally call
Cuckoo-flower to-day, for there can be no doubt that
this is the "lady's-smocks" of the line above,—letting
alone the fact that the "cuckoo-buds" in the song being of
"yellow hue" put the idea out of court. Lord Tennyson's
lines point equally clearly to the *Cardamine pratensis.*
Lady's-smock is said to be a corruption of "Our Lady's
Smock," and to be one of the plants dedicated to the
Virgin, because it comes into blossom about Ladytide;
though as a matter of fact the flower is seldom seen so
early. It is remarkable how many attentions this graceful, but humble and scentless flower has received; and
besides all the poets Isaac Walton mentions it twice:
"Look! down at the bottom of the hill there, in that
meadow, chequered with water-lilies and lady-smocks."[1]
And later: "Looking on the hills, I could behold them
spotted with wood and groves—looking down in the
meadow, could see there a boy gathering lilies and
lady's-smocks, and there, a girl cropping culverkeys and
cowslips, all to make garlands suitable to this present
month of May." It is difficult to be positive about
culverkeys. Columbines, bluebells, primroses and an
orchis have all been called by this name at different
times. The primrose is cut out of the question here
by its colour, for in the poem which has been quoted a

[1] Complete Angler.

little while before Davors sings of "azure culverkeys."
The columbine is rarely found in a wild state and flowers
later in the year, the orchis is hardly "azure," so on the
whole it looks as if the likeliest flower would be the
wild hyacinth.   To return to the lady's-smocks, Gerarde
says they are of "a blushing, white colour," and like
the "white sweet-john."   In the seventeenth century
their titles were various and he gives some of them, and in
doing so he shows an ingenuous, very pleasing clinging
to the names familiar to his youth.   "In English,
cuckowe flowers, in Northfolke, Canterbury bells, at
Namptwich in Cheshire, where I had my beginning,
ladiesmocks which hath given me cause to christen it
after my country fashion."   Parkinson finds that "these
herbes are seldom used eyther as sauce or sallet or in
physick, but more for pleasure to decke up the garlands
of the country-people, yet divers have reported them
to be as affectuall in the scorbute or scurvy as the
water-cresses."   The plant was regarded as an excellent
remedy for these evils by the inhabitants of those
northern countries where salted fish and flesh are largely
eaten.   The leaves are slightly pungent and somewhat
bitter ; and in the early part of the nineteenth century it
was regarded as an ordinary salad herb, so that its reputation in that respect must have risen since Parkinson's
days.

LANGDEBEEFE (*Helminthia echoides*).

Langdebeefe is mentioned with scanty praise.   "The
leaves are onely used in all places that I knew or ever
could learne, for an herbe for the pot among others."
It is difficult to be absolutely certain as to the identity
of the plant, for Gerarde places it with Bugloss, and
Parkinson, among the Hawkweeds.   Mr Britten says,
however, that both writers referred to *Helminthia echoides*,
but that *Echium vulgare*, Viper's Bugloss, is the plant

that Turner called Langdebeefe, and Viper's Bugloss is still called Langdebeefe in Central France. Near Paris, however, *Langue de bœuf* means *Anchusa Italica*. "The leaves," says Gerarde, "are like the rough tongue of an oxe or cow, whereof it took its name," and he gives another instance of the *insouciance* of contemporary physicians. They "put them both into all kindes of medicines indifferently, which are of force and vertue to drive away sorrow and pensiveness of the minde, and to comfort and strengthen the heart." "Both" refers to Bugloss and "little wilde Buglosse," which he has just informed us grows upon "the drie ditch bankes about Pickadilla." Times change!

LIQUORICE (*Glycyrrhiza glabra*).

Gerarde describes two kinds of Liquorice: the first has "woody branches . . . beset with leaves of an over-worne greene colour, and small blew floures of the colour of an English Hyacinth." From the peculiar shape and roughness of the seed-pods it was distinguished by the name of "Hedge-hogge Licorice." This kind was very little used. Common Liquorice resembles it very closely, but has less peculiar seed-vessels.

The cultivation of *licorish* in England began about the year of Queen Elizabeth's reign, and it has been much grown at Pontefract (whence Pontefract lozenges are named), Worksop, Godalming and Mitcham. It must have been once an extremely profitable crop. "There hath been made from fifty Pound to an hundred Pound of an Acre, as some affirm." The caution expressed in the last three words is rather nice. "I. W.," the author of this bit of information (he gives no other signature), published his book in 1681, and was evidently of a very patriotic disposition. He is indignant that "although our English Liquorice exceeds any

Foreign whatsoever," yet we "yearly buy of other Nations," and Parkinson is of much the same opinion: "The root grown in England is of a fame more weake, sweete taste, yet far more pleasing to us than Licorice that is brought us from beyond Sea," which is stronger and more bitter. A later writer prefers English roots on the ground that those imported are often "mouldy and spoiled." "With the juice of Licorice, Ginger and other spices there is made a certaine bread or cakes called Gingerbread, which is very good against the cough." It is not the light in which Gingerbread is usually looked upon. Liquorice administered in many ways was a great remedy against coughs. Boiled in faire water, with Maiden-haire and Figges, it made a "good ptisane drinke for them that have any dry cough," and the "juice of Licoris, artificially made with Hyssoppe water," was recommended against shortness of breath. Extract of Liquorice is to be found in the Pharmacopœia, and it is imported as "Spanish juice." The extract must be made from the *dried* root, or else it will not be so bright when it is strained. Dr Fernie says that Liquorice is added to porter and stout to give thickness and blackness.

LOVAGE (*Ligusticum Scoticum*).

Mr Britten says: In Lyte and other early works, this [name] is applied to *Levisticum officinale*, but in modern British books it is assigned to *Ligusticum Scoticum*. It grows wild near the sea-shore in Scotland and Northumberland. Lovage "has many long and great stalkes of large, winged leaves, divided into many parts, . . . and with the leaves come forth towards the toppes, long branches, bearing at their toppes large umbells of yellow flowers. The whole plant and every part of it smelleth somewhat strongly and aromatically, and of an

hot, sharpe, biting taste. The *Germans* and other
Nations in times past used both the roote and seede
instead of Pepper to season their meates and brothes,
and found them as comfortable and warming." [1] Turner
mentions Lovage amongst his medical herbs and
Culpepper says : " It is an herb of the Sun, under the
sign Taurus. If Saturn offend the throat . . . this is
your cure."

MALLOW (*Malva*).

> With many a curve my banks I fret,
>   By many a field and fallow
> And many a fair by foreland set,
>   With willow, weed and mallow.
> > *The Brook.*—TENNYSON.

> The spring is at the door,
>   She bears a golden store,
> Her maund with yellow daffodils runneth o'er.

> After her footsteps follow
>   The mullein and the mallow,
> She scatters golden powder on the sallow.
> > *Spring Song.*—N. HOPPER.

Parkinson praises mallows both for beauty and virtue.
" The double ones, which for their Bravery are entertained everywhere into every Countrywoman's garden.
The Venice Mallow is called Good-night-at-noone,
though the flowers close so quickly that you shall
hardly see a flower blowne up in the day-time after 9
A.M." Some medical advice follows, in which " All sorts
of Mallowes" are praised. " Those that are of most
use are most common. The rest are but *taken upon credit.*"
The last remark comes quite casually, and apparently
those that were " but taken upon credit," would be
comprehended in the " all sorts " and administered
without hesitation. French Mallows (*Malva crispa*) is

[1] Parkinson.

most highly recommended as an excellent pot-herb!
indeed all wild mallows may be used in that capacity, and
the Romans are said to have considered them a delicacy.

Marsh Mallow (*Althœa officinalis*) has very soothing
qualities, and was, and is, much used by country people
for inflammation outwardly and inwardly. It contains a
great deal of mucilage, in the root particularly. Timbs
says: "Dr Sir John Floyer mentions a posset (hot
milk curdled by some infusion) in which althœa roots
are boiled"; and it must have been a "comforting" one.
In France, the young tops and leaves are used in spring
salads. "Many of the poorer inhabitants of Syria,
especially the Fellahs, the Greeks, and the Armenians,
subsist for weeks on herbs, of which the Marsh Mallow
is one of the most common. When boiled first, and
then fried with onions and butter, they are said to form
a palatable dish, and in times of scarcity, consequent
upon the failure of the crops, all classes may be seen
striving with eagerness to obtain the much desired plant,
which fortunately grows in great abundance."[1] In Job
xxx. 3, 4 we read: "For want and famine they were
solitary, fleeing into the wilderness in former time
desolate and waste. Who cut up mallows by the
bushes." Smith's "Dictionary of the Bible," however,
casts doubt on this mallow being a mallow at all, and
though admitting that it would be quite possible,
decides that the evidence points most clearly to *Atriplex
Halimus.*

Gerarde says the Tree Mallow "approacheth nearer
the substance and nature of wood than any of the others;
wherewith the people of Olbia and Narbone in France
doe make hedges, to sever or divide their gardens and
vineyards which continueth long;" and these hedges
must have been a beautiful sight when in flower.

The Hollyhock, of course, belongs to this tribe, and

[1] Hogg.

was once apparently eaten as a pot-herb, and found
to be an inferior one. It has been put to other uses,
for Hogg says that the stalks contain a fibre, " from
which a good strong cloth has been manufactured, and
in the year 1821 about 280 acres of land near Flint in
Wales were planted with the Common Holyhock, with
the view of converting the fibre to the same uses as
hemp or flax." It was also discovered in the process
of manufacture, that the plant "yields a blue dye, equal
in beauty and permanence to that of the best indigo."
This experiment however successful in results, cannot
have been justified from a commercial point of view,
and was not often repeated, and there is now no trace of
its having been ever tried.

In other languages, the Hollyhock has very pretty
names ; " in low Dutch, it was called *Winter Rosen,* and in
French, *Rose d'outremer.*"

MARIGOLD (*Calendula Officinalis*).

Hark ! hark ! the lark at heaven's gate sings
And Phœbus 'gins to rise,
His steeds to water at those springs
On chalic'd flowers that lies ;
And winking Mary-buds begin
To ope their golden eyes.
Cymbeline, ii. 3.

The marigold that goes to bed wi' the sun,
And with him rises weeping.
Winter's Tale, iv. 3.

The purple Violets and Marigolds
Shall, as a carpet, hang upon thy grave
While summer days do last.
Pericles, iv. 1.

Marigolds on death-beds blowing.
Two Noble Kinsmen. Introd. Song.

The Marigold observes the sun,
More than my subjects me have done.

So shuts the marigold her leaves
At the departure of the sun ;
So from the honeysuckle sheaves
The bee goes when the day is done.

Br. Pastorals, **book iii.**

But, maiden, see the day is waxen old,
And 'gins to shut in with the marigold.

Br. Pastorals, **book i.**

Open afresh your round of starry folds
  Ye ardent marigolds !
Dry up the moisture from your golden lids
  For great Apollo bids
That in these days your praises should be sung.

I stood tiptoe, etc.—KEATS.

The marigold above, t' adorn the arched bar,
The double daisy, thrift, the button batchelor,
Sweet William, sops-in-wine, the campion.

Polyolbion.   Song **xv.**

The crimson darnel flower, the blue bottle and *gold*
Which though esteemed but weeds, yet for their dainty hues
And for their scent not ill, they for this purpose choose.

Ibid.

The yellow kingcup Flora then assigned.
  To be the badges of a jealous mind,
  The orange-tawny marigold.

Br. Pastorals.

The Marigold has enjoyed great and lasting popularity, and though the flower does not charm by its loveliness, the indomitable courage, with which, after even a sharp frost, it lifts up its hanging head, and shows a cheerful countenance, leads one to feel for it affection and respect. In the end of January (1903) here in Devon there were some flowers and opening buds, though ten days before the ice bore for skating. The Latin name refers to its reputed habit of blossoming on the first days of every month in the year, and in a fairly mild winter this is no exaggeration. Marigolds are dedicated to the Virgin, but this fact is not supposed to have had anything to do with the giving of their name, which had probably been bestowed on them before the Festivals in her honour were kept in England, "Though doubt-less," says Mr Friend, "the name of Mary had much to do with the alterations in the name of Marigold, which may be noticed in its history." There is an idea that they were appropriated to her because they were in flower at all of her Festivals; but on this notion other authorities throw doubt. In ancient days Mari-golds were often called Golds, or Goules, or Ruddes; in Provence, a name for them was " *Gauche-fer* [1] (left-hand iron) probably from its brilliant disc, suggestive of a shield worn on the left arm." Chaucer describes Jealousy as wearing this flower : " Jealousy that werede of yelwe guldes a garland"; and Browne calls the "orange-tawny marigold" its badge.

There was a very strong belief that the flowers followed the sun, and many allusions are made to this; amongst them, two melancholy lines which are said to have been drawn from some " Meditations " by Charles I., written at Carisbrooke Castle.

> " The marigold observes the sun,
> More than my subjects me have done."

Shakespeare refers often to this idea, and the flower was obviously " to earlier writers the emblem of con-stancy in affection and sympathy in joy and sorrow, though it was also the emblem of the fawning courtier who could only shine when everything is bright." (Canon Ellacombe). Marigolds have figured in heraldry, for Marguerite of Valois, grandmother of Henri IV., chose for her armorial device a marigold turning towards the sun, with the motto, *Je ne veux suivre que lui seul.* About the fifteenth century the Marigold was called *Souvenir*, and ladies wore posies of marigolds and hearts-ease mingled, that is, a bunch of " happiness stored in

[1] Ingram, " Flora Symbolica."

recollections," a very pretty allegorical meaning. But it
has been the symbol of memories anything but happy, for
curiously enough, this sun's flower means Grief in the
language of flowers, and in many countries is connected
with the idea of death. This thought occurs in Pericles
and in the song in "Two noble Kinsmen." In
America, one name for them is death-flowers, because
there is a tradition that they "sprang upon ground
stained by the life-blood of these unfortunate Mexicans
who fell victims to the love of gold and arrogant
cruelty of the early Spanish settlers in America."[1]
However, to restore the balance of happiness, one learns
that to dream of Marigolds augurs wealth, prosperity,
success, and a rich and happy marriage! In Fuller's
"Antheologia, or the Speech of Flowers"—a most
amusing tale — the Marigold occupies a prominent
place. The scene opens with a dispute in the Flowers'
Parliament between the Tulip and the Rose. "Whilst
this was passing in the *Upper House* of *Flowers,* no less
were the transactions in the *Lower House* of the *Herbs;*
where there was a general acclamation against *Wormwood.*
Wormwood's friends were casually absent that day, making merry at an entertainment, her enemies (let not that
sex be angry for making Wormwood feminine) appeared
in full body and made so great a noise, as if some mouths
had two tongues in them." Wormwood and the Tulip
were eventually both cast out of the garden, and lying
by the roadside addressed themselves to a passing Wild
Boar, telling him of a hole in the hedge, by which he
may creep into the garden and revenge them, and amuse
himself by destroying the flowers. At the moment he
enters, "Thrift, a Flower-Herb, was just courting
Marigold as follows: 'Mistress of all Flowers that
grow on Earth, give me leave to profess my sincerest
affections to you. . . . I have taken signal notice of your

[1] Folkard.

accomplishments, and among other rare qualities, particularly of this, your loyalty and faithfulness to the Sun, . . . but we all know the many and sovereign virtues in your leaves, the *Herb Generall* in all pottage." He then proceeds to praise himself, "I am no gamester to shake away with a quaking hand what a more fixed hand did gain and acquire. I am none of those who in vanity of clothes bury my quick estate as in a winding sheet." The Marigold demurely hung her head and replied, "I am tempted to have a good opinion of myself, to which all people are prone, and we women most of all, if we may believe your opinions of us, which herein I am afraid are too true." But she is not deceived by his flattery. "The plain truth is you love me not for myself, but for your advantage. It is *Golden* the arrear of my *name*, which maketh *Thrift* to be my suitor. How often and how unworthily have you tendered your affections even to a *Penny royal* itself, had she not scorned to be courted by you. But I commend the girl that she knew her own worth, though it was but a *penny*, yet it is a *Royal* one, and therefore not a match for every base *Suitor*, but knew how to value herself; and give me leave to tell you that *Matches* founded on *Covetousness* never succeed." At this point in her spirited reply the Boar approached. "There is no such teacher as extremity; necessity hath found out more Arts than ever ingenuity invented. The Wall Gillyflower ran up to the top of the Wall of the Garden, where it hath grown ever since, and will never descend till it hath good security for its own safety." Other thrilling scenes follow, and finally the Boar is put an end to by the gardener and "a *Guard* of Dogs."

Marigolds stood as a standard of comparison, and Isaac Walton uses the common saying, "As yellow as a Marigold." Among the various titles of different kinds of Marigold Gerarde gives the oddest, for he calls one variety Jackanapes-on-horseback; Fuller calls it the

"Herb-Generall of all pottage," and it was much esteemed in this capacity. Gay says:

Fair is the gillyflour, for gardens sweet,
Fair is the marigold, for pottage meet.

The Squabble.

"The yellow leaves of the flowers are dried and kept throughout Dutchland against winter, to put into broths, in physical potions, and for divers other purposes in such quantity that in some Grocers or Spice Sellers houses are to be found barrels filled with them and retailed by the penny more or less, insomuch that no broths are well made without Marigolds." One is reminded of the childish heroine in Miss Edgeworth's charming story "Simple Susan" and how she added the petals of Marigolds, as the last touch, to the broth she had made for her invalid mother! Parkinson observes that the flowers "green or dryed are often used in possets, broths and drinks as a comforter to the heart and spirits," and that Syrup and Conserve are made of the fresh flowers; also "the flowers of Marigold pickt clean from the heads and pickled up against winter make an excellent Sallet when no flowers are to be had in a garden, which Sallet is nowadays in the highest esteem with Gentles and Ladies of the greatest note." There is a tone of patronage in this last remark which is rather irritating. "Some used to make their heyre yellow with the floure of this herbe," says Turner, and severely censures the impiousness of such an act. A hundred years ago, according to Abercromby, the flowers were chiefly used to flavour broth and to adulterate Saffron, but they must be even less employed now than then.

Dr Fernie says that the flowers of Marigold were much used by American surgeons during the Civil War, in treating wounds, and with admirable results. "*Calendula* owes its introduction and first use altogether to homœopathic practice, as signally valuable for healing wounds, ulcers, burns, and other breaches of the skin surface." Personal experience leads me to suggest that it is an excellent household remedy.

THE CORN MARIGOLD (*Chrysanthemum segetum*) used to be called Guildes, and it was once so rampant that a law was passed by the Scottish Parliament to fine negligent farmers who allowed it to overrun their lands. Hence the old Scots saying—

> The Gordon, the Guild, and the Watercraw
> Are the three worst ills the Moray ever saw.

PENNYROYAL (*Mentha pulegium*).

> Peniriall is to print your love,
>   So deep within my heart,
> That when you look this nosegay on
>   My pain you may impart,
> And when that you have read the same,
>   Consider wel my woe.
> Think ye then how to recompense
>   Even him that loves you so.
> A Handful of Pleasant Delites.
>
> C. ROBINSON.

> Then balm and mint helps to make up
>   My chapter, and for trial,
> Costmary, that so likes the cup,
>   And next it, pennyroyal.
>
> *Muses' Elysium.*

> Lavender, Corn-rose, Pennyroyal sate,
> And that which cats [1] esteem so delicate
> After a while slow-pac'd with much ado,
> Ground pine, with her short legs, crept hither too.
>
> *Of Plants*, book ii.—COWLEY.

In France, Italy, and Spain, the children make a *crêche de noël* at Christmas time; that is, they make a shed with stones and moss, and surround it with evergreens powdered with flour and cotton-wool, to make a little landscape. In and about this shed are placed the *gens*

---

[1] Cat-mint.

de la crêche; little earthen figures representing the Holy
Family, and the Three Kings with their camels, and the
Shepherds with their flocks, the sheep being disposed
among the miniature rocks and bushes. On Christmas
eve, or else sometimes on Twelfth Night, I think, these
are saluted with the music of pipes and carol singing.
De Gubernatis says that the children of Sicily always
put pennyroyal amongst the green things in their *crêches*,
and believe that exactly at midnight it bursts into flower
for Christmas Day.

Other names for it are Pulioll Royal and Pudding-
grasse, " and in the west parts, as about *Exeter*,
Organs." It is still called organs in the " West parts,"
and organ-tea used to be a favourite drink to take out to
the harvesters. In Italy pennyroyal is a protection
against the Evil Eye, and in Sicily, they tie it to the
branches of the fig-tree, thinking that this will prevent
the figs falling before they are ripe. It is there also
offered to husbands and wives who are in the habit of
" falling out" with each other. " The Ancients said that
it causeth Sheepe and Goates to bleate when they are
eating of it." To produce all those wonderful effects,
it must have a great deal of magic about it. Gerarde
says it grows " in the Common neare London, called
Miles End, about the holes and ponds thereof in sundry
places, from whence poore women bring plentie to sell
in London markets." Would that it could be found at
" Miles End " now ! He gives in passing a sidelight on
the comfort in travelling, in the good old days : " If
you have when you are at the sea Penny Royal in great
quantitie, drie and cast it into corrupt water, it helpeth
it much, neither will it hurt them that drinke thereof."
This inevitable state of things, in making a voyage, is
faced with philosophic calm. " A Garland of Pennie
Royal made and worne on the head is good against
headache and giddiness."

PURSLANE (*Portulaca*).

The worts, the purslane and the mess
Of water-cress.

Thanksgiving.—HERRICK.

De la Quintinye thought Purslane " one of the
prettiest *plants* in a *kitchen-garden*, the *red* or *golden* being
the most agreeable to the eye and the more delicate and
difficult to raise than the green. The thick stalks of
Purslain that is to run to seed, are good to pickle in
Salt and Vinegar for Winter Sallads." I do not agree
with him ; the leaves are pretty enough, but thick,
fleshy, and of no special charm. The graceful Coriander
or the lace-like leaves of Sweet Cicely are far more to
be admired. But even Purslane, which looks quite
prosaic, was mixed up with magic long ago, for strewn
about a bed, it used [1] " in olden times to be considered
a protection against evil spirits." Among a vast number
of diseases, for all of which it is highly recommended,
" blastings by lightening, or planets, and for burning
of gunpowder " are named and Turner says, " It helpeth
the teeth when they are an edged," so it had many
uses !

Evelyn finds that " familiarly eaten alone with Oyl
and Vinegar," moderation should be used, but remarks
that it is eminently moist and cooling " especially the
golden," and is " generally entertained in all our sallets.
Some eate of it cold, after it has been boiled, which Dr
Muffit would have in wine for nourishment." Not a
tempting dish, by the sound of it ! The Purslanes are
found from the Cape of Good Hope and South America
to the " frozen regions of the North." The root of
one variety *Leuisia rediviva*, called Tobacco root (because it has the smell of tobacco when cooked), has great
nutritive qualities. It is a native of North America,
and is boiled and eaten by the Indians, and on long

[1] Folkard.

journeys it is of special use, " two or three ounces a day being quite sufficient for a man, even while undergoing great fatigue." (Hogg.)

RAM-CICHES (*Cicer Arietinum*).

Ram-ciches, Ramshead, or Chick Pea, gains the two first names from the curious shape of the seed pods which are " puffed up as it were with winde in which do lie two, or at the most three seeds, small towards the end, with one sharp corner, not much unlike to a Ram's head." Turner says that the plant is very ill for newe fallowed ground and that " it killeth all herbes and most and sounest of all other ground thistel," which seems a loss one could survive. According to Parkinson the seeds are " boyled and stewed as the most dainty kind of Pease there are, by the Spaniards," and he adds that in his own opinion, " they are of a very good relish and doe nourish much." They are still eaten and appreciated by the country people in the south of France and Spain. Like Borage, Ram-ciches is particularly interesting to students of chemistry ; for it is said that " in very hot weather the leaves sparkle with very small tears of a viscous and very limpid liquid, extremely acid, and which has been discovered to be oxalic acid in its pure state." [1]

RAMPION (*Campanula Rapunculus*).

The Citrons, which our soil not easily doth afford,
The Rampions rare as that.
Polyolbion Song, xv.

De Gubernatis tells a most curious story from Calabria almost exactly that of Cupid and Psyche, but it begins

[1] Hogg.

by saying that the maiden, wandering alone in the fields, uprooted a rampion, and so discovered a stair-case leading to a palace in the depths of the earth.

One of Grimm's fairy tales is called after the heroine, *Rapunzel* (Rampion), for she was given this plant's name, and the whole plot hangs on Rampions being stolen from a magician's garden. There is an Italian tradition that the possession of a rampion (as that of strawberries, cherries, or red shoes), would excite quarrels among children, which would sometimes go as far as "murder." Even in a land of quick passions and southern blood, it can hardly be thought that this tradition had much ground to spring from, and I have not heard of it as existing further north. Parkinson says that the roots may be eaten as salad or "boyled and stewed with butter and oyle, and some blacke or long pepper cast on them." The distilled water of the whole plant is excellent for the complexion, and "maketh the face very splendent." Evelyn thought Rampions "much more nourishing" than Radishes, and they are said to have a "pleasant, nutty flavour"; in the winter the leaves as well as the roots make a nice salad. Even if it is not grown for use, it might well, with its graceful spires of purple bells, be put for ornament in shrubberies. Parkinson has said of Honesty, that "some eate the young rootes before they runne up to flower, as Rampions are eaten with vinegar and oyle"; but Evelyn warns us *apropos* of this very plant (with others) how cautiously the advice of the Ancient Authors should be taken by the sallet gatherer (Parkinson was probably quoting from the "Ancients" when he said this); "for however it may have been in their countries, in England *Radix Lunaria* is accounted among the deadly poisons!" One cannot help wondering if Parkinson or Gerarde ever knew those hardy individuals they allude to as "some," and who tried the experiment!

ROCAMBOLE (*Allium Scorodoprasum*).

Rocambole is a kind of garlic, but milder in flavour, and it is a native of Denmark. De la Quintinye seems to confuse it with Shallots (*Allium ascalonium*), as he writes of "Shallots or Rocamboles, otherwise Spanish Garlick." Evelyn, speaking of Garlic as impossible— one cannot help feeling with a smothered wistfulness— says: " To be sure, 'tis not fit for Ladies' Palates, nor those who court them, farther than to permit a light touch in the Dish, with a *Clove* thereof, much better supplied by the gentler *Rocambole*."

ROCKET (*Eruca sativa*).

Various plants claim the name of Rocket, but it was *Eruca sativa* that was used as a salad herb. Parkinson explains the Italian name *Ruchetta* and *Rucola Gentile* thus : " This Rocket Gentle, so-called from the *Italians*, who by that title of Gentle understand anything that maketh one quicke and ready to jest, to play." It is certainly not specially gentle in the ordinary sense of the words, for it has leaves " like those of Turneps, but not neere so great nor rough "; and if eaten alone, " it causeth head-ache and heateth too much." It is, however, good in Salads of Lettuce, Purslane, " and such cold herbes," and Turner observes that " some use the sede for sauce, the whiche that it may last the longer, they knede it with milke or vinegre, and make it into little cakes." It has a strong peculiar smell, and is no longer used in England ; though Loudon says that in some places on the Continent it makes " an agreeable addition to cresses and mustard in early spring." Culpepper found that the common wild Rocket was hurtful used alone, as it has too much heat, but to " hot and choleric persons it is less harmful " (one would have imagined that it would have been the other way) and "for such we may say, a little doth but a little harm, for angry Mars rules them, and he sometimes will be rusty when he meets with fools." This is altogether a dark saying, but it gives little encouragement to those who would make trial of Rocket.

LONDON ROCKET (*Sisymbrium Irio*).

This plant gained its name in a singular way. It is said to have first appeared in London in the spring following the Great Fire, "when young Rockets were seen everywhere springing up among the ruins, where they increased so marvellously that in the summer the enormous crop crowding over the surface of London created the greatest astonishment and wonder."[1]

SAFFRON (*Crocus sativus*).

Nor Cyprus wild vine-flowers, nor that of Rhodes,
Nor Roses oil from Naples, Capua,
   Saffron confected in Cilicia.
Nor that of Quinces, nor of Marjoram,
   That ever from the Isle of Coös came,
   Nor these, nor any else, though ne'er so rare
Could with this place for sweetest smells compare.
                              Br. Pastorals, Book I.

Clown. I must have Saffron to colour the Warden pies.
                              Winter's Tale, iv. 2.

You set Saffron and there came up Wolf's bane.   (Saying to express an action which has an unexpected result.)

Saffron has been of great importance since the earliest days, and it is mentioned in a beautiful passage of the Song of Solomon. "Thy plants are an orchard of Pomegranates, with pleasant fruits, Camphire with Spikenard, Spikenard and Saffron, Calamus and Cinnamon, with all trees of Frankincense, Myrrh and Aloes, with all the chief spices," iv. 13, 14.

[1] Folkard.

Canon Ellacombe says that the Arabic name, *Al Zahafaran* was the general name for all *Croci*, and extended to the *Colchicums*, which were called Meadow Saffrons. It is pointed out by Mr Friend that, further, the flower has given its name to a colour, and had given it in the days of Homer, and he remarks how much more exactly the expression "Saffron-robed" morning describes the particular tints seen sometimes before sunrise (or at sunset) than any other words can do. Saffron Walden in Essex, whose arms are given on page 101, and Saffron Hill in London (which once formed part of the Bishop of Ely's garden), are also obviously named after it, and as is seen in the former case it has given arms to a borough. As to its introduction into England Hakluyt writes (1582): "It is reported at Saffron Walden that a pilgrim proposing to do good to his country, stole a head of Saffron, and hid the same in his Palmer's Staffe, which he had made hollow before of purpose, and so he brought the root into this realme with venture of his life, for if he had been taken, by the law of the countrey from whence it came, he had died for the fact" ("English Voyages," vol. ii.). Canon Ellacombe thinks that it was probably originally brought here in the days of the Romans, and found "in a Pictorial Vocabulary of the fourteenth century, 'Hic Crocus, An^{ee} Safryn,' so that I think the plant must have been in cultivation in England at that time." In the work of "Mayster Ion Gardener," written about 1440, one of the eight parts into which it is divided is wholly devoted to a discourse, "Of the Kynde of Saferowne," which shows that Saffron must have been a good deal considered in his day. The Charity Commission of 1481 mentions two Saffron-gardens; and in the churchwarden's accounts at Saffron Walden, in the second year of Richard III.'s reign, there is an entry, "Payd to John Rede for pyking of Vunc Saffroni, xii." The town accounts of Cambridge show that in 1531 Saffron was grown there; and at Barnwell in the next parish the prior of Barnwell had ten acres.

Some old wills, too, throw some light on the subject. In the will of Alyce Sheyne of Sawstone, in 1527, "a rood of Saffron" is left to her son. In 1530 (1533?) John Rede, also of Sawstone, leaves his godson a "rood of Saffron in Church Field," and William Hockison of Sawstone, bequeathed in 1531, "to Joan, my wife, a rood of Saffron, and to my maid, Marger, and my son, John, half an acre." As may be easily inferred from these legacies, Saffron was very largely grown at Sawstone, and the two adjoining parishes, as well as at Saffron Walden. The first man to introduce it into Saffron Walden to be cultivated on a really large scale was Thomas Smith, Secretary of State to Edward VI., and in 1565, it was grown in abundance. In 1557 Turner speaks of Saffron-growing, as if this was very general, but it must be remembered that he started life in Essex, farmed successively in Suffolk and Norfolk, and returned to his native county to a farm at Fairstead, and having never moved very far from the special home of the industry, he naturally took as an ordinary proceeding, what would have been very unusual in other parts of the country. It can never have been very widely cultivated; for Turner, whose "Herbal" gives an immense deal of information, and who wrote when the industry was in full swing, omits all mention of Saffron, though he speaks of, and evidently knew Meadow Saffron.

This is a strong sign that cultivation must have been confined to certain localities, chiefly in the eastern counties, though in the west it was grown at Hereford and surrounding districts to a very considerable extent. I do not mean to imply that none was grown in neighbouring counties, but the evidence is not easy to get, and I have not gone deeply enough into the subject to find it, but the Saffron of Hereford was famed.

At Black Marston in Herefordshire, in 1506 and again in 1528, leave was granted by the Prioress of Acornbury, to persons to cultivate Saffron extensively.

In 1582, in spite of a continued demand for it, the cultivation of Saffron seems to have decreased, for Hakluyt writes in his " Remembrances for Master S." [what to observe in a journey he is about to undertake]. "Saffron groweth in Syria. . . . But if a vent might be found, men would in Essex (about Saffron Walden) and in Cambridgeshire, revive the trade for the benefit of setting the poore on worke. So would they do in Herefordshire by Wales, where the best of all Englande is, in which place the soil yields the wilde " Saffron" commonly." The soil there still yields the wilde Saffron so commonly that at the present moment it is regarded with disfavour, as being quite a drawback to some pasture lands, but it is no longer grown there for commercial purposes. Neither Gerarde (1596) nor Parkinson (1640) mention Saffron-growing as an industry, but in 1681 "I. W." gives directions for cultivating and drying it. "English Saffron," he says, "is esteemed the best in the world; it's a plant very suitable to our climate and soil." At Saffron Walden it continued to be grown for commerce for over two hundred years, but has now been uncultivated in that locality for more than a century. In Cambridgeshire, however, it flourished to a later date, and the last Saffron grower in England was a man named Knot, who lived at Duxford in Cambridgeshire, and who grew Saffron till the year 1816.

This is Turner's advice for cultivating it.

> When harvest is gone,
> Then Saffron comes on.
> A little of ground,
> Brings Saffron a pound.

The pleasure is fine,
The profit is thine.
Keep colour in drying,
Well used, worth buying.

And also :—

Pare Suffron between the two St Mary's days [1]
Or set or go shift it, that knoweth the ways . . .
In having but forty foot, workmanly dight
Take Saffron enough for a lord or a knight.

August's Husbandry.

From old records it seems to have been grown in
small patches of less than an acre, and to have been
a most profitable crop. " I. W.," in his directions says,
for drying it, "a small kiln made of clay, and with a
very little Fire, and that with careful attendance," is
required. " Three Pounds thereof moist usually making
one of dry. One acre may bear from seven to fifteen
Pound, and hath been sold from 20s. a Pound to £5 a
Pound." The last price sounds as if it existed only in his
imagination, and one cannot really think that it was given
often ! But on one occasion, Timbs says, an even higher
sum was reached, for when Queen Elizabeth paid a visit
to Saffron Walden, the Corporation paid five guineas
for one pound of Saffron to present to her. Though
this was exceptional, the usual prices for it were very
high ; and to show this, and also the enormous amount
that was used in cooking, Miss Amherst quotes from
some old accounts of the Monastery of Durham : " In
1531, half a pound of 'Crocus' or Saffron was bought
in July, the same quantity in August and in November,
a quarter of a pound in September, and a pound and a half
in October." So much for the quantity ; as to the price,
a merchant of Cambridgeshire charged them in 1539-
1540 for 6½ lbs. Crocus, £7, 8s.

Saffron used to be much employed to colour and to
flavour pies and cakes, and it was this reason that Perdita
sent the " Clown " to fetch some, when she was making

[1] July 22nd and August 15th.

"Warden" (Pear) pies for the sheep-shearing. Saffron cakes still prevail in Cornwall, and come over the border into the next county, and a chemist, in Somerset, said quite lately, that thirty years since, he used to sell quantities of Saffron at Easter-time, but that much less is asked for now. It seems to have been specially used in the materials for feasting at this season. Evelyn tells us that the Germans made it into "little balls with honey, which afterwards they dry and reduce to powder, and then sprinkle over salads" for a "noble cordial." For medicinal purposes Saffron is imported, for in spite of "I. W.'s" praise, that grown in England is far from equalling that of Greece and Asia Minor, though in any case it is only now used as a colouring matter. The saying which survives, "So dear as Saffron," to express anything of worth, is a proof of how great its value once was; and it is true that the plant was credited with powers nothing short of miraculous. Perhaps Fuller tells us the most startling news: "In a word, the Sovereign Power of genuine *Saffron* is plainly proved by the Antipathy of the *Crocodiles* thereunto. For the *Crocodile's tears* are never *true* save when he is forced where *Saffron* groweth (when he hath his name of γξοκό-ςπλθ or the Saffron-fearer) knowing himselfe to be all Poison, and it all *Antidote*."

After this, Gerarde's assertion that for those whom consumption has brought "at death's doore, and almost past breathing, that it bringeth breath againe," sounds moderate. On the doctrine of Signatures, Saffron was prescribed for jaundice and measles, and it is also recommended to be put into the drinking water of canaries when they are moulting. Irish women are said to dye their sheets with Saffron, that it may give strength to their limbs. Saffron has long been much esteemed as a dye, and Ben Jonson tells us of this use for it in his days in lines that literally rollick :—

> Give us bacon, rinds of walnuts,
> Shells of cockles and of small nuts,
> Ribands, bells, and saffron'd linen,
> All the world is ours to win in.
>
> *The Gipsies Metamorphosed.*

Gerarde says: "The chives (stamens) steeped in water serve to illumine or (as we say) limme pictures and imagerie," and Canon Ellacombe quotes from an eleventh century work, showing that it was employed for the same purpose then. "If ye wish to decorate your work in some manner, take tin, pure and finely scraped, melt it and wash it like gold, and apply it with the same glue upon letters or other places which you wish to ornament with gold or silver; and when you have polished it with a tooth, take Saffron with which Silk is coloured, moistening it with clear of egg without water; and when it has stood a night, on the following day, cover with a pencil the places which you wish to gild, the rest holding the place of silver."—*Theophilus*, HENDRIE's Translation.

Meadow-Saffron, or *Colchicum*, yields a drug still much prescribed, of which Turner uttered a caution in 1568. He says it is a drug to "isschew." He warns those "syke in the goute" (for whom it was, and is, a standard remedy) that much of it is "sterke poyson, and will strongell a man and kill him in the space of one day." Drugs must, indeed, have been administered in heroic measures at that time—if he really ever heard of such a case at first hand. It is from the corm, or bulb, of the plant that *Colchicum* is extracted.

SAMPHIRE (*Crithium maritimum*).

> *Edgar.*   Half way down
> Hangs one that gathers Samphire, dreadful trade !
> Methinks he seems no bigger than his head.
>
> *King Lear*, iv. 6.

Samphire is St Peter's Herb, and gains the distinction

TITLE-PAGE OF GERARD'S "HERBAL"

either because it grows on sea-cliffs, and so is appropriate to the patron of fishermen, or more probably, because it flourishes on rocks, and its roots strike deep into the crevices. The French call it *Herbe de St Pierre* and *Pierce-Pierre*, from its peculiar way of growing ; and the Italians have the same name, but call it *Finocchio marino* as well ; and this title, translated to Meer-finckell, was also the German and Dutch name, according to Parkinson. It is strongly aromatic, " being of smell delightfule and pleasant, and hath many fat and thicke leaves, somewhat like those of the lesser Purslane . . . of a spicie taste, with a certaine saltness." Gerarde praises it pickled in salads. Edgar's words show that it must have been popular in Elizabethan days, and so it was for more than a hundred years after as " the pleasantest Sauce " ; and Evelyn considered it preferable to "most of our hotter herbs," and " long wonder'd it has not long since been cultivated in the *Potagère* as it is in France. It groweth on the rocks that are often moistened, at the least, if not overflowed with the sea water," a verdict which tallies with the saying that Samphire grows out of reach of the waves, but within reach of the spray of every tide. I have found it growing in much that position on rocks on the seashore in Cornwall. Two other kinds of Samphire, Golden Samphire (*Inula Crithmifolia*) and Marsh Samphire (*Salicornia Herbacea*), are sometimes sold as the true Samphire, but neither of them have so good a flavour.

SKIRRETS (*Sium Sisarum*).

The Skirret and the leek's aspiring kind,
The noxious poppy-quencher of the mind.
The Salad.—COWPER.

" This is that siser or skirret which *Tiberius* the Emperour commanded to be conveied unto him from Gelduba, a castle about the river of Rhine," and which delighted him so much " that he desired the same to be brought unto him everye yeare out of Germanie." Evelyn found them "hot and moist . . . exceedingly whole-some, nourishing and delicate . . . and so valued by the Emperor Tiberius that he accepted them for tribute "— a point that Gerarde's statement hardly brought out. " This excellent root is seldom eaten raw, but being boil'd, stew'd, roasted under the Embers, bak'd in Pies whole, slic'd or in Pulp, is very acceptable to all Palates. 'Tis reported they were heretofore something bitter, see what culture and education effects." On the top of these congratulations, perhaps it is unkind to say the reported bitterness has a very mythical sound, for long before Evelyn's time, the Dutch name for skirret was Suycker wortelen (sugar root), and that Marcgrave has extracted " fine white sugar, little inferior to that of the cane" from it. But from Turner's account there seems to have been formerly some confusion as to the identity of the plant, and one claimant to the title was somewhat bitter, so perhaps this was the cause of the remarks in *Acetaria*. In Scotland, Skirrets were called Crummock. Though few people seem to have appreciated them so much as did our ancestors, they were till lately sometimes boiled and sent to the table, but are now hardly ever seen.

SMALLAGE (*Apium graveolens*).

Smallage is merely wild celery, and all that is interesting about it is Parkinson's description of his first making acquaintance with sweet smallage—our celery, which has been already quoted. He merely says of ordinary smallage that it is " somewhat like Parsley, but greater, greener and more bitter." It grows wild in moist grounds, but is also planted in gardens, and although "his evil taste and savour, doth cause it not to be accepted unto meats as Parsley," yet it has "many good properties both for inward and outward diseases."

STONECROP (*Sedum*).

Stone-crop, Stone-hot, Prick-Madam or Trick-Madam is a *Sedum*, but which *Sedum* the old Herbalists called by these names is not absolutely clear, it was probably *Sedum Telephium* or *Sedum Album*. Evelyn speaks of "Tripe-Madam, *Vermicularis Insipida*," which seems to point to the latter, as that used to be called Worm-grass. He says Tripe-madam is "cooling and moist," but there is another Stone-crop of as pernicious qualities as the former are laudable, Wall-pepper, *Sedum Minus Causticum* (most likely our *Sedum Acre*). This is called by the French, Tricque-Madame, and he cautions the "Sallet-Composer, if he be not botanist sufficiently skilful" to distinguish them by the eye, to "consult his palate," and taste them before adding them to the other ingredients.

SWEET CICELY (*Myrrhis odorata*).

Sweet Cicely or Sweet Chervil was apparently less of a favourite than its romantic name would seem to warrant, for I can find no traditions concerning it. "Chervil" (of which this is a variety) says Gerarde, "is thought to be so called because it delighteth to grow with many leaves, or rather that it causeth joy and gladness." There does not seem much connection between these two interpretations. He continues that "the name *Myrrhus* is also called Myrrha, taken from his pleasant flavour of Myrrh." Sweet Cicely has a very pleasant flavour, with this peculiarity, that the leaves taste exactly as if sugar had just been powdered over them, but personally I have never been able to recognise myrrh in it. It is a pretty plant, with " divers great and fair spread wing leaves, very like and resembling the leaves of Hemlocke . . . but of sweet pleasant and spice-hot taste. Put among herbes in a sallet it addeth a marvellous good rellish to all the rest. Some commend the green seeds sliced and put in a sallet of herbes. The rootes are eyther boyled and eaten with oyle and vinegare or preserved or candid." Sweet Cicely is very attractive to bees, and was often " rubbed over the insides of the hives before placing them before newly-cast swarms to induce them to enter," and in the North of England Hogg says the seeds are used to polish and scent oak floors and furniture.

TANSY (*Tanacetum vulgare*).

Lelipa—Then burnet shall bear up with this
Whose leaf I greatly fancy,
Some camomile doth not amiss
With savory and some tansy.
Muses' Elysium.

The hot muscado oil, with milder maudlin cast
Strong tansey, fennel cool, they prodigally waste.
Polyolbion, Song xv.

The name Tansy comes from *Athanasia*, Immortality, because its flower lasts so long, and it is dedicated to St Athanasius. It is connected with various interesting old customs, and especially with some observed at Easter time. Brand quotes several old rhymes in reference to this.

Soone at Easter cometh Alleluya.
With butter, cheese and a tansay.
From *Douce's Collection of Carols.*

On Easter Sunday be the pudding seen
To which the Tansey lends her sober green.
The Oxford Sausage.

Wherever any grassy turf is view'd,
It seems a tansie all with sugar strew'd.
From *Shipman's Poems.*

The last lines occur in a description of the frost in 1654. None of these quotations refer to the plant alone ; but to that kind of cake or frittter called taansie, and of which Tansy leaves formed an ingredient. Tansy must be "eaten young, shred small with other herbes, or else, the juiyce of it and other herbes, fit for the purpose beaten with egges and fried into cakes (in Lent and in the Spring of the year) which are usually called Tansies." Though Parkinson speaks of their being eaten in Lent (as they no doubt were), the special day that they were in demand was Easter Day, and of this practice Culpepper has a good deal to say. Tansies were then eaten as a remembrance of the bitter herbs eaten by the Jews at the Passover. "Our Tansies at Easter have reference to the bitter herbs, though at the same time 'twas always the fashion for a man to have a gammon of bacon, to show himself to be no Jew." This little glimpse of an old practice comes from Selden's *Table Talk* and the idea of taking this means to declare one's self a Christian is really delightful. I must quote again from Brand to show another very extraordinary Easter Day custom. "Belithus, a ritualist of ancient times, tells us that it was customary in some churches for the Bishops and Archbishops themselves to play with the inferior clergy at hand-ball, and this, as Durand asserts, even on Easter Day itself. Why they should play at hand-ball at this time rather than any other game, Bourne tells us he has not been able to discover; certain it is, however, that the present custom of playing at that game on Easter Holidays for a tansy-cake has been derived from thence." Stool-ball was apparently a most popular amusement and Lewis in his *English Presbyterian Eloquence* criticises the tenets of the Puritans, and observes with disapproval that all games where there is "any hazard of loss are strictly forbidden; not so much as a game of stool-ball for a tansy is allowed." From a collection of poems

called " A Pleasant Grove of New Fancies," 1657,
Brand extracts the following verses :—

> At stool-ball, Lucia, let us play
> For sugar, cakes and wine
> Or for a tansey let us pay,
> The loss be thine or mine.

> If thou, my dear, a winner be,
> At trundling of the ball,
> The wager thou shalt have and me,
> And my misfortunes all.

Let us hope that the stake was handsomer than it
sounds ! Brand quotes another very curious practice in
which Tansies have a share, once existing in the North.
On Easter Sunday, the young men of the village would
steal the buckles off the maidens' shoes. On Easter
Monday, the young men's shoes and buckles were taken
off by the young women. On Wednesday, they are
redeemed by little pecuniary forfeits, out of which an
entertainment, called a Tansey Cake, is made, with dancing. One cannot help wondering how this cheerful, if
somewhat peculiar custom originated ! In course of
time Tansies came to be eaten only about Easter-time
and the practice seems to have acquired at one period
the lustre almost of a religious rite in which superstition had a considerable share. Coles (1656) and
Culpepper (1652) rebel against this and show with
force and clearness the advantages of eating Tansies
throughout the spring. Coles ignores the ceremonial
reasons and says that the origin of eating it in the
spring is because Tansy is very wholesome after the
salt fish consumed during Lent, and counteracts the ill-
effects which "the moist and cold constitution of winter"
has made on people . . . "though many understand it not
and some simple people take it for a matter of superstition to do so." This shows plainly that the idea of eating
Tansies only at Easter, was pretty widely spread. Cul-

pepper as usual is more incisive. He first gives the same
reason that Coles does for eating Tansies in the spring ;
then : " At last the world being over-run with Popery,
a monster called superstition pecks up his head, and . . .
obscures the bright beams of knowledge by his dismal
looks ; (physicians seeing the Pope and his imps, selfish,
began to do so too), and now, forsooth, Tansies must be
eaten only on Palm and Easter Sundays and their neigh-
bour days. At last superstition being too hot to hold, and
the selfishness of physicians walking in the clouds ; after
the friars and monks had made the people ignorant, the
superstition of the time, was found out by the virtue of
the herb hidden and now is almost, if not altogether left
off. Scarcely any physicians are beholden to none so
much as they are to monks and friars ; for wanting of
eating this herb in spring, maketh people sickly in
summer, and that makes work for the physician. If
it be against any man or woman's conscience to eat
Tansey in the spring, I am as unwilling to burthen their
conscience, as I am that they should burthen mine ; they
may boil it in wine and drink the decoction, it will work
the same effect." " The Pope and his imps " is a grand
phrase ! A more militant Protestant than Culpepper it
would be difficult to find, even in these days.

From other writers, it seems that the phase of associ-
ating Tansies exclusively with Easter, must have worn
itself out, for we find many descriptions of them on
distinctly secular occasions. At the Coronation Feast of
James-II. and his Queen, a Tansie was served among the
1445 " Dishes of delicious Viands " provided for it, and
I must quote some of the others :—" Stag's tongues,
cold ; Andolioes ; Cyprus Birds, cold and Asparagus ; a
pudding, hot ; Salamagundy ; 4 Fawns ; 10 Oyster
pyes, hot ; Artichokes ; an Oglio, hot ; Bacon, Gammon and Spinnage ; 12 Stump Pyes ; 8 Godwits ;
Morels ; 24 Puffins ; 4 dozen Almond Puddings, hot ;

Botargo; Skirrets; Cabbage Pudding; Lemon Sallet; Taffeta Tarts; Razar Fish; and Broom Buds, cold." [1] These are only a very few out of an immense variety that are also named.

Many recipes for a "Tansy" exist, and very often have only the slightest resemblance to one another, but this is rather a nice one and is declared by its transcriber to be "the most agreeable of all the boiled Herbaceous Dishes." It consists of: Tansey, being qualify'd with the juices of other fresh Herbs; *Spinach, green Corn, Violet, Primrose Leaves,* etc., at entrance of the spring, and then fry'd brownish, is eaten hot, with the Juice of Orange and Sugar." Isaac Walton speaks of a "Minnow Tansy," which is made of Minnows "fried with yolks of eggs; the flowers of cowslips and of primroses and a little tansy; thus used they make a dainty dish of meat." Our ancestors seem to have had a great love of "batter," for it is a prominent part in very many of their dishes. Mrs Milne Home says, "In Virginia the Negroes make Tansy-tea for colds and at a pinch, Mas'r's cook will condescend to use it in a sauce," but in English cookery, it has absolutely disappeared.

Tansy had many medicinal virtues. Sussex people used to say that to wear Tansy-leaves in the shoe, was a charm against ague.

Wild Tansy looks handsome when it grows in abundance on marshy ground; and, indeed, its feathery leaves are beautiful anywhere, and it has a more refreshing scent than the Garden-Tansy. "In some parts of Italy people present stalks of Wild Tansy to those whom they mean to insult," [2] a proceeding for which there seems neither rhyme nor reason. Turner tells tales of the vanity of his contemporaries, masculine as well as feminine, for he says:

[1] Complete Account of the Coronations of the Kings and Queens of England, J. Roberts.
[2] Folkard.

" Our weomen in Englande and some men that be sunneburnt and would be fayre, eyther stepe this herbe in white wyne and wash their faces with the wyne or ellis with the distilled water of the same."

THISTLE (*Carduus Marianus and Carduus Benedictus*).

Margaret. Get you some of this distilled Carduus Benedictus, and lay it to your heart, it is the only thing for a qualm.
Hero. There thou prick'st her with a thistle.
Beatrice. Benedictus! why Benedictus? you have some moral in this Benedictus.
Margaret. Moral! no, by my troth, I have no moral meaning; I meant plain holy thistle.

Much Ado about Nothing, iii. 4.

That thence, as from a garden without dressing
She these should ever have, and never want.
Store from an orchard without tree or plant . . .
And for the chiefest cherisher she lent
The royal thistle's milky nourishment.

Br. Pastorals, Book i.

The history, legends, and traditions surrounding Thistles in general, make far too large a subject to be entered on here, and only these two varieties can be considered. *Carduus Marianus*, the Milk or Dappled Thistle, has sometimes been called the Scotch Thistle, and announced to be the Thistle of Scotland. As a matter of fact, I believe, that after long and stormy controversy, that honour has been awarded to *Carduus Acanthioides*, but the Milk Thistle's claims have received very strong support, and so it seems most probable, considering the context, that when Browne referred to the "Royal Thistle," it was this one that he meant. This supposition is borne out by Hogg, who writes: " As Ray says, it is more a garden vegetable than a medicinal plant. The young and tender stalks of the root leaves when stripped of their spiny part, are eaten like cardoon, or when boiled, are used as greens. The young stalks, peeled and soaked in water to extract their bitterness, are excellent as a salad. The scales of the involucre are as good as those of the artichoke, and the roots in early spring are good to eat." The seeds supply food to many small birds, and it is from the gold-finch feeding so extensively on them that it has been called *Carduelis*. This partiality of the gold-finch must have been observed in several lands, for the same name occurs in different tongues. In England, it has been called Thistlefinch; in French, *Chardonneret*, and in Italian, *Cardeletto, Cardeto* being a waste covered with thistles. One cannot help remembering the charming line :—

> " As the thistle shakes,
> When three gray linnets wrangle for the seed,"

with the reflection that other birds besides gold-finches have a deep appreciation of it.

But to go back to the Thistle itself, after all these uses made of every part, no wonder that Browne called it a "chiefest cherisher of vital power!" Although, latterly, its reputation in medicine has fallen, in old days, on account of its numerous prickles (Doctrine of Signatures), it was thought good for stitches in the side. Culpepper has further advice : "In spring, if you please to boil the tender plant (but cut off the prickles, unless you have a mind to choke yourself), it will change your blood as the season changeth, and that is the way to be safe."

Carduus Benedictus, called the Holy, or the Blessed Thistle, was considered a great preservative against the plague, and that it was also given for a sudden spasm is shown in the delightful scene between Beatrice and her friends in " Much Ado About Nothing." It follows the *ruse* that they have just played upon her, to persuade her that Benedict is already in love with her, in the hope that she may become enamoured of him, and the play upon the name is very charming. Culpepper says that *Carduus*

Benedictus was good against "diseases of melancholy,"
which is additional evidence that Shakespeare did not
go out of his way to find an imaginary remedy that
would suit that occasion, but with exquisite skill took
a remedy that would have been natural in his time,
and surrounded it with wit. Less than a hundred years
ago a decoction used to be made from its leaves, which
are remarkable for their "intense bitterness," and it was
said to be an excellent tonic; but, like the Milk Thistle,
the Holy Thistle's virtues in medicine are now discredited. The thistle was once dedicated to Thor,
and the bright colour of the flower was supposed to
come from the lightning, and therefore lightning could
not hurt any person or building protected by the flower.
It was used a good deal in magic, and there is an old
rite to help a maiden to discover which, of several
suitors, really loves her best. She must take as many
thistles as there are lovers, cut off their points, give
each thistle the name of a man, and lay them under her
pillow, and the thistle which has the name of the most
faithful lover will put forth a fresh sprout! In East
Prussia, says Mr Friend, there is a strange but simple
cure for any domestic animal which may have an open
wound. It is to gather four red thistle blossoms before
the break of day, and to put one in each of the four
points of the compass with a stone in the middle of
them.

Here ends the list of Herbs, but before finishing the
chapter I must add a few names of buds and berries
which, though not herbs, were often employed as such,
especially to garnish, or to flavour dishes. Evelyn
includes many of these in his *Acetaria*. "The Capreols,
Tendrils and Claspers of Vines," very young, may be
"eaten alone or mingled with other sallet. So may
the 'buds and young Turiones of the Tendrils' of
Hops, either raw, ' but more conveniently being boil'd'

and cold, like asparagus." Elder Flowers, infused in vinegar, are recommended, and " though the leaves are somewhat rank of smell, and so not commendable in sallet . . . they are of the most sovereign virtue, and spring buds and tender leaves excellent and wholesome in pottage at that season of the year." Evelyn experimented with " the large *Heliotrope* or Sunflower (e'er it comes to expand and show its golden face), which, being dress'd as the artichoak, is eaten for a dainty. This I add as a new discovery : I once made macaroons with ripe blanch'd seed, but the *Turpentine* did so domineer over all that it did not answer expectation." This must have been a disappointment to his adventurous spirit ! Broom buds appeared on three separate tables at King James II.'s Coronation feast, and seem to have been popular, when pickled.

Violets were also used, and Miss Amherst quotes from an old cookery book the recipe of a pudding called " Mon amy," which directs the cook to " plant it with flowers of violets and serve it forth." Another recipe is for a dish called " Vyolette !" " Take flowrys of vyolet, boyle hem, presse hem, bray (pound) hem smal." After this they are to be mixed with milk, ' floure of rys,' and sugar or honey, and finally to be coloured with violets. Pine-kernels were sometimes eaten. Shelley says of *Marenghi* :

> " His food was the wild fig or strawberry ;
> The milky pine-nuts which the autumn blast
> Shakes into the tall grass."

And in England Parkinson writes, " The cones or apples are used of divers Vintners in this city, being painted to express a bunch of grapes, whereunto they are very like and are hung up on their bushes, as also to fasten keyes unto them, as is seene in many places. The kernels with the hard shels, while they are fresh, or newly taken out, are used by Apothecaries, Comfitmakers, and Cookes. Of them are made Comfits, Marchpanes and such like, and with them a cunning cook can make divers kech-choses for his master's table." Barberries were used as a garnish to salads and other dishes and sometimes as an ingredient. Evelyn mentions them as an item in " Sallet All-sorts," and Gervase Markham describes the making of " Paste of Genoa," a confection of Quince, and adds, " In this sort you now make paste of Peares, Apples, Wardens, Plummes of all kindes, Cherries, Barberries or whatever fruit you please." He adds this fruit to the ingredients required in making aromatic vinegar, and also directs that a good quantity of whole Barberries, both branches and others," be served with Pike " or any fresh fish whatsoever." Parkinson says, " The leaves are sometimes used in the stead of Sorrell to make sauce for meate, and by reason of their sournesse are of the same quality." The " delicious *confitures d'épine vinette*, for which Rouen is famous," are prepared from them, says Dr Fernie, and there is no doubt that they make an excellent jelly. Formerly they were so much prized that, as Miss Amherst quotes from Le Strange's " Household Accounts," in 1618, 3s. was paid for one pound of them.

Strawberry leaves were used as a garnish and for their flavour. Parkinson tells us that they were " always used among other herbes in cooling drinks," and Markham mentions both them and Violet leaves in his directions to " Smoar a Mallard," and " to make an excellent *Olepotrige*, which is the only principall dish of boyled meate, which is esteemed in all *Spaine*. " For dessert " : The berries are often brought to the table as a rare service, whereunto Cleret wine, creame or milke is added with sugar. The water distilled of the berries is good for the passions of the heart, caused by the perturbation of the spirits being eyther drunk alone or in wine, and

maketh the heart mery." Such a pleasant and easy
remedy against the evils arising from "perturbation of
spirits" is worth remembering! Gerarde and Parkinson
both speak of the prickly strawberry; a plant which is
"of no use for meate" but which has "a small head
of greene leaves, many set thick together like unto a
double ruffe, and is fit for a gentlewoman to wear on
her arme, etc. as a raritie instead of a flower." Gerarde
has a curious little note on its discovery. "Mr John
Tradescant hath told me that he was the first that took
notice of this Strawberry and that in a woman's garden
at Plimouth, whose daughter had gathered and set the
roots in her garden, instead of the common Strawberry,
but she finding the fruit not answer her expectation,
intended to throw it away, which labour he spared her,
in taking it and bestowing it among the lovers of such
vanities." The custom of transplanting wild strawberries was very general.

> Wife, unto thy garden and set me a plot,
> With strawberry rootes of the best to be got.
> Such growing abroade, among thorns in the wood,
> Wel chosen and picked proove excellent food.
> *September's Husbandry.*—Tusser.

Miss Amherst says that in the Hampton Court
Accounts there are "several entries of money paid for
strawberry roots, brought from the wood to the King's
garden." The fact that this is no longer the custom,
may explain the disappointment that some have ex-
perienced, who, in the hope of enjoying "the most
excellent cordial smell" described by Sir Francis Bacon,
have haunted their kitchen gardens when the strawberry leaves are dying, and without reward. The
strawberries grown there at present are not, as in his
day, natives, subjected to civilisation, but are chiefly
of American or Asiatic origin (the first foreign strawberry cultivated in England was *Fragaria virginiana,* and

was introduced from North America in 1629; four years after the Essay on Gardens was first published), and if their leaves have any fragrance, it must be of the faintest possible description. Anyone, however, who passes through a wood, towards evening, especially if it is a mild and slightly damp day in October, may speedily realise how true and admirable was this counsel given by the Great Lord Chancellor.

THE ARMS OF SAFFRON WALDEN.

CHAPTER III

> Now will I weave white violets, daffodils,
>   With myrtle spray,
> And lily bells that trembling laughter fills,
>   And the sweet crocus gay,
> With these blue hyacinth and the lover's rose,
>   That she may wear—
> My sun-maiden—each scented flower that blows
>   Upon her scented hair.
>   Trans. from *Meleager.*—W. M. HARDINGE.

IT is, perhaps, surprising in studying the history of
common English herbs to find how many were the uses
to which they were put by our forefathers. One reason
of their eminence was that no doubt in pre-hygienic
days they were more to be desired, but, besides this,
something " delightful to smell to" seems to have been
a luxury generally appreciated for its own sake. In his
poem of the " Baron's Wars," Michael Drayton, by a
casual reference, shows how much agreeable scents
were valued, and the pains taken to procure them. He
is speaking of Queen Isabella's room.

> The fire of precious wood; the light perfume,
> Which left a sweetness on each thing it shone,
> As ev'rything did to itself assume
> The scent from them, and made the same their own,
> So that the painted flowers within the room
> Were sweet, as if they naturally had grown.
> The light gave colours which upon them fell,
> And to the colours the perfume gave smell.

And in describing the bewilderment of a "young,

OLD LABORATORY AT MR. HOOPER'S, 24 RUSSELL STREET, COVENT GARDEN

THE LARGE STILL IN THE CORNER IS FOR DISTILLING ROSE AND AROMATIC WATERS

THE SMALLER STILL IS FOR DISTILLING SPIRIT ESSENCES

tender maid," led through the magnificent court of some prince, he says she was :—

Amazed to see
The furnitures and states, which all embroideries be,
The rich and sumptuous beds, with tester-covering plumes,
And various as the sutes, *so various the perfumes.*

In a discourse, intended to prove that the magic number five is perpetually appearing in all forms of nature, and that network is an equally ubiquitous design, Sir Thomas Browne mentions *en passant*, the "nosegay nets" of the ancients—that is, nets holding flowers, that were suspended from the head, to provide continuously a pleasant odour for the wearer. It is very nice to find a survival of the belief that scents affect the spirits and may be beneficial to the health, and in "Days and Hours in a Garden," E. V. B. declares herself to be of that opinion. "Sweet Smells . . . have a certain virtue for different conditions of health," she says. "Wild Thyme will renew spirits and vital energy in long walks under an August sun. The pure, almost pungent scent of Tea Rose, Maréchal Neil is sometimes invigorating in any lowness of . . . Sweet Briar promotes cheerfulness . . . Hawthorn is very doubtful and Lime-blossom is dreamy. . . . Apple-blossom must be added to my pharmacopœia of sweet smells. To inhale a cluster of Blenheim orange gives back youth for just half a minute after . . . it is a real, absolute elixir."

The sacristan's garden, devoted to growing flowers and herbs for the service of the church, has been already mentioned, and Henry VI. actually left in his will a garden to be kept for this purpose to the church of Eton College (Nichol's "Wills of the Kings and Queens of England"). After the Reformation the practice of laying fresh green things about the churches was apparently not abandoned, for in 1618, James I. set forth a declaration permitting " Lawfull recreations after divine service, and allowed that women should have leave to carry rushes to the church for the decoring of it according to old custome."[1] Rushes are still strewed on Whitsunday at the church of St Mary Radcliffe, in Bristol, and the day is often called " Rush-Sunday " there in consequence.

In the accounts of St Margaret's, Westminster, there is a payment made for " herbs strewn in the church on a day of thanksgiving " in 1650. Coles (1656) says : " It is not very long since the custome of setting up Garlands in Churches, hath been left off with us, and in some places setting up of *Holly, Ivy, Rosemary, Dayes, Yew*, etc., in Churches at Christmas, is still in use."[2] Later, the custom seems almost entirely to have dropped, and in an article in the *Quarterly* (1842), the writer is torn between pious aspirations and loyalty to the church views of the day : " We cannot but admire the practice of the Church of Rome, which calls in the aid of floral decorations on her festivals. If we did not feel convinced that it was the most bounden duty of the Church of England at the present moment to give no unnecessary offence by restorations in indifferent matters, we should be inclined to advocate, notwithstanding the denunciation of some of the early Fathers, some slight exceptions in the case of our own favourites."

The decorations of English houses were much admired by Dr Levinus Lemmius in 1560, when he visited us. " And beside this, the neate cleanliness, the exquisite finenesse, the pleasaunt and delightfull furniture in every poynt for household, wonderfully rejoiced me ; their chambers and parlours strawed over with sweet herbes refreshed me."[3] Further on, he praises " the sundry sortes of fragraunte floures " about the rooms. Parkinson

[1] Fuller's " Church History," Book X. 1655. [2] " Art of Simpling."
[3] Harrison's " Description of England." Ed. by Furnivall, 1877.

mentions wall-flowers and " the greater-flag " being used
" in nosegayes and to deck up a house," and Newton says
they took branches of willow to trim up their parlours and
dining roomes in summer, and did " sticke fresh greene
leaves thereof about their beds for coolnesse." [1] Sir Hugh
Platt (1653) advised that for summer-time your chimney
may be trimmed with a fine bank of mosse . . . or with
orpin, or the white flower called everlasting . . . And at
either end one of your flower or Rosemary pots. . . . You
may also hang in the roof and about the sides of the
room small pompions or cowcumbers pricked full
of barley, and these will be overgrowne with greene
spires, so as the pompion or cowcumber will not appear.
. . . You may also plant vines without the walls, which
being let in at quarrels, may run about the sides of your
windows, and all over the sealing of your rooms." [2]
Herbs in image were sometimes hung round the room.
Harrison mentions " arras worke, or painted cloths,
wherein either diverse histories, or hearbes, beasts,
knots, and such like are stained." Of flowers
thought specially suitable indoors Tusser (1577) gives a
list : " Herbes, branches, and flowers for windows and
pots," and Bachelor's Buttons, Sweet Briar, and " bottles,
blue, red, and tawney " are among the forty he mentions.
A separate list is set forth of twenty-one " Strewing
Herbs," and this includes Basil, Balm, Marjoram, Tansy,
Germander, and Hyssop. The practice of strewing
the floors with herbs and rushes, however, started long
before his time. " At the Court of King Stephen,
which exceeded in magnificence that of his predecessors
. . . and in houses of inferior rank upon occasions of
feasting, the floor was strewed with flowers. . . .
Becket, in the next reign, according to a contemporary
author (Fitz-Stephen) ordered his hall to be strewed
every day, in the winter with fresh straw or hay, and in

[1] "Herbal of the Bible," 1587.   [2] "The Garden of Eden."

summer with rushes or green leaves, fresh gathered; and this reason is given for it, that such knights as the benches could not contain, might sit on the floor without dirtying their cloaths." [1] The contrast between the pomp of so large a following, and the simplicity of their accommodation affords an odd picture of the mingled stateliness and bareness in the great man's household.

In the reign of Edward I., "Willielmus filius Willielmi de Aylesbury tenet tres virgatus terræ . . . per serjeantiam inveniendi stramen ad lectum Domini Regis et ad straminandum cameram suam et etiam inveniendi Domino Rege cum venerit apud Alesbury in estate stramen ad lectum suam et procter hoc herbam ad juncandam cameram suam." [2] (William, son of William of Aylesbury, holds three roods of land . . . by serjeantry, of finding straw for the bed of our Lord the King and to straw his chamber . . . and also of finding for the King when he should come to Aylesbury in summer straw for his bed, and, moreover, grass or rushes to strew his chamber.) Though grass is the literal translation of *herbam*, it is quite possible, judging from old customs generally, that hay or sweet herbs, may be intended here. "It may be observed further that there is a relique of this custom still subsisting, for at Coronations the ground is strewed with flowers by a person who is upon the establishment called the Herb-Strewer, with an annual salary." From this it appears that there were persons regularly appointed to strew herbs for the royal pleasure, but for what length of time the Herb-Strewer was an official actually living at Court, it is very difficult to discover. At the time of the Coronation of James II. and his Queen, Mary Dowle was "Strewer of Herbes in Ordinary to His Majesty," and among the instructions issued before the ceremony were the following: "Two

[1] "Pegge's *Curalia*."   [2] Blount's "Jocular Tenures," 1679.

breadths of Blue Broad-cloth are spread all along the middle of the Passage from the stone steps in the Hall, to the Foot of the Steps in the Choir, ascending the Theatre, by order of the Lord Almoner of the Day, amounting in all 1220 yards; which cloth is strewed with nine Baskets full of sweet herbs and flowers by the Strewer of Herbs in Ordinary to His Majesty, assisted by six women, two to a Basket, each Basket containing two Bushels." All the details of his Coronation were most carefully considered and finally settled "in solemn conclave in the presence of James II.," says Roberts in his sketch of the *Approaching* Coronation of George II., and "little variation has taken place in the Ceremony since." From a manuscript belonging to Mr Eyston, of East Hundred, Wantage, dated 1702, W. Jones ("Crowns and Coronations") quotes an: "Order for a gown of scarlet cloth, with a badge of Her Majesty's Cypher on it, for the Strewer of Herbs to Her Majesty, as was provided at the last Coronation." This looks as if she played her part in the ceremony of crowning King William and Queen Mary, and was also present at the crowning of Queen Anne, though Roberts, in his "Complete Account of the Coronations of the Kings and Queens of England" does not mention her. In the State Archives is a "Warrant to the Master of the Great Wardrobe for delivering of scarlet cloth to Alice Blizard, herb strewer to Her Majesty," dated 30th November 1713, showing that whether at that date she was continually at Court, or whether her services were confined to the day of Coronation, she was at anyrate officially recognised in the ordinary course of things, and not only when any very great ceremony was imminent. I cannot be sure if the Herb Strewer appeared at the Coronation of George I., but she certainly did at that of George II., and in the full accounts of the Coronation of George IV., which was celebrated with great magnificence, there are most elaborate descriptions of her dress, badge, mantle, etc., and also portraits of her in full attire. From among many applicants, the King chose Miss Fellowes, sister of the Secretary to the Lord Great Chamberlain, for the coveted distinction. " Miss Fellowes wore a gold badge suspended from her neck by a gold chain, with an inscription indicative of her office on one side, and the King's arms beautifully chased on the other. Six young ladies assisted her. Their costume was white, but Miss Fellowes wore, in addition, a scarlet mantle trimmed with gold lace. They were very elegantly dressed in " white muslin, with flowered ornaments. Three large ornamented baskets of flowers were brought in and placed near the ladies," [1] who walked in the front of the Royal Procession. At ten minutes before eleven Miss Fellowes, with her six tributary herb-women heading the grand procession, appeared at the Western Gate of the Abbey. . . . She and her maids and the serjeant porter came no further, but remained at the entrance within the west door. In a beautiful series of coloured plates depicting all the costumes worn at that Coronation, there is one of Miss Fellowes and her " maids." She has a small basket in her left hand ; from her right hand, raised high, she is letting a shower of blossoms fall. Her hair is dressed in short ringlets. All the ladies wore wreaths of flowers, and the " maids" have, as well, long garlands falling over one shoulder and across their white dresses almost to the hem. In a charming letter written by Hon. Maria Twistleton to her cousin, Mrs Eardley Childers, there is one more detail of these ladies. " Gold Baskets of Grecian shape, filled with choicest sweets were ranged at their feet, and as they passed they presented a magnolia to us." [2] A claim to this office was

---

[1] " History of the Coronation of George IV." R. Huish.
[2] Published *Nineteenth Century*, June 1902.

put forward, before the last Coronation, but alas! His Majesty decided to dispense with this picturesque adjunct to the ceremony! Though the strewing of rushes and herbs was a part of the preparations for any household festival, they were a special feature of bridal ceremonies.

> As I have seen upon a bridal day,
> Full many maids clad in their best array,
> In honour of the bride come with their flaskets
> Fill'd full with flowers: others, in wicker-baskets
> Bring from the marish, rushes to o'erspread
> The ground whereon to church the lovers tread.
>
> *Br. Pastorals*, book i.

Drayton, too, alludes to this practice in the "Polyolbion."

> Some others were again as seriously employ'd
> In strewing of those herbs, at bridals us'd that be
> Which everywhere they throw with bounteous hands and free.
> The healthful balm and mint from their full laps do fly.
>
> Song xv.

And gives a long list of wedding flowers, of which Meadow-sweet (sometimes called bridewort) is one. Gilded Rosemary, or sprigs of Rosemary dipped in sweet waters were used, and Brand gives an account of a wedding where the bride was "led to church between two sweet boys with bride-laces and rosemary tied to their silken sleeves."[1] Nosegays, too, were gathered for weddings, and Brand quotes a remarkable and cynical passage from "The Plaine Country Bridegroom," by Stephens: "He shews neere affinitie betwixt marriage and hanging, and to that purpose he provides a great nosegay and shakes hands with everyone he meets, as if he were preparing for a condemned man's voyage." Herrick's lines beginning, "Strip her of spring-time, tender, whimpering maids," are too well known to repeat, but they tell very prettily which flowers were

[1] Popular Antiquities.

appropriated to the married and which to the unmarried.
Dyer tells us that this custom of strewing them is still
kept up in Cheshire, with occasional sad results. Often,
the flowers that were strewn were emblematical, and if
the bride chanced to be unpopular, she stepped her way
to church over flowers whose meanings were the reverse
of complimentary!

Drayton's contemporaries were more amiable.

> Who now a posie pins not in his cap?
> And not a garland baldrick-wise doth wear,
> Some, of such flowers as to his hand doth hap
> Others, such as secret meanings bear.
>
> He, from his lass, him lavender hath sent
> Shewing her love, and doth requital crave,
> Him rosemary, his sweetheart whose intent,
> Is that he her should in remembrance have.
>
> Roses, his youth and strong desire express,
> Her sage, doth show his sovereignty in all;
> The July-flower declares his gentleness;
> Thyme, truth; the pansie, heartsease, maidens' call.
>
> Eclogue ix.

Herbs have pointed proverbs; for instance: "He who
sows hatred, shall gather rue,"—a saying which some
have found to be "ower-true"; and, "The Herb-
Patience does not grow in every man's garden,"—a piece
of wisdom which may be proved only too often. Both
these proverbs turn on a pun, but some herbs are alluded
to in a literal sense. The old Herbalists used to count
Pinks among herbs, and this flower's name is very
commonly heard in the expression: "The pink of
perfection." Mercutio says in *Romeo and Juliet*, "I am
the very pink of courtesy"; a phrase which is wonderfully expressive. Miss Amherst quotes an old ballad to
show that the periwinkle was used as a term of praise,
for in this, a noble lady, a type of excellence, is called,
"The parwink of prowesse." The inelasticity of
modern opinions (on herbs) forbids that I should here

go into the history of this most interesting flower, beloved by Rousseau and endowed by the French with magic power. One of their names for it is, *Violette de Sorcier*. I will only say that the Italians call it the " Flower of the Dead," and place it on graves ; and to the Germans it is the " Flower of Immortality." In England it was much used in garlands, and it was with Periwinkle that Simon Fraser was crowned in mockery, when in 1306 (after he had been taken prisoner, fighting for Bruce), he rode, heavily ironed, through London to the place of execution.

Clove gillyflowers were admitted, till lately, into the herb-garden, so I may mention that among several cases of nominal rent, land being held on the payment of certain flowers or other trifles, " three clove gillyflowers to be rendered on the occasion of the King's Coronation," was once the condition of holding the " lands and tenements of Ham in Surrey." Roses were the flowers most often chosen for such a purpose, and roses and gillyflowers together were paid as rent by St Andrew's Monastery in Northampton at the time of its dissolution under Oliver Cromwell. Blount[1] mentions that Bartholomaus Peyttevyn, of Stony-Aston in Somerset, held his lands on the payment of a " sextary " of Gillyflower wine annually, at Christmastide. A "sextary" contained about a pint and a half, sometimes more. " A still more whimsical tenure was that of a farm at Brookhouse, Penistone, York, for which, yearly, a payment was to be made of a red rose at Christmas and a snowball at mid-summer. Unless the flower of the Viburnum or Guelder-rose, sometimes called Snowball, was meant, the payment bill had been almost impossible in those days when ice-cellars were unknown."[2]

Clove gillyflowers found their way into Heraldry,

[1] "Jocular Tenures."   [2] " History of Signboards."

and appeared as heraldic emblems, and besides them, Guillim mentions " Rosemary, Sweet Marjoram, Betony, Purslane and Saffron," being borne in Coat Armour. But, " because such daintiness and affected adornings better befit ladies and gentlemen than knights and men of valour, whose worth must be tried in the field, not under a rose-bed, or in a garden-plot, therefore the ancient Generous made choice rather of such herbs as grew in the fields, as the Cinque-foil, Trefoil," etc.[1] It is an interesting explanation of the reason that dictated the choice of these two last herbs, often seen in heraldic bearings. One of Guillim's corrections must specially delight all west country people. The Coat of the Baskerviles of Hereford was: Argent, a cheveron, Gules, between three Hurts. " These (saith *Leigh*) appear light blue and come of some violent stroke. But, if I mistake not, he is farr wide from the matter . . . whereas they are indeed a kind of fruit or small round Berry, of colour betwixt black and blue . . . and in some places called Windberries, and in others Hurts or Hurtleberries."   Guillim knew the popular name of Whortleberries better than did his fellow-author. The idea of choosing three bruises as a " charge " does not seem to have struck *Mr Leigh* as being at all odd.

In Saxony Rue has given its name to an Order. A chaplet of Rue borne bendwise on " barrs of the Coat Armour of the Dukedom of Saxony " (till then " Barry of ten, sable and or,") was granted by the Emperor Frederick Barbarossa to Duke Bernard of Anhalt (the first of his house to be Duke of Saxony), at his request, "to difference his arms from his Brothers'," Otho, Marquis of Brandenberg, and Siegfrid, Archbishop of Breme. This took place in the year 1181, but the Order was not founded till more than six centuries had passed, and was then due to Frederick Augustus, first King of

[1] Guillim. " Heraldry."

Saxony, who created the Order of the *Rautenkrone* on the 20th July 1807. In the newspapers of October 24th, 1902, it was announced that the King of Saxony had conferred the Order of the Crown of Rue on the Prince of Wales. Sprigs of Rue are now interlaced in the Collar of the Order of the Thistle, but earlier it was composed of thistles and knots. There is extreme uncertainty as to the origin or this Order, and cold suspicion is thrown on assertions that it was, of old, an established "Fraternity,[1] following the lines of other Orders of Knighthood." The first appearance of a collar is on the gold bonnet pieces struck in 1539, where King James V. is represented with a collar composed alternately of thistle heads and what seem to be knots or links in the form of the figure 8 or of the letter S, and a similar collar is placed round the Royal Arms in another gold piece of the same year. Collars with knots of a slightly different shape appear on Queen Mary's Great Seal and on that of James VI. Ashmole says:[2] "It was thought fit that the collars of both the Garter and Thistle of King Charles I. should be used in Scotland, 1633"; but after that the Order seems to have lapsed, for Guillim (Ed. 1679) puts the "Order of Knights of The Thistle or of St Andrewe's" between the Orders of The Knights of the Round Table and the Knights of the Holy Sepulchre in Jerusalem, and speaks of all their rites and ceremonies in the past tense. This seems as if at that period there was an absolute pause in its chequered career. In 1685 it was "revived" by James II. of Great Britain, who created eight knights, but during the Revolution it lapsed again and "lay neglected till Queen Anne in 1703 restored it to the primitive design of twelve

[1] Sir H. Nicholas. "History of the Orders of Knighthood of the British Empire."
[2] "History of the Most Noble Order of the Garter."

Knights of St Andrew" (Every). "By a statute
passed in 1827 the Order is to consist of the Sovereign
and sixteen Knights" (Burke). Sprigs of Rue do
not make their earliest appearance in the collar till
about 1629 and then on doubtful authority. "Mirœus,
however, states that the Collar was made of Thistles
and Sprigs of Rue; and the Royal Achievements of
Scotland in Sir George Mackenzie's 'Science of
Heraldry' published in 1680, are surrounded by a
Collar of Thistles linked with Sprigs of Rue."
Very shortly before this Guillim had described the
collar as being " composed of thistles, intermixed with
annulets of gold." So the publication of Sir George
Mackenzie's book must be the approximate date of the
introduction of the Rue; the present collar, badge
and robe of the Order are the same as those approved
by Queen Anne. André Favyn[1] gives the reasons
for this choice of plants, though as the Rue made its
first appearance in the collar so much later than the
date he assigns (which is that of Charlemagne) one
cannot help fearing that he drew a little on his imagination. King Achaius took for " his devise the Thistle
and the Rewe. And for the Soule therof, Pour ma
deffence Because the Thistle is not tractable or easily
handled . . . giving acknowledgment thereby, that
hee feared not forraigne Princes his neighbours . . .
as for the Rewe although it be an Herbe and Plant
very meane, yet it is (nevertheless full of admirable
vertues) . . . and serveth to expell and drive serpents
to flight . . . and there is not a more soveraigne
remedy for such as are poisoned." Guillim called
Hungus, King of the Picts, the founder, and says that
he, " the Night before the Battle that was fought betwixt
him and *Athelstane*, King of England, sawe in the skie
a bright Cross in fashion of that whereon St Andrew

[1] " Theater of Honour," 1623.

suffered Martyrdom, and the day proving successful unto *Hungus* in memorial of the said Apparition, which did presage so happy an omen, the Picts and Scots have ever since bore in the Ensigns and Banners the Figure of the said Cross, which is in fashion of a Saltier. And from thence 'tis believed that this Order took its rise, which was about the year of our Lord 810." Both authors are quite positive as to their facts regarding the origin of the Order, but they have hardly one fact in common, not even the founder's name!

It is perhaps not very well known that there was once a French Order of the Thistle, or, as it was sometimes called, " Order of Bourbon." It was instituted by Louis II., third Duke of Bourbon, surnamed the Good Duke, and it consisted six and twenty knights,[1] each of whom "wore a Belt, in which was embroydered the word *Esperance* in capital letters; it had a Buckle of Gold at which hung a tuft like a Thistle; on the Collar also was embroydered the same word *Esperance*, with *Flowers* de Luce of Gold from which hung an Oval, wherein was the Image of the Virgin *Mary*, entowered with a golden sun, crowned with twelve stars of silver and a silver crescent under her feet; at the end of the Oval was the head of a Thistle."

There are other Orders called after flowers, or of which flowers form the badge. Several of the "Christian Orders of Knighthood"—orders instituted for some religious or pious purpose—bore lilies among their tokens, and flowers-de-luce appeared in many. The Order of the Lily or of Navarre was instituted by Prince Garcia in 1048. The Order of the *Looking-Glass* of the Virgin *Mary* was created by " *Ferdinand*, the Infant of *Castile*, upon a memorable victory he had over the *Moors*. The Collar of this Order was composed of Bough-pots, full of Lillies, interlaced with Griffons."

[1] Ross. " View of all Religions," 1653.

Ross and Favyn give most curious accounts of the Order " De la Sainte Magdalaine." This was instituted by a Noble Gentleman of France, who is alternately called John Chesnil or Sieur de la Chapronaye, " Out of a godly Zeal to reclaim the French from their Quarrels, Duels and other sins. . . . The Cross of the Order had at three ends, three Flowers-de-Luce ; the Cross is beset with Palms to shew this Order was instituted to encourage Voyages to the Holy Land, within the Palms are Sunbeams and four *Flowers-de-Luce* to shew the glory of the French Nation." They had a house allotted them near Paris, " wherein were ordinarily five hundred Knights, bound to stay there during two years' probation. . . . The Knights that live abroad shall meet every year at their house called the lodging Royal on Mary Magdalene's Festival Day." The Lay Brothers were to be of good family ; the *Vallets des Chevaliers*, of " honestes *Familles d'Artisans et Mecaniques.*" Their garb was carefully ordered, and they were to take the same vows as their master. Other elaborate arrangements were made—" But this Order, as it began, so it ended in the person of Chesnil." One's breath is taken away, as when, in a dream, one falls and falls to immense depths and awakes with a sudden shock ! Francis, Duke of Bretaigne, created the Order of Bretaigne : " This Order consisteth of five and twenty Knights of the *Ears of Corn*, so called to signifie that Princes should be careful to preserve Husbandry." Favyn, however, finds a much more romantic origin for the name, and tells a long story of a dispute among the gods as to the thing most essential to " les Humains." After lengthy argument, " de sorte que Jupiter toujours favorisant les Dames," he declared victory to rest with Ceres, to whose verdict that of Minerva was joined (Minerva had pleaded the Ox), and so they both triumphed over the others.

In Amsterdam, a literary guild was once named after

a herb, and was called the White Lavender Bloom. Herbs have not appeared on many signboards, but in 1638 the marigold was the sign of " Francis Eglisfield, a bookseller in St Paul's churchyard,"[1] as it still is of Child's Bank—and several signs of the " Rosemary Branch" have been known.

The Blessed Thistle was a much prized herb, and its cousin, the Spear Thistle, makes a game for Scotch children ; it is sometimes called " Marian," and when the flower-heads have turned to " blow-balls " the children puff away the down and call :—

> " Marian, Marian, what's the time of day ?
> One o'clock, two o'clock, its time we were away."

Dandelions are still commoner toys.

Grimmer associations are tied up with the bouquet presented to Judges at the Assizes, for originally this bouquet was a bunch of herbs, given to him to ward off the gaol-fever, that was cheerfully accepted as a matter of course for prisoners.   Thornton, writing in 1810, says of Rue, that it is " supposed to be antipestilential" and hence our benches of judges are " regaled" with its unpleasing odour.   Lupines are not properly to be included here, but Parkinson must be quoted as to a curious use of their seeds.   In Plautus' days, " they were used in Comedies instead of money, when in any scene thereof there was any show of payment."   One is glad he condescends to tell us this detail of ancient stage-plays. Among herbs used for nosegays he mentions Basil, Sweet Marjoram, Maudeline and Costmary, and evidently contemplates their being worn for ornament, and speaking of the prickly strawberry remarks it is " fit for a Gentlewoman to weare on her arme, etc., as a raritie instead of a flower."   Scents were more perpetually to be obtained by carrying a pomander, which was originally an orange

[1] " The History of Signboards."

stuffed with spices, and thought also to be good against infection. Cardinal Wolsey is described as carrying a " very fair orange, whereof the meat or substance was taken out and filled up again with part of a sponge whereon was vinegar, and other confection against the pestilential airs "; evidently some alexiphar-mick, which he " smelt unto " when going into a crowded chamber. Drayton says, in speaking of a well dedicated to St Winifred :—

> The sacred Virgin's well, her moss most sweet and rare
> Against infectious damps, for pomander to wear.
> *Polyolbion.*

The pomander developed into being a little scent-case, elaborately made. Mr Dillon describes a silver one of the sixteenth century which he saw in a collection. It was made to be hung by a chain from the girdle, and though " no larger than a plum, contains eight compartments inscribed as follows: ambra, moscheti (musk), viola, naransi (orange), garofalo (gillyflowers), rosa, cedro, jasmins." Sweet-scented plants were reduced to " sweete pouthers," and many were distilled into " sweete waters " and " sweete washing waters," or helped to make " washing balls." Orange-flower water is spoken of as " a great perfume for gloves, to wash them, or instead of Rose-water," and less expensive distillations must have contented more economical housewives. Parkinson tells us of sweet marjoram being put into " sweete bags," and costmary flowers and lavender tied up in small bundles for their " sweet sent and savour." Regarding " sweet water " there is a delightful description in Ben Jonson's Masque *Chloridia*, " Enter Rain, presented by five persons . . . their hair flagging as if they were wet, and in the hands, balls full of sweet water, which as they dance, sprinkle all the room."

The following entry is made among "Queen Elizabeth's Annual Expences":—

Makers of hearb bowres and planters of
    trees   .   .   .   Fee, £25
Stillers of Waters .   .   ,,   40
John Kraunckwell and his wife, 1584.

Peck's Desiderata.

These offices must have been of considerable importance, for when money went much further than it does nowadays, an annual fee of £40 for "stilling waters" was a high one.

> For never resting time leads summer on
> To hideous winter, and confounds him there ;
> Sap check'd with frost, and lusty leaves quite gone,
> Beauty o'ershow'd, and bareness everywhere.
> Then, were not summer's distillation left,
> A liquid prisoner pent in walls of glass,
> Beauty's effect with beauty were bereft,
> Nor it, nor no remembrance what it was.
> But flower's distill'd, though they with winter meet
> Lese but their show ; their substance still lives sweet.
>
> Sonnet V.—SHAKESPEARE.

Among some charming recipes Mrs Roundell gives a charming one for "Dorothea Roundell's Sweet-Jar." But, perhaps, even sweeter is the next recipe, called simply Sweet-Jar.

Sweet-Jar.

" ½ lb. bay salt, ¼ lb. salt-petre and common salt, all to be bruised and put on six baskets of rose-leaves, 24 bay leaves torn to bits, a handful of sweet myrtle leaves, 6 handfuls of lavender blossom, a handful of orange or syringa blossoms, the same of sweet violets, and the same of the red of clove carnations. After having well stirred every day for a week, add ½ oz. cloves, 4 oz. orris root, ½ oz. cinnamon, and two nutmegs all pounded ; put on the roses, kept well covered up in a china jar and stirred sometimes." The recipe of a delicious *Pot Pourri* made in a country house in Devonshire has also been very kindly sent me :—

Pot Pourri.

" Gather flowers in the morning when dry and lay them in the sun till the evening.

Roses.
Orange flowers.
Jasmine.
Lavender.
Thyme. ⎫
Marjoram. ⎬ In smaller quantities.
Sage. ⎪
Bay ⎭

" Put them into an earthen wide jar, or hand basin, in layers.   Add the following ingredients :—

6 lbs. vi.	Bay Salt.
℥ iv.	Yellow Sandal Wood.
℥ iv.	Acorus Calamus Root.
℥ iv.	Cassia Buds.
℥ iv.	Orris Root.
℥ ii.	Cinnamon.
℥ ii.	Cloves.
℥ iv.	Gum Benzoin.
ʒ i.	Storax Calamite.
℥ i.	ʒ Otto of Rose.
ʒ i.	Musk.
℥ ss.	Powdered Cardamine Seeds.

"Place the rose-leaves, etc., in layers in the jar. Sprinkle the Bay salt and other ingredients on each layer, press it tightly down and keep for two or three months before taking it out."

The following herbs are those which are chiefly valued for their perfume or for their historical associations.

BERGAMOT

BERGAMOT (*Monarda fistulosa*).

It is extraordinary how little comment has been made on the handsome red flowers and fragrant leaves of Red Bergamot, or Bee-Balm—a name which Robinson gives it. Growing in masses, it makes a lovely bit of colour, and a very sweet border. Bergamot was a favourite flower in the posies that country people used to take to church, as Mrs Ewing observes in her story "Daddy Darwin's Dove Cot." The youthful heroine loses her posy of "Old Man and Marygolds" on the way to Sunday school, and is discovered looking for it by an equally youthful admirer. He at once offers to get her some more Old Man. "But Phœbe drew nearer. She stroked down her frock, and spoke mincingly but confidentially. 'My mother says Daddy Darwin has red bergamot i' his garden. We've none i' ours. My mother always says there's nothing like red bergamot to take to church. She says it's a deal more refreshing than Old Men, and not so common." A note gives the information that the particular kind of Bergamot meant here was the Twinflower *Monarda Didyma*. There are several varieties of Monarda.

The only superstition that I have ever heard in any way connected with the plant is, that in Dorsetshire it is thought unlucky, and that if it be kept in a house an illness will be the consequence.

COSTMARY (*Tanacetum Balsamita*).

Coole violets and orpine growing still,
Enbathed balme and cheerfull galingale,
Fresh costmarie and healthfull camomile.

Muiopotmos.

Then balm and mint help to make up
My chaplet and for trial
Costmary that so likes the cup,
And next it penny-royal.

Muses' Elysium.

> Then hot muscado oil, with milder maudlin cast,
> Stroing tansey, fennel cool, they prodigally waste.
>
> *Polyolbion*, Song **xv.**

Costmary or Alecost, and Maudeline (*Balsamita Vulgaris*), have so close a semblance that they may be taken together. The German name for Costmary, *Frauen münze*, supports the natural idea that it was dedicated to the Virgin, but Dr Prior says that the Latin name used to be *Costus amarus*, not *Costus Marie*, and that it was really appropriated to St Mary Magdaleine, as its English name Maudeline declares. Both plants were much used to make " sweete washing water; the flowers are tyed up with small bundles of lavender toppes; these they put in the middle of them, to lye upon the toppes of beds, presses, etc., for the sweet sent and savour it casteth." [1] They were also used for strewing. In France Costmary is sometimes used in salads, and it was formerly put into beer and negus; " hence the name *Alecost*."

GERMANDER (*Teucrium Chamœdrys*).

> Clear hysop and therewith the comfortable thyme,
> Germander with the rest, each thing then in her prime.
>
> *Polyolbion*, Song **xv.**

> Germander, marjoram and thyme,
>   Which used are for strewing,
> With hisop as an herb most prime,
>   Herein my wreath bestowing.
>
> *Muses' Elysium.*

Germander was grown as a border to garden "knots," "though being more used as a strewing herbe for the house than for any other use." [1] Culpepper says it is " a most prevalent herb of Mercury, and strengthens the brain and apprehension exceedingly;" and Tusser includes it amongst his " strewing herbs"; from which statements it may be gathered that the scent was pungent

[1] Parkinson.

but agreeable. It is more often mentioned by old herbalists as "bordering knots" than in any other capacity, in spite of Parkinson's remark, and now is very seldom seen at all. It may, very rarely, be found growing wild. Harrison, when he is declaiming against the over-praising of foreigners, says: "Our common Germander, or thistle benet, is found and knowne to bee so wholesome and of so great power in medicine as any other hearbe," but it is not clear whether he really means Germander, or is not rather thinking of *Carduus Benedictus*..

GILLIFLOWER (*Dianthus Caryophyllus*).

Jeliflowers is for gentlenesse,
Which in me shall remaine,
Hoping that no sedition shal
Depart our hearts in twaine.
As soon the sun shall loose his course,
The moone against her kinde,
Shall have no light if that I do
Once put you from my minde.

CLEMENT ROBINSON.

Come, and I will sing you—
"What will you sing me?"
I will sing you Four, O,
What is your Four, O?
Four it is the Dilly Hour, when blooms the gilly-flower.

Dilly Song.—Songs of the West.

I'll weave my love a garland,
    It shall be dressed so fine,
I'll set it round with roses,
    With lilies, pinks and thyme.

The Loyal Lover.

There stood a gardener at the gate
    And in each hand a flower,
O pretty maid, come in, he said,
    And view my beauteous bower.

The lily it shall be thy smock,
    The jonquil shoe thy feet,
Thy gown shall be the ten-week-stock,
    To make thee fair and sweet.

> The gilly-flower shall deck thy head
> Thy way with herbs, I'll strew,
> Thy stockings shall be marigold
> Thy gloves the vi'let blue.
>
> *Dead Maid's Land.*

Gillyflowers are, of course, now excluded from the nerb-border, but once housewives infused them in vinegar to make it aromatic, and candied them for conserves, and numbered them among their herbs, though that is not the reason that they mentioned here. They have their place, because the general ideas about them are too pretty to leave out. First, they were the token of gentleness, as Robinson's lover asserts most touchingly, and Drayton confirms in his line,

> The July-flower declares his gentleness.

Then Gillyflowers (says Folkard) were represented in some old songs to be one of the flowers that grow in Paradise. He quotes from a ballad called " Dead Men's Songs." This verse:

> The fields about the city faire
> Were all with Roses set,
> Gillyflowers and Carnations faire
> Which canker could not fret.
>
> *Ancient Songs.*—RITSON.

There have been great discussions as to what flower was the original " Gillyflower " spoken of by early writers. Folkard says it was " apparently a kind of pet-name to all manner of plants." Parkinson seems to have called Carnations, Clove- Gillyflowers, and Stocks, the Stock-Gillyflowers, and Wall-flowers, Wall-Gillyflowers. It is generally thought that the earlier writers called the *Dianthus* by this name, and later ones, the *Cheiranthus cheiri*, or *Matthiola*. Some of the names for them show how sadly imagination has waned since the seventeenth century. Think of a new flower being called " Ruffling Robin " or " The lustie Gallant," or " Master Tuggie's

Princess," or "Mister Bradshaw, his dainty Lady." Even "the Sad Pageant" has romance about it, but we can match that by a name for *Hesperides* which, I believe, still survives, "The Melancholy Gentleman." Culpepper calls Gillyflowers, "gallant, fine and temperate," but says, "It is vain to describe a herb so well known." So there we will leave them.

LAVENDER (*Lavandula vera*).

Here's flowers for you,
Hat lavender, mints, savory, marjoram,
The marigold that goes to bed wi' the sun,
And with him rises weeping.
Winter's Tale, iv. 3.

The wholesome saulge and lavender still gray,
Ranke smelling Rue, and cummin good for eyes.
Muiopotmos.

Opening upon level plots
Of crowned lilies standing near
Purple spiked lavender.
Ode to Memory.—TENNYSON.

Lavender is for lovers true,
Which evermore be faine,
Desiring always for to have
Some pleasure for their paine.
C. ROBINSON.

Piscator. "I'll now lead you to an honest ale-house; where we shall find a cleanly room, lavender in the windows and twenty ballads stuck about the wall." *The Complete Angler.*

Lavender is one of the few herbs that has always been in great repute and allusions to it are legion. From the custom of laying it among linen, or other carefully stored goods, a proverb has arisen—Timbs quotes from Earle's *Microcosm*: "He takes on against the Pope without mercy and has a jest still *in Lavender* for Bellarmine." Walton's *Coridon* mentions that "the sheets" smell of lavender in a literal sense, and Parkinson says that it is much put among "apparell." Oil of Lavender is still to be found in the British Pharmacopœia, and some of the

old writers utter serious warnings against "divers rash
and overbold Apothecaries and other foolish women,"
who gave indiscriminately the distilled water, or composition that is made of distilled wine in which flower
seeds have been steeped. Turner suggests using it
in a curious manner. "I judge that the flowers of
Lavander quilted in a cappe and dayly worne are good
for all diseases of the head that come of a cold cause and
that they comfort the braine very well." Dr Fernie says
it is of real use in a case of nervous headache. Lavender
used to be called Lavender Spike or Spike alone, and
French Lavender (*L. Stæchas*) Stickadove or Cassidony,
sometimes turned by country people into Cast-me-down.
La petite Corbeille tells us that the juice of Lavender is a
specific in cases of loss of speech and adds drily, " une
telle propriété suffirait pour rendre cette plante à jamais
precieuse." In Spain and Portugal it is used to strew
churches and it is burned in bonfires on St John's Day,
the day when all evil spirits are abroad. In some
countries it must still possess wonderful qualities!
Tuscan peasants believe that it will prevent the Evil
Eye from hurting children.

The pretty delicately-scented spikes of White Lavender
are less well known than they should be, but like many
other herbs they received more admiration in former days
as has been already said, at the close of the sixteenth
century, a literary guild was called after it. In the
Parliamentary Survey (November 1649) of the Manor
of Wimbledon, "Late parcel of the possessions of
Henrietta Maria, the relict and late Queen of Charles
Stuart, late King of England"—an exact inventory is
made of the house and grounds (in which forty-four
perches of land, called the Hartichoke Garden is named),
and among other things, " very great and large borders
of Rosemary, Rue and White Lavender and great
varietie of excellent herbs" are noticed.

LAVENDER COTTON (*Santolina*).

Lavender Cotton is a little grey plant with " very finely cut leaves, clustered buttons of a golden colour and of a sweet smell and is often used in garlands and in decking up of gardens and houses." The French called it *Petit Cyprez* and *Guarde Robe*, from which it may be inferred that it was one of the herbs laid in chests among furs and robes. Tusser counts it among his "strewing herbes," and it is now chiefly used as an edging to beds or borders.

MEADOW-SWEET (*Spiræa Ulmaria*).

Bring, too, some branches forth of Daphne's hair,
And gladdest myrtle for the posts to wear,
With spikenard weav'd and marjorams between
And starr'd with yellow-golds and meadows-queen.
Pan's Anniversary.—BEN JONSON.

Amongst these strewing herbs, some others wild that grow,
As burnet, all abroad, and meadow-wort they throw.
Polyolbion, Song xv.

She. The glow-room lights, as day is failing
    Dew is falling over the field.
He. The meadow-sweet its scent is exhaling,
    Honeysuckles their fragrance yield.
Together. Then why should we be all the day toiling?
    Lads and lasses, along with me!
She. There's Jack o' Lantern lustily dancing,
    In the marsh with flickering flame.
He. And Daddy long-legs, spinning and prancing,
    Moth and midge are doing the same.
Chorus. Then why should we, etc.
S. BARING-GOULD.

Where peep the gaping speckled cuckoo-flowers
The meadow-sweet flaunts high its showy wreath
And sweet the quaking grasses hide beneath.
Summer.—CLARE.

Shall I strew on thee rose or rue or laurel?
Or quiet sea flower moulded by the sea,
Or simples and growth of meadow-sweet or sorrel.
Ave Atque Vale.—SWINBURNE.

Pale Iris growing where the streams wind slowly
Round the smooth shoulders of untrodden hills,
White meadow-sweet and yellow daffodils.
Phæcia.—N. HOPPER.

Queen of the Meadow and Bridewort are two of this flower's most appropriate names and a very pretty one is that which Gerarde tells us the Dutch give it, *Reinette.* The Herbalists do not say much about the "Little Queen," but what they do say, is in the highest degree complimentary. Gerarde decides: "The leaves and flowers excel all other strong herbes for to deck up houses, to strew in chambers, hall and banquetting houses in the summer time ; for the smell thereof makes the heart merrie, delighteth the senses, neither doth it cause headache" as some other sweet smelling herbes do. Parkinson, who says it "has a pretty, sharp sent and taste," praises it for the same purpose and adds the interesting bit of gossip that " Queen *Elizabeth* of famous memory, did more desire it than any other sweet herbe to strew her chambers withal. A leafe or two hereof layd in a cup of wine, will give as quick and fine a rellish therto as Burnet will," he finishes practically. Turner says that women, in the spring-time, " put it into the potages and mooses." I have known it used medicinally by a Herbalist, and can strongly recommend it as an ingredient for *pôt pourri.* The scent is so sweet and clinging that it is surprising that meadow-sweet is not oftener in request when dried and scented flowers are wanted. The Icelander says that if taken on St John's Day and thrown into water, it will help to reveal a thief, for if the culprit be a man, it will sink, if a woman, it will float.

ROSEMARY (*Rosmarinus officinalis*).

Here's Rosemary for you, that's for remembrance.—

Hamlet, iv. 5.

> Rosemary's for remembrance,
> Between us day and night,
> Wishing that I may always have
> You present in my sight.
>
> C. ROBINSON.

The double daisy, thrift, the button batchelor,
Sweet William, sops-in-wine, the campion ; and to these
Some lavender they put, with rosemary and bays,
Sweet marjoram, with her like sweet basil rare for smell,
With many a flower, whose name were now too long to tell.
Polyolbion, Song **xv.**

Oh, thou great shepheard, Lobbin, how great is thy griefe?
Where bene the nosegays that she dight for thee?
The coloured chaplets wrought with a chiefe,
The knotted rush-rings and gilt rosmarie?
November, Shepheard's Calender.—SPENSER.

Rosemary has always been of more importance than
any other herb, and more than most of them put
together. It has been employed at weddings and
funerals, for decking the church and for garnishing
the banquet hall, in stage-plays, and in " swelling dis-
content," of a too great reality ; as incense in religious
ceremonies, and in spells against magic ; " in sickness
and in health "; eminently as a symbol, and yet for very
practical uses. It is quite an afterthought to regard
it as a plant. In " Popular Antiquities," Brand gives
such an admirable account of it that one would like
to quote in full, but must bear in mind the warning,
quoted from " Eachard's *Observations*," in those pages :
" I cannot forget him, who having at some time or
other been suddenly cur'd of a little head-ache with
a Rosemary posset, would scarce drink out of anything
but Rosemary cans, cut his meat with a Rosemary
knife. . . . Nay, sir, he was so strangely taken up
with the excellencies of Rosemary, that he would needs
have the Bible cleared of all other herbs and only
Rosemary to be inserted." At weddings it was often
gilded or dipped in scented waters, or tied " about
with silken ribbands of all colours." Sometimes for
want of it Broom was used. Mr Friend quotes an
account of a sixteenth century " rustic bridal " at
which " every wight with hiz blu buckeram bridelace
upon a branch of green broom—because Rosemary iz

skant thear—tyed on hiz leaft arm." **A** wedding
sermon by Robert Hacket (1607) is also quoted:
" Rosemary . . . which by name, nature, and continued
use, man challengeth as properly belonging to himselfe.
It overtoppeth all the flowers in the garden, boasting
man's rule. Another property of the Rosemary is, it
affecteth the hart. Let this Rosmarinus, this flower
of men, ensigne of your wisdom, love and loyaltie,
be carried not only in your hands, but in your heads
and harts." Ben Jonson says it was the custom for
bridesmaids to present the bridegroom with " a bunch
of Rosemary, bound with ribands," on his first appearance on his wedding morn. Together with an orange
stuck with cloves, it often served as a little New
Year's gift; and the same author mentions this in his
Christmas Masque. The masque opens by showing
half the players unready, and clamouring for missing
properties; and *Gambol*, one of them, says, of *New
Year's Gift*: " He has an orange and Rosemary, but
not a clove to stick in it." A little later, *New Year's
Gift* enters, " in a blue coat, serving-man-like, with
an orange and a sprig of Rosemary, gilt, on his head."
Wassel comes too, " like a neat sempster and songster,
her page bearing a brown bowl drest with ribands and
Rosemary before her."

For less festive occasions it had other meanings: "As
for Rosmarine, I lett it runne all over my garden walls,
not onlie because my bees love it, but because it is the
herb sacred to remembrance, and therefore to friendship;
whence a sprig of it hath a dumb language that maketh
it the chosen emblem of our funeral wakes and in our
buriall grounds." Sir Thomas More thought this, but
others beside him " lett Rosmarine run all over garden
walls," though perhaps they had less sentiment about it;
Hentzner (*Travels*) (1598) says that it was a custom "exceedingly common in England." At Hampton Court,

ROSEMARY

Rosemary was " so planted and nailed to the walls as to cover them entirely."[1] The bushes were sometimes set " by women for their pleasure,[2] to grow in sundry proportions, as in the fashion of a cart, a peacock or such things as they fancy," or the branches were twined amongst others to make an arbour. Brown refers to this :—

> Within an arbour, shadow'd by a vine
> Mix'd with Rosemary and Eglantine.
> *Br. Pastorals*, book i.

Rosemary was one of the chief funeral herbs. Herrick says :—

> Grow it for two ends, it matters not at all,
> Be't for my bridall or my buriall.

Sprigs of it were distributed to the mourners before they left the house, which they carried to the churchyard and threw on the coffin when it had been lowered into the grave. In *Romeo and Juliet* Friar Laurence says :—

> Dry up your tears and stick your Rosemary
> On this fair corse.

Brand quotes passages from Gay, Dekker, Cartwright, Shirley, Misson, Coles, " The British Apollo " and " The Wit's Interpreter," which connect Rosemary with burials ; and it was also planted on graves.

Coles says it was used with other evergreens to decorate churches at Christmas-time, and Folkard that, " In place of more costly incense, the ancients often employed Rosemary in their religious ceremonies. An old French name for it was *Incensier*. It was conspicuous on a very remarkable occasion in history. In " A Perfect Journall, etc., of that memorable Parliament begun at Westminster, Nov. 3, 1640," is the following passage, " Nov. 28. That afternoon Master Prin and Master Burton came in to London, being met and accompanied

---

[1] Hentzner's " Travels."
[2] Barnaby Googe's " Husbandry " (1578).

with many thousands of horse and foot, and rode with
rosemary and bayes in their hands and hats; which is
generally esteemed the greatest affront that ever was
given to the courts of justice in England." The
"affront" lay in the general rejoicing that attended
this overthrowing of the sentence passed by the Star
Chamber, and the causes which led to this enthusiasm
were these: "Some years before," Prynne, Burton,
and Bastwick had written against the Government and
the Bishops, and for this offence had been sentenced to
pay a fine of £5000 each, to have their ears cut off, to
stand in the pillory and to be imprisoned for life. "All
of which," says Clarendon, "was executed with rigour
and severity enough." "After being first imprisoned
in England," Mr Pyrnne was sent to a castle in the
island of Jersey, Dr Bastwick to Scilly, and Mr Burton
to Guernsey." Bastwick's wife seized the first moment
that the Commons were assembled (in Nov. 1640) to
present a petition, with the result that on the fourth
day after Parliament met, orders for their release were
sent to the Governors of the respective castles. Clarendon, who, of course, had no sympathy, but much dislike for them, admits: "When they came near London,
multitudes of people of several conditions, some on
horseback, others on foot, met them some miles from
the town; very many having been a day's journey; and
they were brought about two of the clocke in the afternoon in at Charing Cross, and carried into the city by
above ten thousand persons with boughs and flowers in
their hands, the common people strewing flowers and
herbs in the ways as they passed, making great noise
and expressions of joy for their deliverance and return;
and in those acclamations, mingling loud and virulent
exclamations against the bishops, "who had so cruelly
persecuted such godly men." An appendix,[1] devoted

[1] "History of the Rebellion,"

to this incident, further describes their entry, " The two branded persons riding first, side by side, with branches of rosemary in their hands, and two or three hundred horse closely following them, and multitudes of foot on either side of them, walking by them, every man on horseback or on foot having bays or rosemary in their hats or hands, and the people on either side of the street strewing the way as they passed with herbs, and such other greens as the season afforded, and expressing great joy for their return." This splendid reception must have revealed very plainly to the Government the mind and temper of the people. Nowadays the exuberance of the mob in greeting popular heroes is much what it seems to have been then, only they do not generally express it in such a pretty way as strewing rosemary and bays.

Culpepper writes that Rosemary was used " not only for physical but civil purposes," and among other uses, was placed in the dock of courts of justice. The reason for this was that among its many reputed medicinal virtues, " it was accounted singular good to expel the contagion of the pestilence from which poor prisoners too often suffered. It was also especially good to comfort the hearte and to helpe a weake memory," and was generally highly thought of. Rosemary is still retained in the pharmacopœia and is popularly much valued as a stimulant to making hair grow. *L'eau de la reine d'Hongrie*, rosemary tops in proof spirit, was once famous as a restorative and is mentioned in Perrault's fairy story of " The Sleeping Beauty." After the princess pricks her hand with the spindle and falls into the fatal sleep, among the means taken to bring back consciousness, " en lui frotte les tempes avec de l'eau de la reine d'Hongrie; mais rien ne lui faisait revenir." Rosemary is also an ingredient in *Eau de Cologne*. Its efficacy in magic is mentioned in another chapter. In the countries where it grows to a " very great height "[1] and the stem is " cloven out into thin boards, it hath served to make lutes, or such like instruments, and here with us carpenter's rules, and to divers other purposes."

RUE (*Ruta graveolens*).

Reverend sirs,
For you there's Rosemary and Rue ; these keep
Seeming and savour all the winter long,
Grace and remembrance to you both.
Winter's Tale, iv. **3.**

Here did she fall a tear ; here, in this place,
I'll set a bank of rue, sour herb of grace ;
Rue, even for ruth, here shortly shall be seen,
In the remembrance of a weeping queen.
Richard II., iii. 4.

There's rue for you, and here's some for me; we may call it herb of grace o' Sundays   O ! you may wear your rue with a difference.
Hamlet, iv. 5.

Michael from Adam's eyes the film 'emoved
. . . then purged with euphrasy and rue,
The visual nerve; for he had much to see.
Paradise Lost, book xi,

He who sows hatred, shall gather rue.
Danish Proverb.

" Ruth was the English name for sorrow and remorse, and *to rue* was to be sorry for anything or to have pity, . . . and so it was a natural thing to say that a plant which was so bitter and had always borne the name *Rue* or *Ruth* must be connected with repentance. It was therefore the Herb of Repentance, and this was soon transformed into the Herb of Grace."[2] Canon Ellacombe's explanation makes clear why rue was often alluded to symbolically, especially by Shakespeare, to whom the thought of repentance leading to grace seems to have been an accustomed one. It has been often stated the actual origin of the name was the fact that rue was

[1] Parkinson.
[2] "Plant-lore and Garden-craft of Shakespeare," Canon Ellacombe.

used to make " the *aspergillum,* or holy-water brush, in
the ceremony known as the *asperges,* which usually pre-
cedes the Sunday celebration of High Mass; but for
this supposition there is no ground." [1] Rue was supposed
to be a powerful defence against witches, and was used
in many spells, and Mr Friend describes a " magic
wreath" in which it is used by girls for divination.
The wreath is made up of Rue, Willow and Crane's-
bill. " Walking backwards to a tree they throw the
wreath over their heads, until it catches on the branches
and is held fast. Each time they fail to fix the wreath
means another year of single blessedness." In the Tyrol,
a bunch of Rue, Broom, Maidenhair, Agrimony and
Ground Ivy will enable the wearer to see witches.
Lupton adds a tribute to its powers of magic : " That [2]
Pigeons be not hunted nor killed of Cats at the
windowes, or at every passage and at every Pigeon's
hole, hang or put little Branches of Rew, for Rew hath
a marvellous strength against wilde Beasts. As Didymus
doth say." Milton refers to a belief, very widely spread,
that Rue was specially good for the eyes, when he says :

> Michael
> . purged with Euphrasie and Rue,
> The visual nerve.

that Adam's eyes should be made clear. (Euphrasie is
Eyebright.) Rue was also an antidote to poison, and
preserved people from contagion, particularly that of
the plague, and was thought to be of great virtue
for many disorders. " Some doe rippe up a beade-rowle
of the vertues of Rue, as Macer the poet and others "
who apparently declared it to be good for almost
every ill. Mr Britten remarks : " It was long, and
probably still is the custom to strew the dock of the
Central Criminal Court at the Old Bailey with Rue.
It arose in 1750, when the contagious disease known

[1] Britten. [2] " Book of Notable Things " (1575).

as jail fever, raged in Newgate to a great extent. It may
be remembered that during the trial of the Mannings
(1849), the unhappy woman, after one of the speeches of
the opposing counsel, gathered up some of the sprigs of
Rue which lay before her, and threw them at his head."

Turner recommends Rue "made hott in the pyll of
a pomegranate" for the "ake of the eares."

SOUTHERNWOOD (*Artemisa Abrotanum*).

Lavender and Sweet Marjoram march away,
Sothernwood and Angelica don't stay,
Plantain, the Thistle, which they blessed call,
And useful Wormwood, in their order fall.
Of Plants, book i.—COWLEY.

I'll give to him,
Who gathers me, more sweetness than he'd dream
Without me—more than any lily could.
I, that am flowerless, being Southernwood.

Shall I give you honesty,
Or lad's love to wear?
Or a wreath less fair to see,
Juniper and Rosemary?
Flaxenhair?

Rosemary, lest you forget,
What was lief and fair,
Lad's love, sweet thro' fear and fret,
Lad's love, green and living yet,
Flaxenhair.
Finnish Bride Song.—N. HOPPER.

Southernwood has many *sobriquets*, among which are
Lads or Boy's Love, Old Man, and Maiden's Ruin ; the
last a corruption of *Armoise du Rône*, Mr Friend says.
The French have contracted the same title to *Auronne*
and also call the plant *Bois de St Jean* and *Citronelle*.
Dutch people used to call it *Averonne* (another form of
the French contraction) and the Germans, *Stab-wurtz*.
The name *Bois de St Jean* is given it, because in some
parts of France it is one of the plants dedicated to St
John the Baptist, and the German title came from their

faith in it as a " singular wound-hearb." Turner considered that the fumes of it being burned, would drive away serpents, and credits it with many valuable properties, chiefly medicinal ; and Culpepper calls it " a gallant, mercurial plant, worthy of more esteem than it hath." It has also been supposed to have great virtue to prevent the hair falling out. In later days Hogg has declared it to have an agreeable, exhilarating smell," and to be " eminently diaphoretic." But Thornton, who loves to shatter all favourite herbal notions, remarks that these good results are chiefly because it " operates on the mind of the patient," and that as a fomentation it is hardly more useful " than cloths wrung out of hot water." So transitory is good report !

WOOD-RUFF (*Asperula Odorata*).

The threstlecoc him threteth oo
A way is huere wynter wo
When woodrove springeth. *Springtide*, 1300.

All that we say, and all we leave unsaid
    Be buried with her . . .
Pansies for thoughts, and wood-ruff white as she,
    And, for remembrance, quiet rosemary.
                                    Elegy.—HOPPER.

The wood-ruff or wood-rowell has its leaves " set about like a star, or the rowell of a spurre," whereby it gains its name. English people also called it Wood-rose and Sweet-Grass ; the French, *Hépatique étoilée*, and the Germans, *Waldmeister* and *Herzfreude*, and they steep it in " *Bohle*," a kind of " cup " made of light wine.

In England it used to be " made up into garlands or bundles and hanged up in houses in the heate of summer, doth very wel attemper the aire, coole and make fresh the place, to the delight and comfort of such as are therein." [1] Wood-ruff was employed to decorate churches, and churchwardens' accounts still exist (at St

[1] Gerarde.

Mary-atte-Hill, London) including wood-ruff garlands and lavender in the expenses incurred in keeping St Barnabas' Day. Johnston says[1]: " The dried leaves are put among linen for their sweet smell, and children put a whorl between the leaves of their books with a like purpose, and many people like to have one neatly dried laid in the case of their watch." Sensible, as well as pretty customs ! It was one of the herbs recommended to " make the hart merrye," and Tusser puts it among his " stilling herbs," thus : " Wood-roffe, for sweet waters and cakes." Country people used to lay it a little bruised to a cut, and its odour of new made hay must have made it a pleasanter remedy than many that they used.

WORMWOOD (*Artemisia Absinthium*).

And none a greater Stoick is, than I ;
The *Stoa's* Pillars on my stalk rely ;
Let others please, to profit is my pleasure.
The love I slowly gain's a lasting treasure.

Of Plants, book i.—COWLEY.

What savour is better, if physic be true,
In places infected than wormwood and rue
It is as a comfort for heart and the brain,
And therefore to have it, it is not in vain.

July's Husbandry.—TUSSER.

Here is my moly of much fame
    In magic often used ;
Mugwort and nightshade for the same,
    But not by me abused

Muses' Elysium.—DRAYTON.

Traditions cluster round *Artemisia Absinthium* and A. Vulgaris, Mugwort. Canon Ellacombe says that the species are called after Diana, as she was supposed to " find them and delivered their powers and leechdom to Chiron the Centaur . . . who named these worts from the name of Diana, Artemis ; " and he thinks therefore that " Dian's bud," spoken of in the *Midsummer Night's*

[1] " Botany of the Eastern Borders " (1853).

Dream was one of them. The plant was of some importance among the Mexicans, and when they kept the festival of Huixtocihuatl, the Goddess of Salt, they began with a great dance of women, who were joined to one another by strings of different flowers, and who wore on their heads garlands of wormwood. This dance continued all night, and on the following morning the dance of the priests began. (*Nineteenth Century*, Sept. 1879.)

According to the ancients, Wormwood counteracts the effects of poisoning by toadstools, hemlock, and the biting of the shrew mouse or sea-dragon; while Mugwort preserves the wayfarer from fatigue, sunstroke, wild beasts, the Evil Eye in man, and also from evil spirits! Lupton says that it is "commonly affirmed that, on Midsummer Eve, there is found at the root of Mugwort a coal which keeps safe from the plague, carbuncle, lightning, and the quartan ague, them that bear the same about them; and Mizaldus, the writer hereof, saith that it is to be found the same day under the Plantain, which is especially and chiefly to be found at noon." [1] Later writers have unkindly insisted that these wonderful "coals" were no more nor less than old dead roots! Gerarde and Parkinson are both dignified and contemptuous over these stories. Gerarde says, "Many other fantasticall devices invented by poets are to be seen in the works of ancient writers. I do of purpose omit them, as things unworthy of my recording or your reviewing." Parkinson is still more severe on "idle superstitions and irreligious relations," and abuses this special "idle conceit," which Gerarde has not deigned to repeat. It is told even by "Bauhinus, who glorieth to be an eye-witnesse of this foppery. But oh! the weake and fraile nature of man! Which I cannot but lament." Turner devotes a great deal of space to

[1] "Notable Things."

the disputes of writers as to the identity of the " true
Ponticke Wormwood," and says that " he himselfe is
certainly accurate on the point, having been taught it by
Gerhardas de Wyck, at that tyme the Emperour's secretary" at Cologne.   " This noble Clerk was afterwards
sent by Charles the fyft, Embassator to the great Turke."

It is from wormwood that *Absinthe* is made; and it
has been used instead of hops in making beer.   It used
to be laid among stuffs and furs to keep away moths
and insects—by its bitterness, ordinary folk supposed,
but Culpepper knew better, and gives an astrological
reason : " I was once in the tower and viewed the wardrobe and there was a great many fine cloaths (I can give
them no other title, for I was never either linen or
woolen draper), yet as brave as they looked, my opinion
was that the moths might consume them.   Moths are
under the dominion of Mars; this herb Wormwood
(also an herb of Mars) being laid among cloaths will
make a moth scorn to meddle with the cloaths as much
as a lion scorns to meddle with a mouse, or an eagle
with a fly."   One would not expect to find a moth a
" martial creature," but evidently he *is*, and this explanation of the working of the law of " sympathies,"
not only tells us so, but kindly shows us a sure means
of safeguarding our goods from an ubiquitous enemy.

Mugwort has many reputed medical virtues, and Dr
Thornton who usually crushes any pretension to such
claims, says it " merits the attention of English physicians, in regard to gout."   It is with this plant that the
Japanese prepare the *Moxa* that they use as a cautery
to a great extent.

Mugwort is said to be a good food for poultry
and turkeys.   De Gubernatis tells a Russian legend
about this plant which they call *Bech*.   Once the Evil
One offended his brother, the Cossack Sabba, who
seized and bound him, and said he should not be

released till he had done him some great service.
Presently, some Poles came close by and made a feast,
and were happy, leaving their horses to graze. The
Cossack Sabba coveted the horses and promised the Evil
One his liberty if he could manage to get them. The
Evil One then sent other demons to the field and caused
Mugwort to spring up, whereupon the horses trotted
away, and as they did so, the Mugwort moaned " *bech,
bech.*" And now when a horse treads on it, the plant
remembers the Pole's horses and still moans " *bech, bech* ! "
for which reason, in the Ukraine it is still called by that
name. It is left untold whether the flight of the horses
was due to the magical nature of the plants, or to their
usual bitterness. The latter is likely enough, as according to Dr Thornton, horses and goats are not fond of it,
and cows and swine refuse it.

Other well-known varieties of Wormwood are *H.
pontica*, Roman wormwood whose leaves are less bitter ;
and *A. Maritima*, sea-wormwood, and *A. Santonica*,
Tartarian wormwood.

Bay (*Laurus Nobilis*).

Then in my lavender I'll lay,
Muscado put among it,
And here and there a leaf of bay,
Which still shall run along it.

Muses' Elysium.

This done, we'll draw lots who shall buy
And gild the bays and rosemary.

Hesperides.—HERRICK.

Down with the rosemary and bays,
Down with the mistletoe,
Instead of holly, now upraise,
The greener box, for show.

Ceremonies for Candlemas Eve.—HERRICK.

A Bay-tree invites criticism, as it is certainly not a
"herb," but it is so often classed with some of them,

especially with rosemary (to whom it seems to have been a sort of twin) that a brief extract from its interesting history must be made.   Herrick's verses show that both for weddings and decorations, rosemary and bays were paired together—bays being also gilded at weddings—and Brand quotes some lines from the " Wit's Interpreter " to show that alike at funerals, they were fellows :—

> Shrouded she is from top to toe,
> With Lillies which all o'er her grow,
> Instead of bays and rosemary.

And Coles says, "Cypresse garlands are of great account at funeralls amongst the gentiler sort, but rosemary and bayes are used by the commons both at funeralls and weddings."   Parkinson's testimony is eloquent: " It serveth to adorn the house of God, as well as of man ; to procure warmth, comfort, and strength to the limmes of men and women by bathings and anoyntings out, and by drinks, etc., inward : to season the vessels wherein are preserved our meates, as well as our drinkes ; to crown or encircle as with a garland the heads of the living, and to sticke and decke forth the bodies of the dead; so that from the cradle to the grave we have still use of, we have still need of it."   No one could give higher praise to its natural virtues, but in other countries, it was endowed with supernatural ones.   "Neyther falling sickness, neyther devyll, wyll infest or hurt one in that place where a bay-tree is.   The Romans call it the Plant of the Good Angell." [1]   On the contrary, the withering of bay-trees was a very ill omen, and a portent of death. Canon Ellacombe says this superstition was imported from Italy, but it seems to have taken root in England. Shakespeare mentions it in *Richard II.*, as if it were no new idea ; and Evelyn tells us, as if he were adding a fresh fact to a store of common knowledge, that in

---

[1] "Book of Notable Things," C. Lupton.

1629, at Padua, before a great pestilence broke out, almost all the Bay-trees about that famous University grew sick and perished.

Sir Thomas Browne deals with another belief : " That bays will protect from the mischief of lightning and thunder is a quality ascribed thereto, common with the fig-tree, eagle and skin of a seal. Against so famous a quality Vicomeratus produceth experiment of a bay-tree blasted in Italy. And, therefore, although Tiberius for this intent did wear laurel upon his temples, yet did Augustus take a more probable course, who fled under arches and hollow vaults for protection." Sir Thomas is very logical.

It is not always clear when Laurel and when Bay is intended, because our Bay-tree was often called Laurel in Elizabethan days. For instance :—

> And when from Daphne's tree he plucks more Baies,
> His shepherd's pipe may chant more heavenly lays.
> Intro. to *Br. Pastorals* by CHRISTOPHER BROOKE.

If one is airily told one may pluck *bays* from a *laurel* bush, it is impossible to know which is really meant, and a certain confusion between the two is inevitable. William Browne, who took, or pretended to take, seriously the view that bays could not be hurt by thunder, brings forward an ingenious theory to account for it. It is that " being the materials of poets ghirlands, it is supposed not subject to any of Jupiter's thunderbolts, as other trees are.

> " Where Bayes still grow (by thunder not struck down),
> The victor's garland and the poet's crown."

Besides being a prophet of evil, the Bay-tree was also a token of joy and triumph. " In Rome, they use it to trim up their *Churches* and *Monasteries* on Solemn *Festivals* . . . as also on occasion of Signal *Victories* and other joyful Tidings; and these *Garlands* made up with *Hobby-*

Horse Tinsel, make a glittering show and rattling Noise when the *Air* moves them"; also, "With the *Leaves* of *Laurel* they made up their *Despatches* and Letters *Laurus involutoe*, wrapt in Bay-leaves, which they sent the Senate from the victorious General." Imagine a "victorious General" now sitting down to label despatches with leaves, signifying triumph! "Ere Reuter yet had found his range," how much better the art of becoming ceremonial was understood.

Finally, the Bay was regarded as a panacea for all ailments, and, therefore, the statue of Æsculapius was crowned with its leaves.

I append to this book a copy of the List of Herbs that Tusser gives in "March's Abstract." It will be seen that he has carefully classified them according to their suitability for stilling, strewing, bough-pots or kitchen.

CHAPTER IV

OF THE GROWING OF HERBS

In March and in April, from morning to night,
In sowing and setting, good housewives delight;
To have in a garden or other like plot,
To trim up their house, and to furnish their pot.

The nature of flowers, dame Physic doth shew;
She teacheth them all, to be known to a few,
To set or to sow, or else sown to remove,
How that should be practised, pain if ye love.

.   .   .   .   .   .

Time and ages, to sow or to gather be bold,
But set to remove, when the weather is cold.
Cut all thing or gather, the moon in the wane,
But sow in encreasing or give it his bane.

Now sets do ask watering, with pot or with dish,
New sown do not so, if ye do as I wish:
Through cunning with dibble, rake, mattock and spade,
By line, and by level, the garden is made.

Who soweth too lateward, hath seldom good seed,
Who soweth too soon little better shall speed,
Apt time and the season, so diverse to hit,
Let aiér and layer, help practice and wit.
Five hundred Points of Good Husbandry.—TUSSER.

THE majority of herbs are not exacting in their require-
ments, but a few foreigners thrive the better for a little
protection as a start. This is the opinion of a successful
gardener on the Herb-Border in an ordinary kitchen-
garden: " As to soil and situation, I used to devote a
border entirely to Herbs, under a privet hedge, facing
north-west, with a rough marly bottom. I had a plant

of most varieties I could get hold of, both Culinary and Medicinal."

Circumstances dictated that my own herbs should grow in a plot, rather overshadowed, and I found that they flourished, though annuals, as a rough rule, do best where they can get plenty of sunshine. In speaking of their cultivation, I have divided them into three groups : Perennials, Biennials and Annuals, and take the Perennials first.

Tansy will grow in almost any soil and may be increased, either in spring or autumn, by slips or by dividing the roots. *Lavender* is not always easy to please and likes a rather poor, sandy soil. When it is rich and heavy, matters are sometimes improved by trenching the ground and putting in chalk about a bushel to a land-yard (16 feet 6 inches by 16 feet 6 inches); lime from a kiln is also used in the same quantity.[1] Broad-leaved and narrow-leaved are the varieties of the purple Lavender usually sold, and, besides these, White Lavender. The narrow-leaved is the hardiest kind and its scent is the strongest; but the white-flowered has a very delicate fragrance. It requires care, but is better able to stand cold in a poor, than in a rich soil. The best way of propagating Lavender is by layering it, and this should be done in the summer; the plants can then be taken off the spring following. The narrow-leaved does not grow well from seed, and all kinds are shy of striking. The best known varieties of *Artemisia*, are *Tarragon, Wormwood*, and *Southernwood*, and they all prefer a dry and rather poor soil. If Tarragon, especially, be set in a wet soil, it is likely to be killed in the winter. Two kinds of Tarragon are usually found in gardens; one has bluish-green, very smooth leaves and the true Tarragon flavour, and is commonly known as French

[1] Neither lime nor chalk must be repeatedly added or the soil will be impoverished.

Tarragon. Russian Tarragon, the other kind, lacks the special flavour, and bears less smooth leaves of a fresher green shade. Runners should be taken from these plants in the spring. Wormwood is satisfied with a shady corner and may be propagated by seeds or cuttings. Southernwood is increased by division of the roots in the spring.

Horehound and *Rue* may be coupled together as liking a shady border and a dry, calcareous soil, and I have always heard that the latter thrives best when the plant has been *stolen*! It is a good thing to cut the bush down from time to time, when it will spring again with renewed vigour. Rue may be grown from seeds or cuttings taken in the spring. Horehound may be grown from seeds or cuttings, but is most usually increased by dividing the roots.

Hyssop, Rosemary, and *Sage* are natives of the south of Europe, and the two first appreciate a light, sandy soil, and not too much sun. Hyssop should be sowed in March or April; rooted off-sets may be taken in these months or in August and September, or cuttings from the stems in April or May, and these should be watered two or three times a week till they have struck. Both Hyssop and Sage are the better for being cut back when they have finished flowering. Loudon[1] says of Rosemary: "The finest plants are raised from seed. Slips or cuttings of the young shoots may be taken in the spring and summer and set in rows, two-thirds into the ground and occasionally watered till they have struck. In the autumn they may be transplanted." There are four kinds of Sage: red, green, small-leaved, or Sage of Virtue, broad-leaved or Balsamic. Gardening books speak of the red variety as being the commonest, though it seems to me that the common green sage is the one oftenest seen in kitchen-gardens. Red Sage

[1] " Encyclopædia of Gardening."

seldom comes " true " from seed but is easily raised by cuttings, and it sometimes succumbs to a hard winter. The other varieties are propagated by seed or by cuttings taken in May or June; the outer shoots should be the ones chosen and they should be put well into the ground and watered. After about three years the plants begin to degenerate and new ones should be set. Three kinds of *Marjoram* are cultivated, *Winter* (*Origánum Heracleoticum*), *Pot* (*O. Onites*) and *Sweet Marjoram* (*O. Marjorana*). The last-named is not a perennial. Winter and Pot Marjoram like a dry, light soil and are best propagated by off-sets, slipping or parting the roots in spring or autumn, but they may be also raised from seed. *Bergamot*, sometimes called Bee Balm, is, Robinson says, of the simplest culture, thriving or flowering in any position or soil. " For its scent alone, or for its handsome crimson flowers it would be well worth cultivating." [1] He adds that the different varieties of *Monarda* are admirably suited to being planted " for naturalization in woods and shrubberies." Bergamot may be increased by division of the roots in the spring or grown from seed.

Balm grows almost too readily and has a terrible habit of spreading in all directions unless severely checked. To propagate it, the roots should be divided, or slips taken either in spring or autumn.

Thyme.—Of the varieties of *Serpyllum* there seems no end, and the number of the species of *Thymus* is still dubious. Twelve kinds of them are offered for sale in an ordinary seed list sent to me the other day, but of these, few are grown in the kitchen-garden. *Common Thyme* or *Lemon Thyme* are the kinds most usually cultivated. Common Thyme has long, narrow-pointed leaves and Lemon Thyme is easily recognised by its scent from the wild Thyme, of which it has generally

[1] "English Flower Garden."

been considered a variety. *Golden* or *Variegated Thyme* (also lemon-scented) makes a pretty and fragrant edging to a flower-bed, but should be cut back when it has done flowering, unless the seed is to be saved, as it becomes straggling and untidy, and there is more danger of its being killed by the frost than if the winter finds it compact and bushy. Thyme is propagated by seed, by taking up rooted side-shoots, or by cuttings taken in the spring. It thrives best in a light, rich earth, and should be occasionally watered till well rooted.

There are two varieties of *Camomile*, the single and the double-flowered; the first is the most valuable in medicine, but the second is the most commonly met with. Camomile grows freely in most soils, but seems naturally to choose gravel and sand. The roots may be divided or, as the gardener before quoted, remarks: " Only let a plant of it go to seed; it will take care of itself." *Costmary* is seldom grown. Loudon says the whole plant has " a peculiarly agreeable odour"; personally, the odour strikes me as exactly resembling that of mint sauce. The plant is rather handsome, with large greyish leaves and small deep-yellow flowers; it likes a dry soil and is increased by division of the roots after the flowering time is over.

Mint, *Peppermint* and *Penny-royal*, demand the same treatment, and all like moisture. They are easily increased by dividing the roots in the spring or autumn, by taking off runners in the autumn, or by cuttings taken in the spring. The cuttings should be planted about half way into the earth. To have really good mint, it should be transplanted about every third year. *Green Mint* is sometimes required in the winter and early spring, and this may be provided by putting a few outside runners in a pot and placing it in bottom heat. "Plant for succession every three weeks, as forced roots soon decay."

Winter Savoury is "propagated by slips or cuttings in April or June, planted in a shady border, and transplanted a foot apart and kept bushy by cuttings." [1]

Fennel has become naturalised and is sometimes found growing wild by the sea; it is usually raised from seed or increased by side off-sets of the roots which may be taken in spring, summer or autumn. *Bugloss* or *Alkanet* grows freely anywhere, but seems to prefer moisture, and it may be increased by division of the roots or grown from seeds.

Of *Mallows* and *Marsh Mallows*, De la Quintinye says, "They ought to be allowed a place in our Kitchen-Gardens . . . they grow of their own accord," but he admits that it is best to "sow them in some bye-place," because of their propensity to spread. They are raised from seed, but cuttings may do well, and off-sets of the root, carefully divided, are satisfactory. *Sweet Cicely* may be increased by dividing the roots. It is well suited to an open shrubbery or wild garden, as well as to a herb-border. *Elecampane* is propagated by off-sets, taken when the plant has done flowering; it likes a moist soil or shade, and sends up tall spikes of bright yellow flowers. This year some of mine were over six feet high.

Angelica, Abercrombie tells us, is an annual-perennial, which means that it must be taken up and newly planted every year to be at all good, though off-sets from the plant would continue to come up of their own accord. It delights in moisture, and flourishes on the banks of running streams, but will do well almost anywhere. Angelica is best raised from seed, which, if sown in August, will grow better than if sown earlier in the year and it will sometimes grow from cuttings. *Liquorice* is "propagated by cuttings of the roots. On account of the depth to which the root strikes when the plant has

---

[1] Abercrombie, "Every Man his own Gardener."

PLANTATION OF LAVENDER

room to flourish, the soil should have a good staple of mould thirty inches or three feet in depth. Taking the small horizontal roots of established plants, cut them into sections six inches long. Having traced out rows a yard asunder, plant the sets along each row at intervals of eighteen inches, covering them entirely with mould."[1]

Saffron will grow in any soil, but prefers a sandy one, and plenty of sun. It is increased by seed, and by off-sets, which must be taken from the bulb when the plant is in a state of rest. As Saffron is an autumn-flowering plant, the time of rest is in the beginning of summer, and the bulb should be taken up when the leaves (which appear in the spring) begin to decay. The parent bulbs should be kept dry for a month and then replanted, that they may have time to "establish themselves" and flower before winter. This should be done once in three years. *Skirrets* are seldom eaten, but occasionally seen; they may be raised from seed, or by off-sets from the roots taken in spring or autumn. *Chives* are propagated by dividing the roots either in spring or autumn, and when the leaves are wanted they should be cut close, and then new ones will grow up in their place.

Sorrel of two kinds is cultivated, *Rumex Acetosa* and *Rumex Scutatus* or *French Sorrel*; Garden Sorrel rejoices in a damp, French Sorrel in a dry, soil. Both are most commonly increased by parting the roots, which may be done either in spring or autumn, and the roots planted about a foot apart and watered. Loudon says: "The finer plants are propagated from seed," which should be sown in March, though it may be sown in any of the spring months, and the plants must be thinned out when they are one or two inches high. When the stalks run up in the summer they should be cut back occasionally.

[1] Abercrombie.

Herb Patience or *Patience Dock* is raised from seed sown in lines and thinned out and the leaves to be eaten must be cut young. *Burnet* is easily raised from seed, or increased by dividing the roots in the spring. All the flower-stalks ought to be cut down, if they are not required for seed. *Dandelion*, it is hardly necessary to say, is only too easily raised from seed or by roots. Loudon says that when wanted for the table, the leaves should be tied together and earthed up, which will blanch them satisfactorily; otherwise, it may be grown blanched by keeping it always in a dark place.

For obvious reasons there are obstacles to the cultivation of *Water-cress*; a very little running water, however, will suffice, and it may be grown from seeds or by setting roots in the shallow stream. It should never be grown in stagnant water. Loudon quotes several authorities on the subject of growing *Samphire*; it is difficult to please, but this treatment was successful at Thames Ditton. The Samphire was " placed in a sheltered, dry situation, screened from the morning sun, protected by litter in the winter, and in the spring the soil was sprinkled with a little powdered barilla, to console it for the lack of its beloved sea-spray." It is raised from seed which should be sown as soon as it is ripe, or the roots may be divided.

In the early part of August, the young shoots should be cut back, and the decayed flower-stems removed, on such plants as hyssop, sage, lavender, and the like, and they will then send out new short shoots, which will make a close, bushy head for the winter. If possible, this should be done in damp weather. In October, the beds should be weeded; if the plants stand at some distance from each other, the earth between should be loosened, and if the beds are old, a little manure would be a great advantage. Amongst close-growing herbs, digging is impossible, but the ground must be hoed, raked and cleaned of weeds.

BIENNIALS.—*Parsley.*—There are many kinds of parsley, and one specially recommended is the triple-curled variety. All parsleys are raised from seed, and it is a good thing to sow one bed in March and a second in June, thus securing a continual supply all through the winter. The plants want well thinning out, and if the weather be very dry, the last sown should have two or three waterings with weak manure water. To protect them from the frost, a reed-hurdle, or even a few branches of fir, may be used, but, of course, a box-frame and light is the best. Parsley likes a deep soil, not too rich; and a good quantity of soot worked into it much improves the plants.

Caraway is raised from seed, which should be sown in the autumn, and it may also be sown in March or April, but the result will not be so good. This plant likes a rich, light soil. *Dill* should be sown in the spring, either broadcast or in drills, six to twelve inches apart. It may be sown in autumn, but this is not very advisable. *Clary* is sown in the end of March or in April, and should be transplanted to six to twelve inches apart, when the plants are two or three inches high; it may also be grown from cuttings.

Rampions should be thinly sowed in April or May in shady borders. If the plant is grown for use, it must not be allowed to flower, and in this case, it should not be sown till the end of May. The plants should be moderately watered at first (and later if the weather be very dry), and when sufficiently grown, they should be thinned out to three or four inches apart. The roots are fit for use in November. *Alexanders* or *Alisanders,* will send up shoots indefinitely, but must be sown afresh every year if wanted for the table. The seed should be sown in drills eighteen inches or more apart, and the plants thinned out to five or six inches distance from each other. When they are well grown they should be earthed up several inches on each side to blanch them.

ANNUALS.—*Anise* and *Coriander* like a warm, dry, light soil. If this is not procurable, anise should be "sown in pots in heat, and removed to a warm site in May."[1] Coriander may be sown in February, if it be mild and dry, and the seeds must be buried half an inch. *Cumin* is rarely seen; but it is advised that it should be sown in a warm, sunny border in March or April.

Sweet Marjoram and *Summer Savory* must both be sowed in light earth, either in drills nine inches apart, or broadcast, when they must be thinned out later on. The plants thinned out may be planted in another bed at six inches distance from each other, and must be watered. *Sweet Basil* and *Bush Basil* are both raised from seed sown in a hot-bed in the end of March, and the young plants should be set a foot apart in a warm border in May. They may be sown in an open border, but there is a risk of their coming up at all, and a certainty, that if they do, the plants will be late and small. Sweet Basil (*Ocymum Basilicum*) is much the largest plant, Bush Basil (*O. Mininum*) being scarcely half the size; both like a rich soil.

Borage is raised from seed, and, if let alone, will seed itself and come up, year after year, in the same place. It likes a dry soil. Gardening books recommend that it should be planted in drills and thinned, but for the sake of the picturesque, it should be dotted about among low-growing herbs in single plants or little clumps. *Marigolds* should be planted in light, dry soil; they may be "sowed in the spring, summer, or autumn, to remain or be transplanted a foot asunder."[2] The outer edge (near the palings) of Regent's Park, close to Hanover Gate, testifies to their power of seeding themselves.

[1] Loudon.   [2] Abercrombie

Authorities differ as to whether *Finocchio* is an annual, but
at anyrate, in England, it must be treated as one.
Finocchio should be sowed in dry, light earth, and must
afterwards be thinned, or the plants transplanted to a
distance of fifteen inches between each.   The swelling
stems "of some tolerable substance" must be earthed
up five or six inches, and will be blanched and tender
in a fortnight's time, and if sowed in successive sowings,
it may be eaten from June till December.

Endive must be sown in successive crops in July and
the early part of August, and this will produce "a
sufficiency to last through the winter and early spring.
If sown earlier it runs to seed the same year; but if
early endive is required, a little white-curled variety
is the best to sow.   The ground should be light and
rich on a dry subsoil"; when sufficiently grown, the
plants should be thinned, and those taken out, transplanted at a distance of ten or twelve inches apart, and
watered occasionally till they are well rooted.   Endive
is more easy to blanch if sowed in trenches than in level
ground.   In wet weather, blanching is best accomplished
by putting a garden-pot over the plant; but, in summer,
it is better to tie the leaves together and earth them
half way up.   The process will take from a week in dry
weather to nearly three weeks in wet, and the plant
must be taken up soon after it is finished, as after a few
days it begins to decay.   In severe frost the bed should
be covered with straw litter.

Chervil is sown in August and September, and can be
used in the same autumn and through the winter; if
successive crops are wanted, it may be sown any time
between the end of February and August.   It should
be sown in shallow drills, and the plants left to grow
as they come up.   When the leaves are two or three
inches high they are ready to be used, and if cut close,
fresh leaves will shoot up in their place. *Lambs' Lettuce*

is appreciated chiefly in the winter; it should be sown in August, and again in September to last through the winter and early spring. Dry fairly mellow soil will suit it, and it may be left to grow as it was sowed.

Rocket.—" This is an agreeable addition to cresses and mustard, early in spring. It should be sown in a warm border in February, and during the next months if a succession is wanted. After the first rough leaf has appeared, thin out the plants."[1] The *Purslanes* are both tender annuals, Green Purslane (*Portulaca olerecea*) being rather hardier than Golden Purslane (*P. sativa*). They should be sowed on hot-beds in February or March; or in a warm border, they may be sowed in drills during fine weather in May. They should be left as they grow, and when the leaves are gathered they must be cut low, and then a fresh crop will appear. Purslane must be watered occasionally in very dry, hot weather.

The above remarks pretend to being no more than bare outlines of the art of growing certain herbs. Many of these have outlived their reputation, and are now cultivated for no practical purpose, but for sentiment's sake, or for their aromatic grace, by those who " take a delight " in such things. To these I hope these sugges-tions may be useful. Any person desiring to bring a special herb to perfection is hardly likely to need reference to one of the many admirable gardening dictionaries, for it is not probable that he would look to an amateur for solid instruction on such points. To con-clude, Leonard Meager[2] gives some pithy directions which it is well to bear in mind :—

" In setting herbs ever observe to leave the tops no more than a handful above the ground, and the roots a foot under the earth.

" Twine the roots of the herbs you set, unless too

---

[1] Loudon.   [2] " New Art of Gardening."

brittle.   Gather herbs when the sap is full in the top of them.   Such herbs as you intend to gather for drying, to keep for use all the winter, do it about Lammas-tide ; dry them in the shade that the sun draw not out their vertue, but in a clear air and breezy wind, that no mustiness may taint them."

Cut all herbs just before they flower, except where the flower heads are wanted—lavender or camomile, for instance.   These should be cut just before the flowers are fully open.

CHAPTER V

OF HERBS IN MEDICINE

When bright Aurora gilds the eastern skies,
I wake and from my squalid couch arise . . .
Be this my topic, this my aim and end,
Heav'n's will to obey and seek t' oblige a friend . . .
Some herbs adorn the hills—some vales below,
Where limpid streamlets in meanders flow,
Here's Golden Saxifrage, in vernal hours,
Springs up when water'd well by fertile showers:
It flourishes in bogs where waters beat,
The yellow flowers in clusters stand complete.
Adorn'd with snowy white, in meadows low,
White Saxifrage displays a lucid show : . . .
Why should my friends in pining grief remain,
Or suffer with excruciating pain ?
The wholesome medicines, if by heaven blest,
Sure anodynes will prove and give them rest. . . .
Here's Tormentilla, with its searching parts,
Expels the pois'nous venom from our hearts . . .
Wood-betony is in its prime in May,
In June and July does its bloom display,
A fine, bright red does this grand plant adorn,
To gather it for drink I think no scorn ;
I'll make a conserve of its fragrant flowers,
Cephalick virtues in this herb remain,
To chase each dire disorder from the brain.
Delirious persons here a cure may find
To stem the phrensy and to calm the mind.
All authors own wood-betony is good,
'Tis king o'er all the herbs that deck the wood ;
A king's physician erst such notice took
Of this, he on its virtues wrote a book.
                    The Poor Phytologist.—JAMES CHAMBERS.

THE old herbalists used so many herbs and found
each one good for so many disorders that one is filled

CHELSEA PHYSIC GARDEN

with wonder that patients ever died, till one examines into the prescriptions and methods generally, and then one is more astonished that any of them recovered. I shall not mention any prescriptions here, excepting the celebrated antidote to all poison, Venice Treacle. This included seventy-three ingredients, and was evolved from an earlier and also famous nostrum, the *Mithridaticum*, originated by Mithridates, King of Pontus. Of course, this "treacle" was in no way connected with the sugary syrup we call by this name, but is a corruption of the Latin—*Theriaca*, a counter poison. Venice Treacle is an extreme example of the multitude of conflicting elements that were massed together and boldly administered in ancient remedies. The memory of it still clings about a wayside plant, *Erysimum cheiranthoides*, better known as Treacle-Mustard, which has gained its English name from the fact that its seeds were used in this awe-inspiring compound.

Anyone who is interested in ancient remedies can easily gain much information from Culpepper or Salmon. Either herbal can be procured at a low price (in a cheap edition) from any second-hand bookseller, and Salmon's wild statements, especially about animals, and Culpepper's biting wit, make them amusing reading. It is more instructive to examine the principles that animated the practice, and from one, the Doctrine of Signatures took form—a doctrine widely believed in, and of great influence. Coles [1] expounds it with great clearness: "Though Sin and Sattan have plunged mankinde into an Ocean of Infirmities . . . yet the mercy of God, which is over all His workes, maketh . . . herbes for the use of man, and hath not onely stamped upon them a distinct forme, but also given them particular Signatures, whereby a man may read, even in legible characters, the use of them. . . . Viper's

[1] "Art of Simpling."

Bugloss hath its stalks all to be speckled like a snake or viper, and is a most singular remedy against poyson and the sting of scorpions. . . . Heart Trefoyle is so called, not onely because the leafe is triangular, like the heart of a man, but also because each leafe contains the perfection of the heart, and that in its proper colour, viz., in flesh colour. It defendeth the heart. . . . The leaves of Saint John's Wort seem to be pricked or pinked very thick with little holes like the pores of a man's skin. It is a soveraigne remedy for any cut in the skin." This was a view very generally shared. William Browne says :

> In physic by some signature
> Nature herself doth point us out a cure.

And again :

> Heaven hath made me for thy cure,
> Both the physician and the signature.
> *Br. Pastorals*, book iii.

Drayton's *Hermit* pursued a development of this theory. He merely accepted the conclusions of earlier authorities who had made discoveries about the properties of plants and had named them accordingly.

> Some (herbs) by experience, as we see,
> Whose *names express their natures.*
> *Muses' Elysium.*

It was, naturally, more simple to administer all-heal, for a wound; hore-hound, for "mad dogge's biting," and so on, than to decipher the signature from the plant, himself, and so he and many others, prescribed the herbs, with more reference to their names, than unprejudiced attention to results.

The planets were another determining factor in the choice of remedies. Each plant was dedicated to a planet and each planet presided over a special part of the body, therefore, when any part was affected, a herb belonging to the planet that governed that special part must,

as a rule, be used.   Thus, Mercury presided over the
brain, so for a headache or " Folly and Simplicity (the
Epidemicall diseases of the Time) " one of Mercury's
herbs must be chosen.   Mercurial herbs were, as a rule,
refreshing, aromatic and of " very subtle parts."   The
planets seem usually to have caused, as well as cured the
diseases in their special province, and therefore their own
herbs, brought about the cure "by sympathy."   But sometimes, a planet would cause a disorder in the province
ruled by another planet, to whom the first was in opposi-
tion, and in this case the cure must be made " by antipathy."   Thus the lungs are under Jupiter, to whom
Mercury is opposed, therefore in any case of the lungs
being affected, the physician must first discover whether
Jupiter or Mercury were the agent and if the latter, the
remedy must be " antipathetical " ; it must be from one
of Mercury's herbs.   Sometimes where a planet had
caused a disease in the part it governed, an " antipathetical " cure, by means of an adversary's herbs, was
advised ; for instance Jupiter is opposed to Saturn, so
Jupiter's herbs might be given for toothache or pains in
the bones caused by Saturn, for the bones are under
Saturn's dominion.   An antipathetical remedy, however,
Culpepper does not recommend for common use, for
" sympathetical cures strengthen nature ; antipathetical
cures, in one degree or another, weaken it."   Besides
this, the position of the planet had to be considered,
the " House " that it was in, and the aspect in which
it was to the moon and other planets.
   " A benevolent Planet in the sixth, cures the disease
without the help of a Physitian.
   "A malevolent Planet there causeth a change in the
disease, and usually from better to worse.
   "A malevolent in the Ascendant threatens death, and
makes the sick as cross-grained as *Bajazet* the Turkish
Emperor when he was in the Iron Cage."

This is from Culpepper's " Astrological Judgment of Diseases "; in his " Herbal " he gives definite directions :

" Fortify the body with herbs of the nature of the Lord of the Ascendant, 'tis no matter whether he be a Fortune or Infortune in this case.

" Let your medicine be something antipathetical to the Lord of the Sixth.

" If the Lord of the Tenth be strong, make use of his medicines.

" If this cannot well be, make use of the medicines of the Light of Time."

Turning to the herbs appropriated to the special planets, we find that those of Mars were usually strong, bright and vigorous, and cured ills caused by violence, including the sting of " a martial creature, imagine a wasp, a hornet, a scorpion." Yellow flowers were largely dedicated to the Sun or Moon, radiant, bright-yellow ones to the Sun ; these of paler, fainter hues to the Moon. Flowers dedicated to either were good for the eyes, for the eyes are ruled by " the Luminaries." Jupiter's herbs had generally, " *Leaves* smooth, even, slightly cut and pointed, the veins not prominent. *Flowers* graceful, pleasing bright, succulent." The herbs of Venus were those with many flowers, of bright or delicate colours and pleasant odours. Saturn, who is almost always looked upon as being unfavourable, had only plants, whose leaves were " hairy, dry, hard, parched, coarse,"[1] and whose flowers were " gloomy, dull, greenish, faded or dirty white, pale red, invariably hirsute, prickly and disagreeable."

One does not know how much modern physicians care about propitiating Jupiter, but certainly they make an effort in that direction every time that they do, as did the Ancients, and write Rx—thus making his sign—at the top of a prescription. The small attention paid by

[1] Folkard.

doctors to herbs is often supposed to be a modern development, but hear Culpepper in 1652 ! " Drones lie at home and eat up what the bees have taken pains for. Just so do the college of physicians lie at home and domineer and suck out the sweetness of other men's labours and studies, themselves being as ignorant in the matter of herbs as a child of four years old, as I can make appear to any rational man by their last dispensatory."

It was not unnatural that the Herbalists should maintain the superiority of vegetable over mineral drugs, and Gerarde expresses his opinions in the introduction to his "Herbal." " I confesse blind Pluto is nowadays more sought after than quick-sighted Phœbus, and yet this dusty metall, . . . is rather snatched of man to his own destruction. . . . Contrariwise, in the expert knowledge of herbes what pleasure still renewed with varietie ? What small expence ? What security ? And yet what an apt and ordinary meanes to conduct men to that most desired benefit of health ? "

Many herbs have been expunged from modern Pharmacopœias. Perhaps we have no use for them now that we, in England, no longer live in perpetual terror of the bitings of sea-hares, scorpions or tarantulas, as our forefathers seem to have done ! In Harrison's " Description of England," the habit of preferring foreign, to native herbs, is rebuked. " But herein (the cherishing of foreign herbs) I find some cause of just complaint, for that we extoll their uses so farre that we fall into contempt of our owne, which are, in truth, more beneficiall and apt for us than such as grow elsewhere, sith (as I said before) everie region hath abundantly within his own limits whatsoever is needfull and most convenient for them that dwell therein." Probably there are to-day some thinkers of this stamp, as well as others who will hold anything valuable as long as it has been fetched from " overseas."

Russell gives instructions, in his " Boke of Nurture,"
how to " make a Bath medicinable," by adding herbs,—
mallow, hollyhocks and fennel being among the number.
And he directs that herbs " sweet and greene " should be
hanged round the room " when the Master will have a
bath "; a proceeding which was evidently something of a
ceremony.

To-day, there is an unfortunate tendency among the
poor, to desert herbs, *not* for " doctor's medicine," but
for any quackery they may chance to see "on the paper"
and some of these remedies are advertised to cure nearly
as many and diverse diseases, as any of the compounds
prescribed by the Ancients.   Consequently, one usually
hears of the uses of herbs in the past tense.   There is a
curious poem (published at Ipswich, 1796) called the
" Poor Phytologist, or the Author Gathering Herbs," by
James Chambers, Itinerant Poet, which gives the names
and virtues of the simples most prized at that date.   He
was a pedlar, who wandered about the country, always
accompanied by several dogs, and he added to his " pre-
carious mode of existence, the art of making nets and
composing acrostics."   I have quoted some of his lines
at the beginning of this chapter, but few of the herbs he
mentions are in popular use now, at least in the west of
England.   Betony occurs in some old village recipes
still employed, though its vaunted powers have been
declared vain by science.   Amongst those that I have
known, or have heard of, through personal friends, as
being still, or quite recently in use, are the following :—
Dandelion, Centaury, Meadow-Sweet and Wild-Sage are
used as " bitters."   By *Wild*-Sage, *Wood*-Sage is usually,
if not always, meant.   Dandelion is, of course, in the
British Pharmacopœia ; and Wood-Sage, though not
officinal, is asked for by some chemists.   Bear's foot
(Hellebore) has five finger-like leaves, but one finger is
bad and must be torn off.   Angelica is a wonderful herb ;

Parkinson put it in the fore-front of all medicinal plants
and it holds almost as high a place among village herbalists
to-day. Among many other virtues, the dried leaves are
said to have great power to reduce inflammation if steeped
in hot water and applied to the affected part. Mallows,
especially Marsh-Mallows, retain their old reputation for
relieving the same ill and the well-known *Pâtés de
Guimauve* are made from their roots. Elder, beloved by
all herbalists, still keeps its place in the British
Pharmacopœia, and the cooling effects of Elder-Flower
Water, none can deny. In the country, Elder leaves
and buds are most highly valued and are used in drinks,
poultices and ointments. Hyssop, or as some call it
I-sop, is sometimes used. Primrose, Poor Man's Friend,
and Comfrey are together made into an ointment, but
White Comfrey should be used when the ointment is for
a woman, Red-flowered Comfrey when it is for a man.
"Poor Man's Friend" in this case is Hedge-Garlic, but
the name is sometimes given to Swine's Cress (*Lapsana
Communis*). The juice of House-Leek, mixed with cream
relieves inflammation and particularly the irritation
which follows vaccination in an arm "taking beautifully." *Probatum est.* Penny-pies or Penny-wort (*Cotyledon
Umbilicus*) is said to be equally efficacious, especially
used with cream, and when simmered with the "sides
of the pan," have been known to heal, where linseed poultices failed to do good. When the leaf of
Penny-wort is applied to a wound, one side draws, the
other side heals. Wormwood is often in request
by brewers. Marigold-tea is a widely administered
remedy for the measles, and is one of the few
remedies which everybody seems to know. Very often
families appear to have their own special formula, and
even where the chief herbs in different prescriptions to relieve the same ailment are identical, the
lesser herbs vary. Saffron was also recommended for

measles; both probably on the " Doctrine of Colour Analogy" referred to the rash.   An old Herbalist told me that he considered Marigolds nearly as good as Saffron and "more home-grown, so to speak."   Dr Primrose, a physician in the reign of Charles II., who wrote a book on " Popular Errors in Physick," inveighs against the custom then in vogue of covering " the sick [with measles or small-pox] with red cloaths, for they are thought by the affinitie of the colour to draw the blood out to them, or at least some suppose that it is done by force of imagination.   And not onely the people, but also very many physicians use them."   Marigold-tea is at anyrate a better survival as " treatment " than this system!   Meadow-Saffron is still officinal, and is well known in the form it is usually dispensed, Tincture of Colchicum.   Broom has a place in the pharmacopœia, and is also a popular remedy.   Furze is not officinal, but a preparation made from it, Ulexine, is mentioned in a well-known medical dictionary.   An infusion of Furze-blossom used to be given to children to drink in scarlet fever.   Camomile is officinal, and the great authority, Dr Schimmelbusch recently recommended it as a mouth-wash, for disinfecting the muscous membrane after cases of operation in the mouth.   In a fomentation Camomile heads are a recognised anodyne; and Wild Camomile and Red Pimpernel are given locally for asthma, it is said, with great success.   Boy's love, (Southernwood), Plantain leaves, Black Currant leaves, Elder buds, Angelica and Parsley, chopped, pounded, and simmered with clarified butter, make an ointment for burns or raw surfaces.   A maker of this particular oint-ment near Exeter, died a year or two ago, but up to her death it was much in request.   Butter is always better for making ointments than lard, because cows feed on herbs, and all herbs are good for something.   Sage poultices and sage gargle are very good for sore

PLANTATION OF POPPIES (*P. Somniferum*)

throats, better than some of the gargles that "the gentlemen" prescribe (so a Herbalist told me), and red sage is better than green. Rosemary has long been celebrated for making the hair grow. Water-cress is very good for the blood, and the expressed juice has been known to prove a wonderful cure for rheumatism. A lady told me of a case she knew in Berkshire, where a man was absolutely crippled till he tried this remedy, and afterwards quite recovered his power to move and a very good degree of strength. Water-cress was one of the plants from which Count Mattei extracted his vegetable electricity. Parsley, freshly gathered and laid on the forehead is good for a headache, and if put in a fold of muslin and laid across inflamed eyes, it is said to be beneficial. Endive tea is cooling and is given to "fever" patients, and the dry leaves of lovage infused in white wine were good for ague. An infusion of Raspberry leaves, Agrimony, and Barberry-bark was good for consumptive patients, and Cowslip and Cucumber were made into a wash to make the complexion "splendent," to use an old expression. Coltsfoot is still given for coughs ; Sweet Marjoram was administered for dropsy, Alderberries for boils ; Arb-Rabbit (Herb-Robert) made into poultices for "inflammation ;" Brook-lime, given for St Anthony's Fire, and Brown Nut, made into a decoction, was taken hot just before going to bed, for a cold. Groundsel, Docks, Hay-Maids (Ground-Ivy), Feather-Few, Chicken-Weed, Hedge-Garlic or Hedge-Mustard, I have also heard recommended at different times. The Blessed Thistle is a useless ingredient in a good herb-ointment for burns. Amongst the last named plants are several not strictly to be called "herbs," but they and others I shall mention are "simples," and as such they fitly find a place among medicinal herbs. Foxglove and Belladonna, of course, are among the most important drugs in the Pharma-

copœia, and both the fruits and leaves of Hemlock
have also a place there. Foxglove, called in Devonshire, Cowflop, is recommended as an application to
heal sores, and one woman told me that it should
always be gathered on the north side of the hedge.
It is interesting to note that the Italians have a proverb, " Aralda, tutte piaghe salda" (Foxglove heals
all sores). Cliders (Goose-grass, *Galium aparine*) was
much given for tumours and cancers, and is praised
by other than merely village sages. Dr Fernie quotes
the testimony of several doctors who used it with
success, and adds, " some of our trading druggists now
furnish curative preparations made from the fresh herb."

> No ear hath heard, no tongue can tell,
> The virtues of the pimpernel.

This most popular plant, amongst other uses, is put into
poultices. Bacon mentions it as a weather prophet.
" There is a small red flower in the stubble-fields, which
country people call the wincopipe, which if it open in
the morning, you may be sure of a fine day to follow." [1]
The virtues of Betony are set forth by the " Poor Phytologist," and he is quite right in saying that it was once
esteemed a most sovereign remedy for all troubles
connected with the brain. It was, in fact, so far
extolled that an adage was once current :—

> " Sell your coat and buy betony."

In Italy there are two modern sayings, one a pious aspira-
tion, " May you have more virtues than Betony " ; and
the other an allusion, " Known as well as Betony."
Though the reputation of this plant has quite withered,
that of horehound is in a more flourishing state, and
it is still, I believe, considered of real use for coughs.
Violet leaves are now becoming a fashionable remedy

[1] "Natural History." Cent. IX.

in the hands of amateur doctors, who prescribe them for cancer. In the Highlands, it is said, they were used for the complexion, and a recipe is translated from the Gælic, " Anoint thy face with goat's milk in which violets have been infused, and there is not a young prince on earth who will not be charmed with thy beauty." The Greater Celandine was once dedicated to the sun, and it is still recommended as being good for the eyes, though not by members of the faculty. The following advice was given me by an old Cornish woman, but I am almost sure the flower she spoke of was the Lesser Celandine. This probably arose from a confusion of the two flowers, as I have never heard or seen the Lesser Celandine elsewhere commended for this purpose. " Take celandines and pound them with salt. Put them on some rag, and lay it on the inside of the wrist on the side of whichever eye is bad. Change the flowers twice a day, and go on applying them till the eye is well. Put enough alum to curdle it, into some scalded milk. Bathe the eyes with the liquid and apply the curds to the place."

Green Oil made after the following recipe has often proved beneficial for slight burns and scalds, and smells much nicer than the boracic ointment usually ordered for such injuries. It is also recommended for fresh wounds and bruises. " Take equal quantities of sage, camomile, wormwood and marsh-mallows, pick them clean and put them into sweet oil and as much of it as will cover the herbs ; if a quart add a quarter of a pound of sugar, and so on in proportion. Let them stand a week without stirring, then put them into the sun for a fortnight, stir them every day. Strain them with a strong cloth very hard, and set it on a slow fire with some red rose-buds and the young tops of lavender, let them simmer on a slow fire for two hours, strain off the oil, and put to it a gill of brandy. (If some hog's lard be poured upon the herbs, they will keep and make an excellent poultice for any kind of sore.)

The oil should be applied *immediately* to any kind of bruise or burn. It will prevent all inflammation and heal the wound. The time to begin making it is when the herbs are in full vigour, which depends much on the season being early; in general the middle of May is about the time, as the rose-buds and lavender would not be ready sooner than the middle of June.

Mrs Milne Home gives the ingredients of the *Tisane de Sept Fleurs*, which, she says, is often prescribed by French doctors for colds and sleeplessness—

" Bouillon blanc.	Mullein.
Tilleul.	Lime.
Violette.	Violet.
Coquelicot.	Poppy.
Pied de chat.	Tussilago.
Guimauve.	Mallow.
Mauve.	Another sort of mallow."

I think Mauve means mallow, Guimauve, marsh-mallow. Beyond these simples that I have mentioned as being in popular use, various English plants and herbs are used not much (if at all) by country people, but by medical men, and a few of those included in the British Pharmacopœia may be remarked on here.

Hops are used in the form of *Infusum Lupuli*. They have long had the reputation of inducing sleep, and George III. slept on a hop-pillow. To prevent the hops crackling (and producing exactly the opposite effect) it is advised that a little alcohol should be sprinkled on them. To eat poppy-seed was thought a safe means of bringing drowsiness. " But," says Dr Primrose (about 1640), " Opium is now brought into use, the rest [of soporifics] being layd aside. Yet the people doe abhorre from the use thereof and avoyd it as present poyson, when notwithstanding being rightly prepared, and administered in a convenient dose, it is a very harm- lesse and wholesome medicament.   The Ancients indeed thought it to bee poyson, but that is onely when it is taken in too great a quantity."   One wonders what ex- periences "the people" went through to learn this terror of the drug !   Gerarde and Parkinson both commend it as a medicine that " mitigateth all kinde of paines," but say that it must be used with great caution.   Browne refers to the poppy's power of soothing.

> "Where upon the limber grass
> Poppy and mandragoras,
> With like simples not a few
> Hang for ever drops of dew.
> Where flows Lèthe without coil,
> Softly like a stream of oil.
> Hie thee, thither, gentle Sleep."
>   In *The Inner Temple Masque.*

It is from the seed of the White Poppy (*Papaver somni- ferum*) that opium is prepared, and that procured from poppies grown in England is quite as good, and often purer, than opium imported from the East.   The first poppies that were cultivated in this country for the pur- pose were grown by Mr John Ball of Williton about 1794.   Timbs quotes : " 'Cowley Plantarium.   In old time the seed of the white poppy parched was served up as a dessert.'   By this we are reminded that white poppy seeds are eaten to this day upon bread made exclusively for Jews.   The 'twist' bread is generally prepared by brushing over the outside upper crust with egg and sprinkling upon it the seeds."   In Germany, *Mond-kuchen*, a kind of pastry in which poppy seeds are mixed, is still a favourite dish.   *Mond-blumen* (moon-flowers) is a name not unnaturally given to poppies, as they have been emblems of sleep ever since the Greeks used to repre- sent their deities of Sleep, Death and Night as crowned with them.

> " The water-lily from the marish ground
>   With the wan poppy,"

were both dedicated to the moon.

Gentian is greatly valued and largely prescribed by our doctors, but Parkinson raises a curious echo from a time when, it is generally supposed, people were less " nice " than they are to-day. " The wonderful wholesomeness of Gentian cannot be easily knowne to us, by reason our daintie tastes refuse to take thereof, for the bitternesse sake, but otherwise it would undoubtedly worke admirable cures." Valerian was, and is officinal, but seldom finds its way into " pottage " nowadays. Gerarde, however, writes: " It hath been had (and is to this day among the poore people of our Northerne parts) in such veneration amongst them, that no broths, pottage or physicall meats are worth anything if Setwall were not at an end: whereupon some woman Poet or other hath made these verses:

> " They that will have their heale,
>   Must put Setwall in their keale (kail)."

The herbalist speaks of "Garden Valerian or Setwall" as if they were one and the same, but Mr Britten says that Setwall was not *Valeriana officinalis* but *V. pyrenaica*. All varieties seem to have been used as remedies, and in Drayton's charming " Eclogue," of which Dowsabel is the heroine, he shows that it was used as an adornment.

> " A daughter, ycleapt Dowsabel,
>   A maiden fair and free,
>   And for she was her father's heir,
>   Full well she was ycond the leir,
>   Of mickle courtesy.
>   The silk well couth she twist and twine
>   And make the fine march-pine,
>   And with the needle-work ;
>   And she couth help the priest to say
>   His mattins on a holy day
>   And sing a psalm in kirk . . .

A FIELD OF ENGLISH ACONITE

The maiden in a morn betime,
Went forth when May was in the prime.
To get sweet setywall,
The honeysuckle, the harlock,
The lily and the ladysmock,
To deck her summerhall."

The summary of Dowsabel's education is so delightful, that though it was irrelevant, I could not refrain from quoting it. Aconite, Wolfsbane, or Monkshood (*Aconitum Napellus*) was held in wholesome terror by the old herbalists, who described it as being most venomous and deadly. Gerarde says, " There hath beene little heretofore set downe concerning the virtues of the Aconite, but much might be said of the hurts that have come thereby." Parkinson chiefly recommends it to " hunters of wild beastes, in which to dippe the heads of their arrows they shoote, or darts they throw at the wild beastes which killeth them that are wounded speedily"; but, he says, it may be used in outward applications. Aconite was first administered internally by Stoerck, who prescribed it for rheumatism, with good results, and it is now known to be sedative to the heart and respiratory organs, and to reduce temperature.

Other English-grown plants in the Pharmacopœia are : Anise, Artemisia maritima (Wormwood), Uvæ Ursi (Bearberries), Coriander, Caraway, Dill, Fennel, Flax (Linseed), Henbane, Wych-Hazel, Horse-Radish, Liquorice, Lavender, Mint, Mezereon, Musk, Mustard, Arnica, Pyrethrum, Rosemary, Squills, Saffron and Winter-green. In the making of Thymol, a preparation in common hospital use, *Monarda punctata* (Bergamot), Oil of Thyme and *Carum copticus* are used.

The following plants are not yet to be found in the Pharmacopœia, which includes those only that have been tried by very long experience, but leading physicians have prescribed these drugs with success. *Convalleria,* from Lily of the Valley ; *Salix nigra,* from the Willow ; *Savin,*

Juniper; *Rhus*, Sumach; *Aletris*, Star-Grass; *Lycopo-dium*, Club-Moss; *Grindelia*; from Larkspur, Oil of *Stavesacre*; and from Broom, *Spartein*.

There are two plants that I do not like to omit, for their history's sake, though their power to do good is no longer believed in, Plantain and Lungwort. The first was considered good for wounds in the days of Chaucer, and Shakespeare mentions it.

> *Romeo.*   Your plantain leaf is excellent for that.
> *Benvolio.*   For what, I pray thee?
> *Romeo.*   For your broken shin.
> > *Romeo and Juliet*, I. 2, 51.

Lungwort (*Pulmonaria officinalis*) owes its name and its reputation to the white spots on the leaves, which were thought to be the "signature," showing that it would cure infirmities and ulcers of the lungs. It is remarkable how many popular names this flower has. Gerarde tells us that the leaves are used among pot-herbes, and calls it Cowslips of Jerusalem, Wild Com-frey and Sage of Bethlem; and other country names are, Beggar's Basket, Soldiers and Sailors, Adam and Eve, and in Dorset, Mary's Tears. The name Adam and Eve arose from the fact that some of the flowers are red and others blue: red, in earlier days, being usually associated with men and blue with women. One of Drayton's prettiest verses alludes to it.

> "Maids, get the choicest flowers, a garland and entwine;
> Nor pink, nor pansies, let there want, be sure of eglantine.
> > See that there be store of lilies,
> > (Call'd of shepherds daffadillies)
> > With roses, damask, white, and red, the dearest fleur-de-lis,
> The cowslip of Jerusalem, and clove of Paradise."
> > *Eclogue III*

CHAPTER VI

OF HERBS AND MAGIC

" And first, her fern-seed doth bestow
The kernel of the mistletow,
And here and there as Puck should go,
    With terror to affright him.

The nightshade straws to work him ill,
There with her vervain and her dill,
That hindreth witches of their will,
    Of purpose to dispight him.

Then sprinkled she the juice of rue,
That groweth underneath the yew,
With nine drops of the midnight dew
    From lunary distilling."
           Nymphidia.—DRAYTON.

" Trefoil, vervain, John's wort, dill,
Hinders witches of their will."
          Guy Mannering.

Amongst the account-books of the Physic Garden in Chelsea, there is one on whose fly-leaf is scrawled a list of " Botanical Writers before Christ." It begins :

Zoroaster.
Orpheus.
Moses.
Solomon.
Homer.
Solon.

Names that one hardly expects to find grouped together, and especially not under this heading. The vegetable world, however, has attracted writers since the earliest times, and in the days when supernatural agencies were almost always brought forward to account for uncomprehended phenomena, it was not marvellous that misty lore should lead to the association of plants and magic. The book of nature is not always easy to read, and the older students drew from it very personal interpretations. Some herbs were magical because they were used in spells and sorceries ; others, because they had power in themselves. For instance, Basil, the perfume of which was thought to cause sympathy between two people, and in Moldavia they say it can even stop a wandering youth upon his way and make him love the maiden from whose hand he accepts a sprig. The Crocus flower, too, belongs to the second class, and brings laughter and great joy, and so it is with others. Plants were also credited with strong friendships and " enmities " amongst themselves. " The ancients " held strong views about their " sympathies and antipathies," and this sympathy or antipathy was attributed to individual likes and dislikes. " Rue dislikes Basil," says Pliny, " but Rue and the Fig-tree are in a great league and amitie " together. Alexanders loveth to grow in the same place as Rosemary, but the Radish is " at enmetie " with Hyssop. Savory and Onions are the better for each other's neighbourhood, and Coriander, Dill, Mallows, Herb-Patience and Chervil " love for companie to be set or sowne together." Bacon refers to some of these, but he took a prosaic view and thought these predilections due to questions of soil !

Being credited with such strong feelings amongst themselves, it is easier to understand how they were supposed to sympathise with their " environment." Honesty, of course, grew best in a very honest man's garden. Where Rosemary flourishes, the mistress rules. Sage will fade with the fortunes of the house and revive again as they recover; and Bay-trees are famous, but melancholy prophets.

> *Captain*—'Tis thought the king is dead; we will not stay,
> The Bay-trees in our country are all wither'd.
>
> *Richard II.* ii. 4.

From this, it is not a great step to acknowledge that particular plants have power to produce certain dispositions in the mind of man. So, the possession of a Rampion was likely to make a child quarrelsome : while, on the contrary, eating the leaves of Periwinkle " will cause love between a man and his wife." Laurel greatly " composed the phansy," and did " facilitate true visions," and was also " efficacious to inspire a poetical fury " (Evelyn). Having admitted the power of herbs over mental and moral qualities, we easily arrive at the recognition of their power in regard to the supernatural. If, as Culpepper tells us, " a raging bull, be he ever so mad, tied to a Fig-tree, will become tame and gentle ; " or if, as Pliny says, any one, " by anointing himself with Chicory and oile will become right amiable and win grace and favour of all men, so that he shal the more easily obtain whatsoever his heart stands unto," it is not much wonder that St John's Wort would drive away tempests and evil spirits, four-leaved Clover enable the wearer to see witches, and Garlic avert the Evil Eye. Thus many herbs are magical " in their own right," so to speak, apart from those that are connected with magic, from being favourites of the fairies, the witches, and, in a few cases, the Evil One !

De Gubernatis quotes from a work on astrology attributed to King Solomon, and translated from the Hebrew (?) by Iroé Grego (published in Rome, 1750), with indignant comments on the " pagan " methods of the Church in dealing with sorceries. Directions how to make an *aspersoir pour exorcisme* are given in it, which, teaching, he says, simply add to the peasant's existing load of superstition. Vervain, Periwinkle, Sage, Mint, Valerian, Ash and Basil are some of the plants chosen. " Tu n'y ajouteras point l'Hysope, mais le Romarin " (Rosemary). It is odd that Hyssop should be excluded, because it has always been a special defence against powers of darkness. In Palermo (again according to De Gubernatis), on the day of St Mark, the priests mount a hill in procession and bless the surrounding country, and the women gather quantities of the Hyssop growing about, and take it home to keep away from their houses the Evil Eye, and " toute autre influence magique." Rosemary is celebrated, from this point of view, as from others. It was, say the Spaniards, one of the bushes that gave shelter to the Virgin Mary in the flight into Egypt, and it is still revered. Borrow, in " The Bible in Spain," notices that, whereas in that country it is *Romero*, the Pilgrim's Flower, in Portugal it is called *Alecrim*, a word of Scandinavian origin (from *Ellegren*, the Elfin plant), which was probably carried south by the Vandals. Other authorities think that " Alecrim " comes from the Arabians. The reference to Rosemary occurs in a delightful passage. Borrow was staying at an inn, when one evening " in rushed a wild-looking man mounted on a donkey. . . . Around his *sombrero*, or shadowy hat, was tied a large quantity of the herb, which in English is called Rosemary. . . . The man seemed frantic with terror, and said that the witches had been pursuing him and hovering over his head for the last two leagues." On making inquiries, Borrow was told that the herb was " good against witches and mischances on the road." He treats this view with great scorn, but says : " I had no time to argue against this superstition," and with charming *naïveté* admits that, notwithstanding his austerity, when, next morning at departure, some sprigs of it were pressed upon him by the man's wife for his protection, " I was foolish enough to permit her to put some of it in my hat." The Sicilians thought that it was a favourite plant of the fairies, and that the young fairies, taking the form of snakes, lie amongst the branches. Dill, able to "hinder witches of their will," was used in spells *against* witches, besides being employed by them. There was a strong belief that plants beloved by magicians, and powerful for evil in their hands, were equally powerful to avert evil when used in charms against witchcraft. Lunary, or Honesty, is another plant with a double edge. In France it is nicknamed *Monnaie du Pape* and *Herbe aux Lunettes*, and its shining seed-vessels have many pet names in English. "It has a natural power of dispelling evil spirits," quotes Mr Friend, and explains this verdict by pointing that Lunary with its great silver disks, called after the the moon, is disliked and avoided by evil spirits, who fear the light and seek darkness. Rue is used by witches and against them; in some parts of Italy a talisman against their power is made by sewing up the leaves in a little bag and wearing it near the heart. If the floor of a house be rubbed with Rue it is certain that all witches must fly from it. In Argentina grows the Nightmare flower, *Flor de Pesadilla*. The witches of that region extract from it a drug which causes nightmare lasting all night long, and they contrive to give it to whoever they wish to torment. Besides these, Pennyroyal and Henbane, Chervil and Vervain, Poppies, Mandrakes, Hemlock and Dittany were specially used by witches in making spells. Valerian, Wormwood, Elder, Pimpernel, Angelica, and all yellow flowers growing in hedgerows are antagonistic to them. Their dislike to yellow flowers may have arisen from these being often dedicated to the sun, and being therefore repellent to lovers of gloom and mystery. Angelica preserved the wearer from the power of witches or spells, and is,

I think, the only herb quoted by Gerarde as a power against witchcraft. He does not condescend generally to consider superstitions other than medical. Of the herbs dedicated to the Evil One are Yarrow, sometimes known as the Devil's Nettle; Ground-Ivy, called his Candlestick, and Houseleek, which he has rather unjustly appropriated. Mr Friend explains that in Denmark, "Old Thor" is a polite euphemism, and that the Houseleek really belonged to Thor, but has been passed on through confusion between the two. Yarrow or Milfoil has been used for divination in spells from England to China.

> " There's a crying at my window and a hand upon my door,
> And a stir among the Yarrow that's fading on the floor,
> The voice cries at my window, the hand on my door beats on,
> But if I heed and answer them, sure hand and voice are gone."
>
> MAY EVE.

Johnston[1] says: "Tansy and Milfoil were reckoned amongst plants averse to fascination; but we must retrograde two centuries to be present at the trial of Elspeth Reoch, who was supernaturally instructed to cure distempers by resting on her right knee while pulling 'the herb callit malefour' betwixt her mid-finger and thumbe, and saying of, 'In nomen Patris, Filii, et Spiritus Sancti.'"

Johnston gathers his information from Dalzell on the "Darker Superstitions of Scotland."

Wormwood is in some parts of Europe called the "Girdle of St John," it has so much power against evil spirits. Cumin is much disliked by a race of Elves in Germany, called the Moss-People. Dyer[2] tells us that the life of each one is bound up with the life of a tree, and if the inner bark of this is loosened, the elf dies. Therefore their precept is:—

[1] " Botany of the Eastern Borders " (1853).
[2] " Folk-Lore of Plants."

RAMPION

" Peel no tree,
Relate no dream,
Bake no cumin in bread,
So will Heav'n help thee in thy need."

On one occasion when a loaf baked with Cumin was given as an offering to a forest-wife, she was heard screaming—

" They've baken for me Cumin bread
That on this house brings great distress."

The unhappy giver at once began to go downhill, and was soon reduced to abject misery! Elecampane is in Denmark called Elf-Dock. Flax-flowers are a protection against sorcery. " Flax [1] is supposed to be under the protection of the goddess Hulda, but the plant's blue blossom is more especially the flower of Bertha, whose blue eyes shine in its calyx, and whose distaff is filled by its fibres. . . . It was the goddess Hulda who first taught mortals the art of growing flax, of spinning, and of weaving it. . . . Between Kroppbühl and Unterlassen, is a cave which is believed by the country people to have been the entrance to Queen Hulda's mountain palace. Twice a year she passed through the valley, scattering blessings around her path—once in summer, when the blue flowers of the Flax were brightening the fields, and again during the mysterious " twelve nights " immediately preceding our Feast of Epiphany, when, in ancient days, gods and goddesses were believed to visit the earth." The Bohemians have a belief that if seven-year-old children dance among flax, they will become beautiful. From the little Fairy-Flax " prepared and manufactured by the supernatural skill, the ' Good People ' were wont in the olden time to procure their requisite supplies of linen," writes Johnston.

Wild Thyme is specially beloved by fairies and elves, and Fox-gloves and Wood-sorrel are also favourites,—

[1] Folkard.

Fox-gloves, being called in Ireland, Fairy-cap, and Wood-sorrel, known in Wales as Fairy-bells.

Among plants that have magic powers in themselves are two varieties of Pimpinella; the Anise and the Burnet Saxifrage. The first averts the Evil Eye, and the second is called in Hungary, "Chaba's Salve," because it is said that its virtues were discovered by King Chaba, who after a furious battle cured 15,000 of his soldiers with it. In Iroé Grego's book, it is advised that the sword of a magician should be bathed in the blood of a mole, and the juice of Pimpinella. De Gubernatis says that in Germany and in Rome, Endive-seed is sold as a love-philtre, and when wanted for this reason, the plant must be uprooted not with the hand but with a bit of gold, or stag's horn (which symbolise the disk and rays of the sun) on one of the *jours des Apôtres*, June 27th, St Peter's Day, or July 25th, St James' Day.

The Mustard-tree is called in Sanscrit, the Witch, for when Hindus want to discover a witch, they light lamps during the night, and fill vessels with water,[1] into which they gently drop Mustard-seed oil, pronouncing the name of every woman in the village. If, during the ceremony, as they pronounce the name of a woman, they notice the shadow of a female in the water, it is a sure sign that such a woman is a witch. Mugwort laid in the soles of the boots, will keep a man from weariness, though he walk forty miles. Wreaths of Camomile flowers hung up in a house on St John's Day will, it is said in Prussia, defend it against thunder, and Wild Thyme and Marjoram laid by milk in a dairy will prevent it being "turned" by thunder. The root of Tarragon held between the teeth will cure toothache, and the name Réséda, the family name of Mignonette, is supposed to be derived from the verb " to assuage,"

[1] Folkard.

for it was a charm against so many evils. If a sprig of Basil were left under a pot, it would, in time, turn to scorpions! It is a strange plant altogether. The ancient Greeks thought that it would not grow unless when the seed was sown railing and abuse should be poured forth at the same time. Much blossom on the broom foretells a plentiful harvest of corn. " Les anciens " according to *La petite Corbeille* believed that a pot of Gilly-flowers, growing in a window, would fade if the master of the house died; and similar curious sympathies in Sage and Honesty and Rosemary have already been noticed.

There is a belief in the West Country that no girl who is destined to be an old maid, can make a myrtle grow. Mr Friend does not mention this, but he does tell us that a flowering myrtle is one of the luckiest plants to have, and it is often difficult to grow; and he generously presents us with the receipt that he had heard given to make sure of its flowering. The secret is, while setting the slip, to spread the tail of one's dress, and *look proud!*

To transplant Parsley is very unlucky, and to let Rhubarb run to seed will bring death into the family before a year is out. These beliefs are still active. One hears also that no one will have any luck with young chickens if they bring any blossom (of fruit-trees) into the house, which is, indeed, an unlucky thing to do at any time.

There was a fairly recent case in Gloucestershire, which showed that the idea still survives that if flower-seeds are sowed on Palm Sunday, the flowers will come out double.

Though Elder is not a herb, it cannot be omitted here, for every inch of an Elder-tree is connected with magic. This is especially the case in Denmark. First of all there is the Elder-tree Mother, who lives in the tree and watches for any injury to it. Hans

Andersen tells a charming story about her and the
pictures that she sometimes brings. It may happen, that
if furniture is made of the wood, Hylde-Moer may follow
her property and haunt and worry the owners, and
there is a tradition that, once when a child was put in a
cradle of Elder-wood, Hylde-Moer came and pulled it by
the legs and would give it no peace till it was lifted out.
Permission to cut Elder wood must always be asked
first, and not till Hylde-Moer has given consent by keeping silence, may the chopping begin. He who stands
under an Elder-tree at midnight on Midsummer-Eve will
chance to see Toly, the King of the Elves, and all his
retinue go by. "The pith of the branches when cut in
round, flat shapes, is dipped in oil, lighted, and then put
to float in a glass of water; its light on Christmas Eve is
thought to reveal to the owner all the witches and
sorcerers in the neighbourhood." [1] The Russians believe
that Elder-trees drive away evil spirits, and the
Bohemians go to it, with a spell, to take away fever.
The Sicilians think that sticks of its wood will kill
serpents and drive away robbers better than any other,
and the Serbs introduce a stick of Elder into their wedding ceremonies to bring good luck. In England it was
thought that the Elder was never struck by lightning;
and a twig of it tied into three or four knots, and carried
in the pocket, was a charm against rheumatism. A
cross made of Elder, and fastened to cow-houses and
stables, was supposed to keep all evil from the animals.
Canon Ellacombe, in the Tyrol, says: "An Elder bush,
trimmed into the form of a cross, is planted in a new-
made grave, and if it blossoms, the soul of the person
lying beneath it is happy." Sir Thomas Browne takes
the "white umbrella or medical bush of Elder as an
epitome of the order arising from five main stems, quin-
cuncially disposed and tolerably maintained in their

[1] Folkard.

sub-divisions." The number 5, and its appearance in
works of Nature, must have occupied his mind at one
time to a very great extent, judging from his writings.
There is a saying that :—

> An eldern stake and a black thorn ether (hedge)
> Will make a hedge to last for ever.

And it is a common tradition that an Elder stake will last
in the ground longer than an iron bar the same size.
Several very different musical instruments have been
alike named "Sambuke," because they were all made
out of Elder-wood. Elder-berries have also wonderful
properties. In Styria, on "Bertha Night (6th January),
the devil goes about with special virulence. As a safe-
guard persons are recommended to make a magic circle,
in the centre of which they should stand, with Elder-
berries gathered on St John's night. By doing this, the
mystic Fern-seed may be obtained, which possesses the
strength of thirty or forty men. There are no instructions as to why or how the desired Fern-seed should
arrive, and all the proceedings are somewhat mysterious."

The most extraordinary collection of charms and
receipts is to be found in an old book, called *Le petit
Albert*; probably the contents are largely gleaned from
out the wondrous lore set forth by Albertus Magnus.
A charm—it must be a charm, for a mere recipe could
hardly achieve such results, "pour s'enrichir par la
pêche des poissons" is made by mixing Nettles, Cinquefoil,
and the juice of Houseleek, with corn boiled in water of
Thyme and Marjoram, and if this composition is put into
a net, the net will soon be filled with fish. Cinquefoil
appears in many spells, particularly as a magic herb in
love-divinations, and also against agues! Some parts of
the book shed a lurid light on the customs of the day, as
for instance, recipes "to render a man or woman insen-
sible to torture." Here is a less ghastly extract. "Je
quitte des matières violentes pour dire un Mot de Paix.

J'ai lû dans le très curieux livre des Secrets du Roi Jean d'Arragon, que si aucun dans le mois de septembre, ayant observé le temps que le soleil est entré au signe de la Vierges a soin de cueillir de la fleur Soucy (Marigold) qu'a été appellé par les Anciens, Epouse du Soleil, and si on l'enveloppe dedans des feuilles de Laurier avec un dent de Loup, personne ne pourra parler mal de celui qui les portera sur luy et vivra dans un profonde paix et tranquillité avec tout le monde." There is an odd, little passage about the supernatural beings who inhabit the four elements, Salamanders, Nymphs, Sylphs, and Gnomes, and the practices of Lapland miners to obtain " la bienveillance des Gnomes." This is managed through observing their love of perfumes. Each day of the week a certain perfume was burnt for them and these odours had an elaborate formula, compiled with reference to the planets. Thus Sunday's perfume is " sous les auspices du soleil," and contains Saffron and Musk ; Monday's is made of the Moon's special plants and includes the seed of the White Poppy ; and the ingredients for each are equally appropriate to the ruling planet. Mars has Hellebore and Euphorbia in his perfume ; Venus, dried roses, red coral, and ambergris; and Saturn, black poppy seeds, Mandrake roots and Henbane. In an English translation (there are many editions of *Le petit Albert*) fifteen magical herbs of the Ancients are given, but I will only quote two.

" The eleventh hearbe is named of the Chaldees Isiphilon . . . or Englishmen, Centory . . . this hearbe hath a marvellous virtue, for if it be joined with the blood of a female lapwing or black plover and put with oile in a lamp, all they that compasse it about shall believe themselves to be witches, so that one shall believe of another that his head is in heaven and his feete on earth."

" If ∴ the fourteenth hearbe, smallage, be bounden to an oxe's necke, he will follow thee whithersoever thou wilt go." The last instructions lead one to agree with the poet:

" I would that I had flourished then,
    When ruffs and raids were in the fashion,"

and when views of mine and thine were less rigid than they are to-day.

CHAPTER VII

OF HERBS AND BEASTS

Here may'st thou range the goodly, pleasant field,
And search out simples to procure thy heal,
What sundry virtues, sundry herbs do yield,
    'Gainst grief which may thy sheep or thee assail.
                                Eclogue vii.—DRAYTON.

And tryed time yet taught me greater thinges ;
    The sodain rising of the raging seas,
The soothe of byrdes by beating of their winges,
    The powre of herbes, both which can hurt and ease ;
And which be wont t' enrage the restless sheepe,
And which be wont to worke eternal sleepe.
                        Shepheard's Calendar.—SPENSER.

And did you hear wild music blow
All down the boreen, long and low,
The tramp of ragweed horses' feet,
And Una's laughter wild and sweet.
                The Passing of the Shee.—N. HOPPER.

HERBS and animals may appear linked together in many
aspects, but there are two in which I specially wish to
look at them—first, glancing at the old traditions that
tell of beasts and birds themselves having preferences
among herbs; secondly, the human reasoning, which
decreed that certain plants must benefit or affect special
creatures. The glamour of magic at times hovers over
both. Ragwort is St James's Wort (the French call it
Jacobée), and St James is the patron saint of horses,
therefore Ragwort is good for horses, and has even
gained the name of the Staggerwort, from being often
prescribed for " the staggers." This is a good speci-

men of the reasoning, but there is romance about the plant which is far more attractive. Besides being good for horses, it is actually the witches' own horse! There is a high granite rock called the Castle Peak, south of the Logan Rock in Cornwall, where, as tales run, witches were specially fond of gathering, and thither they rode on moonlight nights on a stem of Ragwort. In Ireland, it is the fairies ride it, and there it is sometimes called the Fairy's Horse.

> Reach up to the star that hangs the lowest,
> Tread down the drift of the apple blow,
> Ride your ragweed horse to the Isle of Wobles.

Ragwort is specially beloved by the Leprehauns, or Clauricanes, the little fairy cobblers, who are sometimes seen singing or whistling over their work on a tiny shoe. They wear " deeshy-daushy " leather aprons, and usually red nightcaps.

> Do you not catch the tiny clamour,
> Busy click of an elfin hammer,
> Voice of the Lepracaun singing shrill,
> As he merrily plies his trade.
>
> W. B. Yeats.

There is a very nice legend of the Field of Boliauns, which turns on the belief that every Leprehaun has a hidden treasure buried under a ragwort. And if anyone can catch the little man, and not for one second take his eyes off him until the plant is reached, the Leprehaun must show him exactly where to dig for it. In the Isle of Man, they used to tell of another steed, not the fairies' horse, but a fairy or enchanted horse, ridden by mortals. If anyone on St John's Eve, they said, trod on a plant of St John's Wort after sunset, the horse would spring out of the earth, and carry him about till sunrise, and there leave him wherever they chanced at that moment to be.

William Coles [1] speaks with great decision as to the

1 " Art of Simpling."

various remedies which animals find for themselves. "If the Asse be oppressed with melancholy, he eats of the herbe *Asplenium* . . . so the wilde Goats being shot with Darts or Arrows, cure themselves with Dittany, which Herb hath the power to worke them out of the Body and to heale up the wound." Gerarde adds that the "Deere in Candie" seek the same remedy, and Parkinson remarks of Hemp Agrimony, "It is sayd that hunters have observed that Deere being wounded by the eating of this herbe have been healed of their hurts." Drayton's *Hermit* refers to dictam or dittany.

> And this is dictam which we prize
> Shot shafts and darts expelling.

Shelley is less definite. He only laments:

> The wounded deer must seek the herb no more
> In which its heart cure lies.

Goats do not seek Sea-Holly as a remedy, but it has a startling effect upon them if, by accident, they touch it. "They report that the herb Sea-Holly (*Eryngium maritimum*), if one goat take it into her mouth, it causeth her first to stand still, and afterwards the whole flocke, untill such time as the Shepherd take it forth of her mouth, as Plutarch writeth."[1] However much these wild theories may exceed facts as to animals curing themselves, they are not altogether without reason, for the instinct of beasts leading them to healing herbs has often been noticed. Evelyn says: "I have heard of one Signior *Jaquinto*, Physician to Queen *Anne* (Mother of the Blessed *Martyr*, Charles the First), and was so to one of the *Popes*. That observing the *Scurvy* and *Dropsy* to be the Epidemical and Dominent Diseases of this Nation, he went himself into the *Hundreds* of *Essex* (reputed the most unhealthy County of this *Island*), and us'd to follow the Sheep and Cattell

[1] Gerarde.

on purpose to observe what Plants they chiefly fed upon; and of those *Simples* compos'd an excellent *Electuary* of extraordinary Effects against those Infirmities.

" Thus we are told, that the Vertue of the Cophee was discover'd by marking what the *Goats* so greedily brutted upon. So *Æsculapius* is said to have restor'd dismember'd *Hippolitus* by applying some simples, he observ'd a *Serpent* to have us'd another dead *Serpent*." The last instance sounds mythical! But goats have really more than once led mankind to some useful bit of knowledge. There is a Chilian plant, *Boldo*, a tincture of the leaves of which are frequently administered in France for hepatic complaints, and this is the history of the discovery of its virtues. " The goats in Chili had been for many years subject to enlargement of the liver, and the owners of the flocks had begun to despair of them as a source of revenue, until it was observed that certain flocks were exempt from the complaint, whilst others in adjacent districts continued subject to it. It was ultimately discovered that the goats browsing in fields where *Boldo* grew were never a prey to hepatic diseases, and the herb became gradually known and used, first by South American and then by French druggists." *Boldo* is little used in England.

Sheep seek Dandelions; and Miss Anne Pratt quotes an agricultural report, describing how some weakly lambs were moved into a field full of Dandelions in flower, and how rapidly the conspicuous blossoms were devoured. Finally, as the flowers grew fewer and fewer, the lambs were seen pushing one another away from the coveted plants, and in this field they speedily gained in health and strength. *Valerianella Olitaria* is said to be a favourite food of lambs, and so gains its name of Lambs' Lettuce. Shepherds and flocks have always been favourite subjects for poetry, and Drayton touches them very prettily:—

> When the new wash'd flock from the river side,
> Coming as white as January's snow,
> The ram with nose-gays bears his horns in pride,
> And no less brave the bell-wether doth go.

Nep or Cat-mint is said to have a great attraction for cats. Of which there is this old rime :—

> If you set it, the catts will eate it,
> If you sow it, the catts won't know it.[1]

The weasel, with a grand knowledge of counter-poisons, " arms herself with eating of Rue," *before* fighting a serpent. Folkard says that in the north of England there is a tradition that when hops were first planted there, nightingales also made their first appearance, and he adds that both have long since disappeared, north of the Humber. In other parts of England there is an idea (quite a false one) that nightingales will only sing where cowslips flourish. The cuckoo is connected with both plants and minerals. In some parts of Germany, Mr Friend writes, the call of the cuckoo is thought to reveal mines, and the cuckoo's bread, the purple orchis, grows most abundantly where rich veins of metal lie beneath. There is a story about the plantain, a plant with a most interesting legendary history, in which the cuckoo appears. Once the Plantain or Waybread was a maiden, always watching for her absent lover, and at last she was changed into the plant that almost always grows by the road-side. And now every seventh year the plantain becomes a bird, either the Cuckoo or the Cuckoo's servant, the Dinnick.

The Yellow Rattle is sometimes called Gowk's Siller, and Gowk may mean either the Cuckoo or a fool, so they may quarrel for it. Johnston seems to think that the siller belongs rather to the fool, for he remarks: " the capsules rattle when in seed . . . being like the fool unable to conceal its wealth." The Swallow restored sight

[1] Coles.

to the eyes of her young, when any evil had befallen them, by the help of Celandine. And it was for this reason, says Gerarde, that the flower gained its name, *Chelidonium,* swallow-herbe, and not because it "first springeth at the coming of the swallows or dieth when they goe away." . . . Celsus doth witnesse that it will restore "the sight of the eies of divers young birds . . . and soonest of all of the sight of the swallow." The eagle, when he wishes his sight to be particularly keen, rubs his eyes with the wild Lettuce, and the hawk follows his example, but chooses Hawk-weed with equal success. Doves and pigeons find that Vervain cures dimness of vision and goldfinches and linnets and some other birds turn to eyebright. "The purple and yellow spots which are upon the flowers of eyebright very much resemble the diseases of the eyes or bloodshot."[1] There is a very wide belief in a magic plant called Spring-wort or Spring-wurzel of which Folkard gives an interesting description. "Pliny," he says, "records the superstition concerning it, almost in the same form in which it is now found in Germany. If anyone touches a lock with it, the lock, however strong, must yield. In Switzerland it is carried in the right pocket to render the bearer invulnerable to dagger or bullet; and in the Hartz mountains it is said to reveal treasures. One cannot easily find it oneself, but generally the wood-pecker (according to Pliny also the raven, in Switzerland, the Hoopoe, in the Tyrol, the swallow) will bring it under the following circumstances. When the bird has temporarily left its nest this must be stopped up with wood. The bird then flies away to find the Spring-wurzel and will open the nest by touching it with the root. Meantime a fire or a red cloth must be placed near by, which will so frighten the bird that it will let the

[1] "Adam in Eden," Coles.

magical root fall." *Le petit Albert*, to procure Spring-wort suggests tying up a magpie's nest with new cords, but merely says that she brings *une herbe* to release her nestlings, without giving its name.

Several legends are attached to the Wood-pecker. Amongst others there is an idea that the root of the Peony is good for epilepsy, but should a Wood-pecker be in sight when the patient tastes it he would be forthwith struck blind! In Piedmont there is a little plant called the Herb of the Blessed Mary, which is fatal to birds, and there it is said that when young wild birds are caught and caged their parents bring them a sprig of it, that death rather than imprisonment may be their lot. De Gubernatis speaks of an oriental bird of greater resource, the *Paperone*, for when *his* little ones are imprisoned he seeks and brings a root which breaks the iron bars and releases them. Parkinson tells of an Indian herb which " cast to the birds causeth as many as take it to fall downe to the ground as being stoned for a time, but if any take it too greedily it will kill them, if they bee not helped by cold water put on their heads, but Dawes above all other birds are soonest kild thereby." There is a suggestion of comedy in this picture of a seventeenth century herbalist in a foreign land pouring cold water on the heads of wild birds.

"The raven, when he hath killed the chameleon, and yet perceiving he is hurt and poisoned by him, flyeth for remedy to the Laurell," which "represseth and extinguisheth the venom," says Pliny.[1] The elephant, under the same circumstances, recovers himself by eating "wild Olive, the only remedy he hath of this poison . . . The storke, feeling himself amisse, goeth to the herbe Organ for remedy," and Parkinson quotes Antigonas as saying that ring-doves cured their wounds

[1] Philemon Holland's Translation.

FENNEL

with the same plant. Stock-doves, jays, merles, black-
birds and ousels recover "their appetite to meate,"
by eating bay leaves; and ducks, geese and other
waterfowl seek endive or chicory. Of course, chickweed and goosegrass have gained their names as
the result of similar observations, more modern, and
possibly more accurate. Elder-berries are eaten by
birds, but they are said to have serious effects on
chickens.

Lizards cure themselves of the biting of serpents with
calaminth, and the tortoise cautiously eats a "kind of
sauorie or marjerome" before the battle. Sir Francis
Bacon mentions that, "the snake loveth fennel; that the
toad will be much under sage; that frogs will be in
cinquefoil"; though he unromantically doubts that the
virtue of these herbs is the cause of these preferences.
Turner also remarks on the toad's liking for sage, and
says: "Rue is good to be planted among Sage, to
prevent the poison which may be in it by toads fre-
quenting amongst it, but Rue being amongst it they
will not come near it." A toad recovers itself by means
of the plantain from the poison of the spider, and
Bullein[1] tells us of the frog's fondness for the *Scabiosa*,
under whose leaves they will "shadow themselves from
the heate of the daie, poppyng and plaiying under these
leaves, which to them is a pleasant Tent or Pavillion."
The reputed venom of toads was sometimes said to be
sucked from camomile, of all plants!

Pliny wrote of the serpent, that waking in the
spring, she finds that during the winter her sight
has become "dim and dark, so that with the herbe
Fennell she comforteth and anointeth her eies," and
having cast her coat, "appeareth fresh, slick and yong
again."

If camomile furnishes venom for toads, it seems to

[1] Bullein's "Bulwarke; or, Booke of Simples," 1562.

provide nourishment for fishes.   William Browne says
of some nymphs :—

> Another from her banks, in sheer good will,
> Brings nutriment for fish, the camomile.

Isaac Walton observes that, "Parsley and Garden
earth recovers and refreshes sick fish." The Alder or
Aul is indirectly connected with trout in a Herefordshire
rhyme :—

> When the bud of the Aul is as big as the trout's eye,
> Then that fish is in season in the River Wye.

Among other counsels *Piscator* speaks of the perch's
tastes.   "And he hath been observed by some not
usually to bite till the mulberry-tree buds—that is to
say, till extreme frosts be past in the spring. . . . Some
think [of grayling] that he feeds on water-thyme, and
smells of it at his first taking out of the water."   A pike
has a liking for lavender, and the directions for trying
for this fish with a dead bait begin : "Dissolve gum of
ivy in oil of spike [lavender], and then anoint the bait
with it.   Wheat boiled in milk and flavoured with
Saffron is a choice bait for Roach and Grayling, and
Mulberries and those Blackberries which grow upon
briars, be good baits for Chubs and Carps."   Gerarde says
that Balm rubbed over hives will keep the bees there,
and cause others to come to them, and Parkinson thought
that the "leaves or rootes of *Acorus* (sweet-smelling
Flagge) tyed to a hive" would have the same effect.

To turn to the herbs prescribed by men for beasts,
we find that Spenser alludes to two of them :—

> Here grows *melampode* everywhere
> And *terebinth* good for gotes.
> July—*Shepheard's Calendar.*

A marginal note suggests that the latter meant the
"turpentine tree."   "The tree that weepeth turpentine"
is mentioned by Drayton, and we may suppose that both
poets referred to the same tree, the Silver Fir (*Pinus*

picra). Melampode was hellebore or bear's foot, a
very important plant, and it was much used in magic.
A cynical French verse says:—

L'ellébore est la fleur des fous,
On l'a dédie a maints poètes.

Once people blessed their cattle with it to keep them
from evil spells, and "for this purpose it was dug up
with certain attendant mystic rites : the devotees first
drawing a circle round the plant with a sword, and then
turning to the east and offering a prayer to Apollo and
Æsculapius for leave to dig up the root."[1] In the old
French romance, *Les Quatre Fils Aymon*, the sorcerer,
Malagis or Maugis, when he wishes to make his way, un-
challenged, through the enemy's camp, scatters powdered
hellebore in the air as he goes. Both the Black and the
White Hellebore, Parkinson says, are known to be very
poisonous, and the white hellebore was used by hunters
to poison arrows, with which they meant to kill
"wolves, foxes, dogs," etc. Black Hellebore was used
to heal and not to hurt, and "a piece of the roote being
drawne through a hole made in the eare of a beast
troubled with cough, or having taken any poisonous
thing, cureth it, if it be taken out the next day at the
same houre." This writer believes that White Hellebore would be equally efficacious in such a case, but
Gerarde recommends the Black Hellebore only as being
good for beasts. He says the old Farriers used to "cut
a slit in the dewlap and put in a bit of Beare-foot, and
leave it there for daies together." *Verbascum thapsis* was
called Bullock's Lungwort, from the resemblance of its
leaf to a dewlap, and on the Doctrine of Signatures was
therefore given to cattle suffering from pneumonia.

Samoclas, or Marchwort, was a strange herb which
used to be put in the drinking-troughs of cattle and
swine to preserve their health. But to obtain this

[1] Timbs.

desirable result it had to be "gathered fasting, and with the left hand, without looking back, when it was being plucked."[1] Gervase Markham mentions a curious evil among cattle. He says if a shrew-mouse run over a beast "it feebleth his hinder parts and maketh him unable to go. The cure is to draw him under, or beat him with a Bramble, which groweth at both ends in the furrowes of corne lands." Markham was a noted authority on Husbandry and Farriery in the early part of the seventeenth century, and he gives advice for the various ills afflicting horses. For nightmare he prescribed balls composed of Aniseed, Liquorice and Garlic, and other ingredients. For toothache, Ale or Vinegar, in which Betony has been seethed ; and loose teeth are to be rubbed with the leaves of Elecampane, which will "fasten" them. Stubwort (wood-sorrel), "lapped in red Dock leafe and roasted in hot cinders, will eat away the dead flesh in a sore," and any "splint, iron, thorne or stub " may be drawn out by an application of Yarrow, Southernwood, Cummin-seed, Fenugreek and Ditany, bruised with black soap. Horse Mint, Wormwood and Dill are other herbs recommended by this author.

Gerarde says that the leaves of Arsmart (*Persicaria*) rubbed on the back of a tired horse, and a " good handfull or two laid under the saddle, will wonderfully refresh him ; " and *Le petit Albert* gives a recipe for making a horse go further in one hour than another would go in eight. You must begin by mingling a handful of "Satyrion" in his oats, and anointing him with the fat of a deer ; then when you are mounted and ready to start " vous lui tournerez la têté du coté de soleil levant et vous penchant sur son oreille gauche vous prononçerez trois fois à voix basse les paroles suivantes et vous partirez aussi tôt : *Gaspar, Melchior, Merchisard.* T'ajonte à cecy que si vous suspenderez au col du cheval les

[1] Timbs.

grosses dents d'un loup qui aura étè tué en courant, le cheval ne sera pas fatigue de sa course." No doubt these proceedings were carried out by the traveller with an air of mystery, and must have impressed the by-standers, but one wonders what the rider thought of them after an hour's journeying? Satyrion is a kind of orchis. There was a herb called *Sferro Cavallo* which was supposed to be able to break locks or draw off the shoes of the horses that passed over it. Sir Thomas Browne speaks of it in his "Popular Errors," and laughs the idea to scorn, and "cannot but wonder at Matthiolus, who, upon a parallel in Pliny, was staggered into suspension" [of judgment]. This plant was probably the Horse-shoe Vetch, whose seed-vessels, being in the shape of horse-shoes, may have given rise to the superstition; but Grimm thought it was the *Euphorbia Lathyris*. The same belief is found in different countries, referred to other plants; the French thought that Rest Harrow had this marvellous property, and Culpepper tells the same tale about the Moonwort (*Botrychium Lunaria*), which had the country name of Unshoe-the-Horse. "Besides, I have heard com-menders say that in White Down in Devonshire, near Tiverton, there were found thirty horse-shoes, pulled off from the feet of the Earl of Essex's horses, being then drawn up in a body, many of them being but newly shod, and no reason known, which caused much admira-tion, and the herb described usually grows upon heaths." One would hardly have thought that "admiration" was the feeling evoked, but perhaps nobody concerned was pressed for time!

Hound's Tongue (*Cynoglossum officinale*) was believed to have the remarkable property that it will "tye the tongues of Houndes, so that they shall not bark at you, if it be laid under the bottom of your feet."

In Markham's advice about domestic animals, he

alludes to a " certaine stage of madnesse " which attacks
rabbits, and says that the cure is Hare-Thistle (*Sonchus
oleraceus*). The " Grete Herbal " called this plant the
"Hare's Palace." " For yf the hare come under it, he
is sure that no best can touche hym."

These statements lead one to feel that once upon
a time, the world was much more like the world
of Richard Jefferies than it is, and that " wood
magic" was nearer to our forefathers than to our-
selves. Nowadays, when everything travels more
quickly along the road of life, the eyes of ordinary
mortals get confused with the movement and the
jostling and they do not see the pretty by-play that
goes on in the bushes by the way, nor peer into the
depths of the woodland beyond. In this they lose
a good deal, but no one can " put back the clock,"
and one must feel grateful that the idylls of the forest
are still being acted, and that there are still men whose
vision is quick enough to catch sight of them, and whose
pens have the cunning to put before others the glimpses
that they themselves have caught.

A legend exists about the Cormorant, the Bat, and the
Bramble—quite inconsequent, but not wholly out of
place here, so it shall serve as a conclusion.

Once the Cormorant was a wool merchant and he
took for partners the Bat and the Bramble. They
freighted a large ship with wool, but she was wrecked
and then they were bankrupt. Ever since that, the
Cormorant is diving into the deep, looking for the lost
ship; the Bat skulks round till midnight, so that he
may not meet his creditors, and the Bramble catches
hold of every passing sheep to try and make up for
his loss by stealing wool. No doubt, you have often
noticed their ways, but did you ever before know their
reasons ?

TUSSER'S LIST

SEEDS AND HERBS FOR THE KITCHEN.

1. Avens.
2. Betony.
3. Bleets or beets, white or yellow.
4. Bloodwort.
5. Bugloss.
6. Burnet.
7. Borrage.
8. Cabbages, remove in June.
9. Clary.
10. Coleworts.
11. Cresses.
12. Endive.
13. Fennel.
14. French Mallows.
15. French Saffron, set in August.
16. Lang de beef.
17. Leeks, remove in June.
18. Lettuce, remove in May.
19. Longwort (*Lungwort*).
20. Liverwort (probably *Agrimonia Eupatoria*).
21. Marigolds, often cut.
22. Mercury (*Chenopodium Bonus Henricus*).
23. Mints, at all times.
24. Nep (*Nepeta Cataria*).
25. Onions, from December to March.
26. Orache or arache, red and white. (*Atriplex hortensis*).
27. Patience.
28. Parsley.
29. Penny-royal.
30. Primrose.
31. Poret (*a leek or small onion according to some writers, Garlick*).
32. Rosemary, in the spring time, to grow south or west.
33. Sage, red or white.
34. English Saffron, set in August.
35. Summer Savory.
36. Sorrell.
37. Spinage.
38. Succory.
39. Siethes (*Chives*).
40. Tansey.
41. Thyme.
42. Violets of all sorts.

Herbs and Roots for Salads and Sauce.

1. Alexanders at all times.
2. Artichokes.
3. Blessed Thistle, or Carduus Benedictus.
4. Cucumbers, in April and May.
5. Cresses, sow with lettuce in the spring.
6. Endive.
7. Mustard-seed, sow in the spring, and at Michaelmas.
8. Musk, Mellion, in April and May.
9. Mints.
10. Purslane.
11. Radish, and after remove them.
12. Rampions.
13. Rocket, in April.
14. Sage.
15. Sorrell.
16. Spinage, for the summer.
17. Sea-holy.
18. Sparage, let grow two years and then remove.
19. Skirrets, set these plants in March.
20. Succory.
21. Tarragon, set in slips in March.
22. Violets of all colours.

These buy with the penny
Or look not for any.

1. Capers.
2. Lemons.
3. Olives.
4. Oranges.
5. Rice.
6. Samphire.

Herbs and Roots, to Boil or to Butter.

1. Beans, set in winter.
2. Cabbages, sow in March and after remove.
3. Carrots.
4. Citrons, sow in May.
5. Gourds, in May.
6. Navews, sow in June (*Brassica Napus*).
7. Pompions, in May.
8. Parsnips, in winter.
9. Runcival Pease, set in winter.
10. Rapes, sow in June.
11. Turnips, in March and April.

Strewing Herbs of all Sorts.

1. Basil, fine and busht, sow in May.
2. Balm, set in March.
3. Camomile.
4. Costmary.
5. Cowslips and Paggles.
6. Daisies of all sorts.
7. Sweet Fennell.

TUSSER'S LIST 203

8. Germander.
9. Hyssop, set in February.
10. Lavender (*Lavendula vera*).
11. Lavender Spike (*L. spica*).
12. Lavender Cotton.
13. Marjoram, knotted, sow or set in the spring.
14. Maudeline.
15. Pennyroyal.
16. Roses of all sorts, in January and September.
17. Red Mints.
18. Sage.
19. Tansy.
20. Violets.
21. Winter Savory.

HERBS, BRANCHES, AND FLOWERS FOR WINDOWS.

1. Bays, sow or plant in January.
2. Bachelor's Buttons.
3. Bottles, blue, red, and tawny.
4. Columbines.
5. Campions.
6. Cowslips (*Tusser here meant Oxlips*).
7. Daffodils or Daffodondillies.
8. Eglantine or Sweet-Brier.
9. Fetherfew.
10. Flower Amour, sow in May (*Amaranthus*).
11. Flower de Luce.
12. Flower-Gentle, white and red (*Amaranthus*).
13. Flower Nice.
14. Gillyflowers, red, white, and Carnations, set in spring and at harvest in pots, pails, or tubs, or for summer, in beds.
15. Holyoaks, red, white, and Carnations (*Hollyhocks*).
16. Indian Eye, sow in May, or set in slips in March (*Dianthus Plumarius*).
17. Lavender of all sorts.
18. Larksfoot (*Larkspur*).
19. Laus tibi (*Narcissus Poeticus*).
20. Lillium Convallium.
21. Lilies, red and white, sow or set in March and September.
22. Marigolds, double.
23. Nigella Romana.
24. Pansies, or Heartsease.
25. Paggles, green and yellow (*Cowslips*).
26. Pinks of all sorts.
27. Queen's Gilliflowers (*Hesperis Matronalis*).
28. Rosemary.
29. Roses of all sorts.
30. Snapdragon.
31. Sops in wine (Pinks).
32. Sweet Williams.
33. Sweet Johns (*Dianthus Barbatus*).

34. Star of Bethlehem (*Orni-thogalum Umbellatum*).
35. Star of Jerusalem (*Trago-pogon pratensis*).
36. Stock Gilliflowers of all sorts.
37. Tuft Gilliflowers.

38. Velvet flowers, or French Marigolds (*Tagetes patula*).
39. Violets, yellow and white.
40. Wall Gilliflowers of all sorts.

HERBS TO STILL IN SUMMER.

1. Blessed Thistle.
2. Betony.
3. Dill.
4. Endive.
5. Eyebright.
6. Fennel.
7. Fumitory.
8. Hyssop.
9. Mints.
10. Plantane.
11. Roses, red and damask.

12. Respies (*Rubus Idæus*).
13. Saxifrage (*Pimpinella saxi-fraga* or *Saxifraga gran-ulata*, or perhaps, *Carum Carvi*).
14. Strawberries.
15. Sorrel.
16. Succory.
17. Woodroffe, for sweet waters and cakes.

NECESSARY HERBS TO GROW IN THE GARDEN FOR PHYSIC, NOT REHEARSED BEFORE.

1. Anise.
2. Archangel (*Angelica*).
3. Betony.
4. Chervil.
5. Cinquefoil (*Potentilla reptans*).
6. Cummin.
7. Dragons (*Arum Macu-latum*).
8. Dittary or garden ginger (*Lepidium Latifolium*).
9. Gromwell seed (*Litho-spernum officinale*).
10. Hart's tongue.
11. Horehound.

12. Lovage.
13. Liquorice.
14. Mandrake.
15. Mugwort.
16. Peony.
17. Poppy.
18. Rue.
19. Rhubarb.
20. Smallage.
21. Saxifrage.
22. Savin.
23. Stitchwort.
24. Valerian.
25. Woodbine.

Thus ends in brief,
Of herbs the chief,
To get more skill,
Read whom ye will;
Such mo to have,
Of field go crave.

AUTHORS REFERRED TO

ABERCROMBIE, " Every Man his own Gardener."
AMHERST (Hon. Alicia), " A History of Gardening in England."
ASHMOLE, " History of the Most Noble Order of the Garter."
BACON, " Sylva Sylvarum ; or, a Naturall Historie."
BLOUNT, " Fragmenta Antiquitatis ; or Jocular Tenures."
BRAND, " Popular Antiquities."
BRITTEN, " A Dictionary of English Plant Names."
BROWNE (Sir Thomas), " Vulgar Errors."
CLARENDON, " History of the Rebellion."
COLES, " Art of Simpling."
CULPEPPER, " The English Physitian."
　　　,, 　" Astrological Judgment of Diseases."
DE GUBERNATIS, *La Mythologie des Plantes.*
DE LA QUINTINYE, " The Compleat Gard'ner."
DILLON, *Nineteenth Century,* April 1894.
DYER (Thistleton), " The Folk-Lore of Plants."
ELLACOMBE (Canon), " The Plant-Lore and Garden-Craft of Shakespeare."
EVELYN (J.), " Acetaria, a Discourse of Sallets," 1699.
FAVYN (André), *Le Théâtre d'honneur et de Chevalries,* 1620.
　　,,　　　,,　" Theatre of Honour."
FERNIE, " Herbal Simples."
FOLKARD, " Plant-Lore, Legends and Lyrics."
FRIEND, " Flowers and Flower-Lore."
FULLER, " Church History."
　　,, " Antheologia ; or, the Speech of Flowers."
GERARDE, " The Herball," 1596.
THE " Grete Herball," 1516.
GUILLIM, " Heraldry."
HAKLUYT's Voyages, " Remembrances for Master S.," 1582.
HARRISON's " Description of England."

" History of Signboards."

Hogg, " The Vegetable Kingdom and its Products."

Huish, " History of the Coronation of George IV."

Ingram, *Flora Symbolica.*

I. W., *i.e.* John Worlidge, *Systema Agriculturæ*, printed (London) for Thos. Dring, 1681.

Jones, " Crowns and Coronations."

Lambert (Miss), *Nineteenth Century*, September 1879, and May 1880.

Le Petit Albert, from the " Secrets of Albertus Magnus, of the Virtues of Herbs, Stones and Certaine Beasts," 1617.

Loudon, " Encyclopædia of Gardening."

Lupton, " Book of Notable Things," 1575.

Markham (Gervase), " The Complete Housewife."

Meager, " The New Art of Gardening," 1697.

Newton, " An Herbal of the Bible," 1587.

Nicholas (Sir N. H.), " History of the Orders of Knighthood of the British Empire.

Parkinson, *Paradisi in Sole, Paradisus terrestris,* 1629.

„ " Theatre of Plants," 1640.

Peck, *Desiderata Curiosa.*

Pegge's *Curalia.*

Platt (Sir Hugh), " The Garden of Eden," 1653.

Pliny's " Natural History," Trans. by Philemon Holland.

Quarterly Review, June 1842.

Rhind, " History of the Vegetable Kingdom."

Roberts (H.), " Complete Account of the Coronations of the Kings and Queens of England."

Robinson, " English Flower-Garden."

Ross, " View of all Religions," 1653.

Selden, " Table Talk."

Smith, " Dictionary of the Bible."

Thornton, " Family Herbal."

Timbs, " Things Not Generally Known."

Tusser, " Five Hundred Points of Good Husbandry," 1577.

Walton (Isaac), " The Complete Angler."

INDEX OF PLANTS

A CATALOGUE OF SELECTED DOVER BOOKS
IN ALL FIELDS OF INTEREST

A CATALOGUE OF SELECTED DOVER BOOKS
IN ALL FIELDS OF INTEREST

AMERICA'S OLD MASTERS, James T. Flexner. Four men emerged unexpectedly from provincial 18th century America to leadership in European art: Benjamin West, J. S. Copley, C. R. Peale, Gilbert Stuart. Brilliant coverage of lives and contributions. Revised, 1967 edition. 69 plates. 365pp. of text.

21806-6 Paperbound $2.75

FIRST FLOWERS OF OUR WILDERNESS: AMERICAN PAINTING, THE COLONIAL PERIOD, James T. Flexner. Painters, and regional painting traditions from earliest Colonial times up to the emergence of Copley, West and Peale Sr., Foster, Gustavus Hesselius, Feke, John Smibert and many anonymous painters in the primitive manner. Engaging presentation, with 162 illustrations. xxii + 368pp.

22180-6 Paperbound $3.50

THE LIGHT OF DISTANT SKIES: AMERICAN PAINTING, 1760-1835, James T. Flexner. The great generation of early American painters goes to Europe to learn and to teach: West, Copley, Gilbert Stuart and others. Allston, Trumbull, Morse; also contemporary American painters—primitives, derivatives, academics—who remained in America. 102 illustrations. xiii + 306pp.

22179-2 Paperbound $3.00

A HISTORY OF THE RISE AND PROGRESS OF THE ARTS OF DESIGN IN THE UNITED STATES, William Dunlap. Much the richest mine of information on early American painters, sculptors, architects, engravers, miniaturists, etc. The only source of information for scores of artists, the major primary source for many others. Unabridged reprint of rare original 1834 edition, with new introduction by James T. Flexner, and 394 new illustrations. Edited by Rita Weiss. 6⅝ x 9⅝.

21695-0, 21696-9, 21697-7 Three volumes, Paperbound $13.50

EPOCHS OF CHINESE AND JAPANESE ART, Ernest F. Fenollosa. From primitive Chinese art to the 20th century, thorough history, explanation of every important art period and form, including Japanese woodcuts; main stress on China and Japan, but Tibet, Korea also included. Still unexcelled for its detailed, rich coverage of cultural background, aesthetic elements, diffusion studies, particularly of the historical period. 2nd, 1913 edition. 242 illustrations. lii + 439pp. of text.

20364-6, 20365-4 Two volumes, Paperbound $5.00

THE GENTLE ART OF MAKING ENEMIES, James A. M. Whistler. Greatest wit of his day deflates Oscar Wilde, Ruskin, Swinburne; strikes back at inane critics, exhibitions, art journalism; aesthetics of impressionist revolution in most striking form. Highly readable classic by great painter. Reproduction of edition designed by Whistler. Introduction by Alfred Werner. xxxvi + 334pp.

21875-9 Paperbound $2.25

VISUAL ILLUSIONS: THEIR CAUSES, CHARACTERISTICS, AND APPLICATIONS, Matthew Luckiesh. Thorough description and discussion of optical illusion, geometric and perspective, particularly; size and shape distortions, illusions of color, of motion; natural illusions; use of illusion in art and magic, industry, etc. Most useful today with op art, also for classical art. Scores of effects illustrated. Introduction by William H. Ittleson. 100 illustrations. xxi + 252pp.

21530-X Paperbound $1.50

A HANDBOOK OF ANATOMY FOR ART STUDENTS, Arthur Thomson. Thorough, virtually exhaustive coverage of skeletal structure, musculature, etc. Full text, supplemented by anatomical diagrams and drawings and by photographs of undraped figures. Unique in its comparison of male and female forms, pointing out differences of contour, texture, form. 211 figures, 40 drawings, 86 photographs. xx + 459pp. 5⅜ x 8⅜. 21163-0 Paperbound $3.00

150 MASTERPIECES OF DRAWING, Selected by Anthony Toney. Full page reproductions of drawings from the early 16th to the end of the 18th century, all beautifully reproduced: Rembrandt, Michelangelo, Dürer, Fragonard, Urs, Graf, Wouwerman, many others. First-rate browsing book, model book for artists. xviii + 150pp. 8⅜ x 11¼. 21032-4 Paperbound $2.00

THE LATER WORK OF AUBREY BEARDSLEY, Aubrey Beardsley. Exotic, erotic, ironic masterpieces in full maturity: Comedy Ballet, Venus and Tannhauser, Pierrot, Lysistrata, Rape of the Lock, Savoy material, Ali Baba, Volpone, etc. This material revolutionized the art world, and is still powerful, fresh, brilliant. With *The Early Work*, all Beardsley's finest work. 174 plates, 2 in color. xiv + 176pp. 8⅛ x 11.

21817-1 Paperbound $3.00

DRAWINGS OF REMBRANDT, Rembrandt van Rijn. Complete reproduction of fabulously rare edition by Lippmann and Hofstede de Groot, completely reedited, updated, improved by Prof. Seymour Slive, Fogg Museum. Portraits, Biblical sketches, landscapes, Oriental types, nudes, episodes from classical mythology—All Rembrandt's fertile genius. Also selection of drawings by his pupils and followers. "Stunning volumes," *Saturday Review*. 550 illustrations. lxxviii + 552pp. 9⅛ x 12¼. 21485-0, 21486-9 Two volumes, Paperbound $6.50

THE DISASTERS OF WAR, Francisco Goya. One of the masterpieces of Western civilization—83 etchings that record Goya's shattering, bitter reaction to the Napoleonic war that swept through Spain after the insurrection of 1808 and to war in general. Reprint of the first edition, with three additional plates from Boston's Museum of Fine Arts. All plates facsimile size. Introduction by Philip Hofer, Fogg Museum. v + 97pp. 9⅜ x 8¼. 21872-4 Paperbound $1.75

GRAPHIC WORKS OF ODILON REDON. Largest collection of Redon's graphic works ever assembled: 172 lithographs, 28 etchings and engravings, 9 drawings. These include some of his most famous works. All the plates from *Odilon Redon: oeuvre graphique complet*, plus additional plates. New introduction and caption translations by Alfred Werner. 209 illustrations. xxvii + 209pp. 9⅛ x 12¼.

21966-8 Paperbound $4.00

DESIGN BY ACCIDENT; A BOOK OF "ACCIDENTAL EFFECTS" FOR ARTISTS AND DESIGNERS, James F. O'Brien. Create your own unique, striking, imaginative effects by "controlled accident" interaction of materials: paints and lacquers, oil and water based paints, splatter, crackling materials, shatter, similar items. Everything you do will be different; first book on this limitless art, so useful to both fine artist and commercial artist. Full instructions. 192 plates showing "accidents," 8 in color. viii + 215pp. 8⅜ x 11¼.   21942-9 Paperbound $3.50

THE BOOK OF SIGNS, Rudolf Koch. Famed German type designer draws 493 beautiful symbols: religious, mystical, alchemical, imperial, property marks, runes, etc. Remarkable fusion of traditional and modern. Good for suggestions of timelessness, smartness, modernity. Text. vi + 104pp. 6⅛ x 9¼.
                                               20162-7 Paperbound $1.25

HISTORY OF INDIAN AND INDONESIAN ART, Ananda K. Coomaraswamy. An unabridged republication of one of the finest books by a great scholar in Eastern art. Rich in descriptive material, history, social backgrounds; Sunga reliefs, Rajput paintings, Gupta temples, Burmese frescoes, textiles, jewelry, sculpture, etc. 400 photos. viii + 423pp. 6⅜ x 9¾.   21436-2 Paperbound $3.50

PRIMITIVE ART, Franz Boas. America's foremost anthropologist surveys textiles, ceramics, woodcarving, basketry, metalwork, etc.; patterns, technology, creation of symbols, style origins. All areas of world, but very full on Northwest Coast Indians. More than 350 illustrations of baskets, boxes, totem poles, weapons, etc. 378 pp.
                                               20025-6 Paperbound $2.50

THE GENTLEMAN AND CABINET MAKER'S DIRECTOR, Thomas Chippendale. Full reprint (third edition, 1762) of most influential furniture book of all time, by master cabinetmaker. 200 plates, illustrating chairs, sofas, mirrors, tables, cabinets, plus 24 photographs of surviving pieces. Biographical introduction by N. Bienenstock. vi + 249pp. 9⅞ x 12¾.   21601-2 Paperbound $3.50

AMERICAN ANTIQUE FURNITURE, Edgar G. Miller, Jr. The basic coverage of all American furniture before 1840. Individual chapters cover type of furniture—clocks, tables, sideboards, etc.—chronologically, with inexhaustible wealth of data. More than 2100 photographs, all identified, commented on. Essential to all early American collectors. Introduction by H. E. Keyes. vi + 1106pp. 7⅞ x 10¾.
                                     21599-7, 21600-4 Two volumes, Paperbound $7.50

PENNSYLVANIA DUTCH AMERICAN FOLK ART, Henry J. Kauffman. 279 photos, 28 drawings of tulipware, Fraktur script, painted tinware, toys, flowered furniture, quilts, samplers, hex signs, house interiors, etc. Full descriptive text. Excellent for tourist, rewarding for designer, collector. Map. 146pp. 7⅞ x 10¾.
                                               21205-X Paperbound $2.00

EARLY NEW ENGLAND GRAVESTONE RUBBINGS, Edmund V. Gillon, Jr. 43 photographs, 226 carefully reproduced rubbings show heavily symbolic, sometimes macabre early gravestones, up to early 19th century. Remarkable early American primitive art, occasionally strikingly beautiful; always powerful. Text. xxvi + 207pp. 8⅜ x 11¼.   21380-3 Paperbound $3.00

ALPHABETS AND ORNAMENTS, Ernst Lehner. Well-known pictorial source for decorative alphabets, script examples, cartouches, frames, decorative title pages, calligraphic initials, borders, similar material. 14th to 19th century, mostly European. Useful in almost any graphic arts designing, varied styles. 750 illustrations. 256pp. 7 x 10. 21905-4 Paperbound $3.50

PAINTING: A CREATIVE APPROACH, Norman Colquhoun. For the beginner simple guide provides an instructive approach to painting: major stumbling blocks for beginner; overcoming them, technical points; paints and pigments; oil painting; watercolor and other media and color. New section on "plastic" paints. Glossary. Formerly *Paint Your Own Pictures.* 221pp. 22000-1 Paperbound $1.75

THE ENJOYMENT AND USE OF COLOR, Walter Sargent. Explanation of the relations between colors themselves and between colors in nature and art, including hundreds of little-known facts about color values, intensities, effects of high and low illumination, complementary colors. Many practical hints for painters, references to great masters. 7 color plates, 29 illustrations. x + 274pp.
20944-X Paperbound $2.50

THE NOTEBOOKS OF LEONARDO DA VINCI, compiled and edited by Jean Paul Richter. 1566 extracts from original manuscripts reveal the full range of Leonardo's versatile genius: all his writings on painting, sculpture, architecture, anatomy, astronomy, geography, topography, physiology, mining, music, etc., in both Italian and English, with 186 plates of manuscript pages and more than 500 additional drawings. Includes studies for the Last Supper, the lost Sforza monument, and other works. Total of xlvii + 866pp. 7⅞ x 10¾.
22572-0, 22573-9 Two volumes, Paperbound $10.00

MONTGOMERY WARD CATALOGUE OF 1895. Tea gowns, yards of flannel and pillow-case lace, stereoscopes, books of gospel hymns, the New Improved Singer Sewing Machine, side saddles, milk skimmers, straight-edged razors, high-button shoes, spittoons, and on and on . . . listing some 25,000 items, practically all illustrated. Essential to the shoppers of the 1890's, it is our truest record of the spirit of the period. Unaltered reprint of Issue No. 57, Spring and Summer 1895. Introduction by Boris Emmet. Innumerable illustrations. xiii + 624pp. 8½ x 11⅝.
22377-9 Paperbound $6.95

THE CRYSTAL PALACE EXHIBITION ILLUSTRATED CATALOGUE (LONDON, 1851). One of the wonders of the modern world—the Crystal Palace Exhibition in which all the nations of the civilized world exhibited their achievements in the arts and sciences—presented in an equally important illustrated catalogue. More than 1700 items pictured with accompanying text—ceramics, textiles, cast-iron work, carpets, pianos, sleds, razors, wall-papers, billiard tables, beehives, silverware and hundreds of other artifacts—represent the focal point of Victorian culture in the Western World. Probably the largest collection of Victorian decorative art ever assembled— indispensable for antiquarians and designers. Unabridged republication of the Art-Journal Catalogue of the Great Exhibition of 1851, with all terminal essays. New introduction by John Gloag, F.S.A. xxxiv + 426pp. 9 x 12.
22503-8 Paperbound $4.50

A HISTORY OF COSTUME, Carl Köhler. Definitive history, based on surviving pieces of clothing primarily, and paintings, statues, etc. secondarily. Highly readable text, supplemented by 594 illustrations of costumes of the ancient Mediterranean peoples, Greece and Rome, the Teutonic prehistoric period; costumes of the Middle Ages, Renaissance, Baroque, 18th and 19th centuries. Clear, measured patterns are provided for many clothing articles. Approach is practical throughout. Enlarged by Emma von Sichart. 464pp.   21030-8 Paperbound $3.00

ORIENTAL RUGS, ANTIQUE AND MODERN, Walter A. Hawley. A complete and authoritative treatise on the Oriental rug—where they are made, by whom and how, designs and symbols, characteristics in detail of the six major groups, how to distinguish them and how to buy them. Detailed technical data is provided on periods, weaves, warps, wefts, textures, sides, ends and knots, although no technical background is required for an understanding. 11 color plates, 80 halftones, 4 maps. vi + 320pp. 6⅛ x 9⅛.   22366-3 Paperbound $5.00

TEN BOOKS ON ARCHITECTURE, Vitruvius. By any standards the most important book on architecture ever written. Early Roman discussion of aesthetics of building, construction methods, orders, sites, and every other aspect of architecture has inspired, instructed architecture for about 2,000 years. Stands behind Palladio, Michelangelo, Bramante, Wren, countless others. Definitive Morris H. Morgan translation. 68 illustrations. xii + 331pp.   20645-9 Paperbound $2.50

THE FOUR BOOKS OF ARCHITECTURE, Andrea Palladio. Translated into every major Western European language in the two centuries following its publication in 1570, this has been one of the most influential books in the history of architecture. Complete reprint of the 1738 Isaac Ware edition. New introduction by Adolf Placzek, Columbia Univ. 216 plates. xxii + 110pp. of text. 9½ x 12¾.
                                        21308-0 Clothbound $10.00

STICKS AND STONES: A STUDY OF AMERICAN ARCHITECTURE AND CIVILIZATION, Lewis Mumford.One of the great classics of American cultural history. American architecture from the medieval-inspired earliest forms to the early 20th century; evolution of structure and style, and reciprocal influences on environment. 21 photographic illustrations. 238pp.   20202-X Paperbound $2.00

THE AMERICAN BUILDER'S COMPANION, Asher Benjamin. The most widely used early 19th century architectural style and source book, for colonial up into Greek Revival periods. Extensive development of geometry of carpentering, construction of sashes, frames, doors, stairs; plans and elevations of domestic and other buildings. Hundreds of thousands of houses were built according to this book, now invaluable to historians, architects, restorers, etc. 1827 edition. 59 plates. 114pp. 7⅞ x 10¾.
                                        22236-5 Paperbound $3.00

DUTCH HOUSES IN THE HUDSON VALLEY BEFORE 1776, Helen Wilkinson Reynolds. The standard survey of the Dutch colonial house and outbuildings, with constructional features, decoration, and local history associated with individual homesteads. Introduction by Franklin D. Roosevelt. Map. 150 illustrations. 469pp. 6⅝ x 9¼.   21469-9 Paperbound $3.50

THE ARCHITECTURE OF COUNTRY HOUSES, Andrew J. Downing. Together with Vaux's *Villas and Cottages* this is the basic book for Hudson River Gothic architecture of the middle Victorian period. Full, sound discussions of general aspects of housing, architecture, style, decoration, furnishing, together with scores of detailed house plans, illustrations of specific buildings, accompanied by full text. Perhaps the most influential single American architectural book. 1850 edition. Introduction by J. Stewart Johnson. 321 figures, 34 architectural designs. xvi + 560pp.

22003-6 Paperbound $3.50

LOST EXAMPLES OF COLONIAL ARCHITECTURE, John Mead Howells. Full-page photographs of buildings that have disappeared or been so altered as to be denatured, including many designed by major early American architects. 245 plates. xvii + 248pp. 7⅞ x 10¾. 21143-6 Paperbound $3.00

DOMESTIC ARCHITECTURE OF THE AMERICAN COLONIES AND OF THE EARLY REPUBLIC, Fiske Kimball. Foremost architect and restorer of Williamsburg and Monticello covers nearly 200 homes between 1620-1825. Architectural details, construction, style features, special fixtures, floor plans, etc. Generally considered finest work in its area. 219 illustrations of houses, doorways, windows, capital mantels. xx + 314pp. 7⅞ x 10¾. 21743-4 Paperbound $3.50

EARLY AMERICAN ROOMS: 1650-1858, edited by Russell Hawes Kettell. Tour of 12 rooms, each representative of a different era in American history and each furnished, decorated, designed and occupied in the style of the era. 72 plans and elevations, 8-page color section, etc., show fabrics, wall papers, arrangements, etc. Full descriptive text. xvii + 200pp. of text. 8⅜ x 11¼.

21633-0 Paperbound $4.00

THE FITZWILLIAM VIRGINAL BOOK, edited by J. Fuller Maitland and W. B. Squire. Full modern printing of famous early 17th-century ms. volume of 300 works by Morley, Byrd, Bull, Gibbons, etc. For piano or other modern keyboard instrument; easy to read format. xxxvi + 938pp. 8⅜ x 11.

21068-5, 21069-3 Two volumes, Paperbound $8.00

HARPSICHORD MUSIC, Johann Sebastian Bach. Bach Gesellschaft edition. A rich selection of Bach's masterpieces for the harpsichord: the six English Suites, six French Suites, the six Partitas (Clavierübung part I), the Goldberg Variations (Clavierübung part IV), the fifteen Two-Part Inventions and the fifteen Three-Part Sinfonias. Clearly reproduced on large sheets with ample margins; eminently playable. vi + 312pp. 8⅛ x 11. 22360-4 Paperbound $5.00

THE MUSIC OF BACH: AN INTRODUCTION, Charles Sanford Terry. A fine, nontechnical introduction to Bach's music, both instrumental and vocal. Covers organ music, chamber music, passion music, other types. Analyzes themes, developments, innovations. x + 114pp. 21075-8 Paperbound $1.25

BEETHOVEN AND HIS NINE SYMPHONIES, Sir George Grove. Noted British musicologist provides best history, analysis, commentary on symphonies. Very thorough, rigorously accurate; necessary to both advanced student and amateur music lover. 436 musical passages. vii + 407 pp. 20334-4 Paperbound $2.25

JOHANN SEBASTIAN BACH, Philipp Spitta. One of the great classics of musicology, this definitive analysis of Bach's music (and life) has never been surpassed. Lucid, nontechnical analyses of hundreds of pieces (30 pages devoted to St. Matthew Passion, 26 to B Minor Mass). Also includes major analysis of 18th-century music. 450 musical examples. 40-page musical supplement. Total of xx + 1799pp.
(EUK) 22278-0, 22279-9 Two volumes, Clothbound $15.00

MOZART AND HIS PIANO CONCERTOS, Cuthbert Girdlestone. The only full-length study of an important area of Mozart's creativity. Provides detailed analyses of all 23 concertos, traces inspirational sources. 417 musical examples. Second edition. 509pp. (USO) 21271-8 Paperbound $3.50

THE PERFECT WAGNERITE: A COMMENTARY ON THE NIBLUNG'S RING, George Bernard Shaw. Brilliant and still relevant criticism in remarkable essays on Wagner's Ring cycle, Shaw's ideas on political and social ideology behind the plots, role of Leitmotifs, vocal requisites, etc. Prefaces. xxi + 136pp.
21707-8 Paperbound $1.50

DON GIOVANNI, W. A. Mozart. Complete libretto, modern English translation; biographies of composer and librettist; accounts of early performances and critical reaction. Lavishly illustrated. All the material you need to understand and appreciate this great work. Dover Opera Guide and Libretto Series; translated and introduced by Ellen Bleiler. 92 illustrations. 209pp.
21134-7 Paperbound $1.50

HIGH FIDELITY SYSTEMS: A LAYMAN'S GUIDE, Roy F. Allison. All the basic information you need for setting up your own audio system: high fidelity and stereo record players, tape records, F.M. Connections, adjusting tone arm, cartridge, checking needle alignment, positioning speakers, phasing speakers, adjusting hums, trouble-shooting, maintenance, and similar topics. Enlarged 1965 edition. More than 50 charts, diagrams, photos. iv + 91pp. 21514-8 Paperbound $1.25

REPRODUCTION OF SOUND, Edgar Villchur. Thorough coverage for laymen of high fidelity systems, reproducing systems in general, needles, amplifiers, preamps, loudspeakers, feedback, explaining physical background. "A rare talent for making technicalities vividly comprehensible," R. Darrell, *High Fidelity*. 69 figures. iv + 92pp. 21515-6 Paperbound $1.00

HEAR ME TALKIN' TO YA: THE STORY OF JAZZ AS TOLD BY THE MEN WHO MADE IT, Nat Shapiro and Nat Hentoff. Louis Armstrong, Fats Waller, Jo Jones, Clarence Williams, Billy Holiday, Duke Ellington, Jelly Roll Morton and dozens of other jazz greats tell how it was in Chicago's South Side, New Orleans, depression Harlem and the modern West Coast as jazz was born and grew. xvi + 429pp.
21726-4 Paperbound $2.00

FABLES OF AESOP, translated by Sir Roger L'Estrange. A reproduction of the very rare 1931 Paris edition; a selection of the most interesting fables, together with 50 imaginative drawings by Alexander Calder. v + 128pp. 6½x9¼.
21780-9 Paperbound $1.25

AGAINST THE GRAIN (A REBOURS), Joris K. Huysmans. Filled with weird images, evidences of a bizarre imagination, exotic experiments with hallucinatory drugs, rich tastes and smells and the diversions of its sybarite hero Duc Jean des Esseintes, this classic novel pushed 19th-century literary decadence to its limits. Full unabridged edition. Do not confuse this with abridged editions generally sold. Introduction by Havelock Ellis. xlix + 206pp. 22190-3 Paperbound $2.00

VARIORUM SHAKESPEARE: HAMLET. Edited by Horace H. Furness; a landmark of American scholarship. Exhaustive footnotes and appendices treat all doubtful words and phrases, as well as suggested critical emendations throughout the play's history. First volume contains editor's own text, collated with all Quartos and Folios. Second volume contains full first Quarto, translations of Shakespeare's sources (Belleforest, and Saxo Grammaticus), Der Bestrafte Brudermord, and many essays on critical and historical points of interest by major authorities of past and present. Includes details of staging and costuming over the years. By far the best edition available for serious students of Shakespeare. Total of xx + 905pp. 21004-9, 21005-7, 2 volumes, Paperbound $5.25

A LIFE OF WILLIAM SHAKESPEARE, Sir Sidney Lee. This is the standard life of Shakespeare, summarizing everything known about Shakespeare and his plays. Incredibly rich in material, broad in coverage, clear and judicious, it has served thousands as the best introduction to Shakespeare. 1931 edition. 9 plates. xxix + 792pp. (USO) 21967-4 Paperbound $3.75

MASTERS OF THE DRAMA, John Gassner. Most comprehensive history of the drama in print, covering every tradition from Greeks to modern Europe and America, including India, Far East, etc. Covers more than 800 dramatists, 2000 plays, with biographical material, plot summaries, theatre history, criticism, etc. "Best of its kind in English," New Republic. 77 illustrations. xxii + 890pp. 20100-7 Clothbound $7.50

THE EVOLUTION OF THE ENGLISH LANGUAGE, George McKnight. The growth of English, from the 14th century to the present. Unusual, non-technical account presents basic information in very interesting form: sound shifts, change in grammar and syntax, vocabulary growth, similar topics. Abundantly illustrated with quotations. Formerly Modern English in the Making. xii + 590pp. 21932-1 Paperbound $3.50

AN ETYMOLOGICAL DICTIONARY OF MODERN ENGLISH, Ernest Weekley. Fullest, richest work of its sort, by foremost British lexicographer. Detailed word histories, including many colloquial and archaic words; extensive quotations. Do not confuse this with the Concise Etymological Dictionary, which is much abridged. Total of xxvii + 830pp. 6½ x 9¼. 21873-2, 21874-0 Two volumes, Paperbound $5.50

FLATLAND: A ROMANCE OF MANY DIMENSIONS, E. A. Abbott. Classic of science-fiction explores ramifications of life in a two-dimensional world, and what happens when a three-dimensional being intrudes. Amusing reading, but also useful as introduction to thought about hyperspace. Introduction by Banesh Hoffmann. 16 illustrations. xx + 103pp. 20001-9 Paperbound $1.00

POEMS OF ANNE BRADSTREET, edited with an introduction by Robert Hutchinson. A new selection of poems by America's first poet and perhaps the first significant woman poet in the English language. 48 poems display her development in works of considerable variety—love poems, domestic poems, religious meditations, formal elegies, "quaternions," etc. Notes, bibliography. viii + 222pp.

22160-1 Paperbound $2.00

THREE GOTHIC NOVELS: THE CASTLE OF OTRANTO BY HORACE WALPOLE; VATHEK BY WILLIAM BECKFORD; THE VAMPYRE BY JOHN POLIDORI, WITH FRAGMENT OF A NOVEL BY LORD BYRON, edited by E. F. Bleiler. The first Gothic novel, by Walpole; the finest Oriental tale in English, by Beckford; powerful Romantic supernatural story in versions by Polidori and Byron. All extremely important in history of literature; all still exciting, packed with supernatural thrills, ghosts, haunted castles, magic, etc. xl + 291pp.

21232-7 Paperbound $2.00

THE BEST TALES OF HOFFMANN, E. T. A. Hoffmann. 10 of Hoffmann's most important stories, in modern re-editings of standard translations: Nutcracker and the King of Mice, Signor Formica, Automata, The Sandman, Rath Krespel, The Golden Flowerpot, Master Martin the Cooper, The Mines of Falun, The King's Betrothed, A New Year's Eve Adventure. 7 illustrations by Hoffmann. Edited by E. F. Bleiler. xxxix + 419pp.

21793-0 Paperbound $2.25

GHOST AND HORROR STORIES OF AMBROSE BIERCE, Ambrose Bierce. 23 strikingly modern stories of the horrors latent in the human mind: The Eyes of the Panther, The Damned Thing, An Occurrence at Owl Creek Bridge, An Inhabitant of Carcosa, etc., plus the dream-essay, Visions of the Night. Edited by E. F. Bleiler. xxii + 199pp.

20767-6 Paperbound $1.50

BEST GHOST STORIES OF J. S. LEFANU, J. Sheridan LeFanu. Finest stories by Victorian master often considered greatest supernatural writer of all. Carmilla, Green Tea, The Haunted Baronet, The Familiar, and 12 others. Most never before available in the U. S. A. Edited by E. F. Bleiler. 8 illustrations from Victorian publications. xvii + 467pp.

20415-4 Paperbound $2.50

THE TIME STREAM, THE GREATEST ADVENTURE, AND THE PURPLE SAPPHIRE— THREE SCIENCE FICTION NOVELS, John Taine (Eric Temple Bell). Great American mathematician was also foremost science fiction novelist of the 1920's. *The Time Stream,* one of all-time classics, uses concepts of circular time; *The Greatest Adventure,* incredibly ancient biological experiments from Antarctica threaten to escape; The *Purple Sapphire,* superscience, lost races in Central Tibet, survivors of the Great Race. 4 illustrations by Frank R. Paul. v + 532pp.

21180-0 Paperbound $2.50

SEVEN SCIENCE FICTION NOVELS, H. G. Wells. The standard collection of the great novels. Complete, unabridged. *First Men in the Moon, Island of Dr. Moreau, War of the Worlds, Food of the Gods, Invisible Man, Time Machine, In the Days of the Comet.* Not only science fiction fans, but every educated person owes it to himself to read these novels. 1015pp.

20264-X Clothbound $5.00

LAST AND FIRST MEN AND STAR MAKER, TWO SCIENCE FICTION NOVELS, Olaf Stapledon. Greatest future histories in science fiction. In the first, human intelligence is the "hero," through strange paths of evolution, interplanetary invasions, incredible technologies, near extinctions and reemergences. Star Maker describes the quest of a band of star rovers for intelligence itself, through time and space: weird inhuman civilizations, crustacean minds, symbiotic worlds, etc. Complete, unabridged. v + 438pp. 21962-3 Paperbound $2.00

THREE PROPHETIC NOVELS, H. G. WELLS. Stages of a consistently planned future for mankind. *When the Sleeper Wakes,* and *A Story of the Days to Come,* anticipate *Brave New World* and *1984,* in the 21st Century; *The Time Machine,* only complete version in print, shows farther future and the end of mankind. All show Wells's greatest gifts as storyteller and novelist. Edited by E. F. Bleiler. x + 335pp. (USO) 20605-X Paperbound $2.00

THE DEVIL'S DICTIONARY, Ambrose Bierce. America's own Oscar Wilde— Ambrose Bierce—offers his barbed iconoclastic wisdom in over 1,000 definitions hailed by H. L. Mencken as "some of the most gorgeous witticisms in the English language." 145pp. 20487-1 Paperbound $1.25

MAX AND MORITZ, Wilhelm Busch. Great children's classic, father of comic strip, of two bad boys, Max and Moritz. Also Ker and Plunk (Plisch und Plumm), Cat and Mouse, Deceitful Henry, Ice-Peter, The Boy and the Pipe, and five other pieces. Original German, with English translation. Edited by H. Arthur Klein; translations by various hands and H. Arthur Klein. vi + 216pp. 20181-3 Paperbound $1.50

PIGS IS PIGS AND OTHER FAVORITES, Ellis Parker Butler. The title story is one of the best humor short stories, as Mike Flannery obfuscates biology and English. Also included, That Pup of Murchison's, The Great American Pie Company, and Perkins of Portland. 14 illustrations. v + 109pp. 21532-6 Paperbound $1.00

THE PETERKIN PAPERS, Lucretia P. Hale. It takes genius to be as stupidly mad as the Peterkins, as they decide to become wise, celebrate the "Fourth," keep a cow, and otherwise strain the resources of the Lady from Philadelphia. Basic book of American humor. 153 illustrations. 219pp. 20794-3 Paperbound $1.25

PERRAULT'S FAIRY TALES, translated by A. E. Johnson and S. R. Littlewood, with 34 full-page illustrations by Gustave Doré. All the original Perrault stories— Cinderella, Sleeping Beauty, Bluebeard, Little Red Riding Hood, Puss in Boots, Tom Thumb, etc.—with their witty verse morals and the magnificent illustrations of Doré. One of the five or six great books of European fairy tales. viii + 117pp. 8⅛ x 11. 22311-6 Paperbound $2.00

OLD HUNGARIAN FAIRY TALES, Baroness Orczy. Favorites translated and adapted by author of the *Scarlet Pimpernel.* Eight fairy tales include "The Suitors of Princess Fire-Fly," "The Twin Hunchbacks," "Mr. Cuttlefish's Love Story," and "The Enchanted Cat." This little volume of magic and adventure will captivate children as it has for generations. 90 drawings by Montagu Barstow. 96pp. (USO) 22293-4 Paperbound $1.95

THE RED FAIRY BOOK, Andrew Lang. Lang's color fairy books have long been children's favorites. This volume includes Rapunzel, Jack and the Bean-stalk and 35 other stories, familiar and unfamiliar. 4 plates, 93 illustrations x + 367pp.
21673-X Paperbound $1.95

THE BLUE FAIRY BOOK, Andrew Lang. Lang's tales come from all countries and all times. Here are 37 tales from Grimm, the Arabian Nights, Greek Mythology, and other fascinating sources. 8 plates, 130 illustrations. xi + 390pp.
21437-0 Paperbound $1.95

HOUSEHOLD STORIES BY THE BROTHERS GRIMM. Classic English-language edition of the well-known tales — Rumpelstiltskin, Snow White, Hansel and Gretel, The Twelve Brothers, Faithful John, Rapunzel, Tom Thumb (52 stories in all). Translated into simple, straightforward English by Lucy Crane. Ornamented with head-pieces, vignettes, elaborate decorative initials and a dozen full-page illustrations by Walter Crane. x + 269pp.
21080-4 Paperbound $2.00

THE MERRY ADVENTURES OF ROBIN HOOD, Howard Pyle. The finest modern versions of the traditional ballads and tales about the great English outlaw. Howard Pyle's complete prose version, with every word, every illustration of the first edition. Do not confuse this facsimile of the original (1883) with modern editions that change text or illustrations. 23 plates plus many page decorations. xxii + 296pp.
22043-5 Paperbound $2.00

THE STORY OF KING ARTHUR AND HIS KNIGHTS, Howard Pyle. The finest children's version of the life of King Arthur; brilliantly retold by Pyle, with 48 of his most imaginative illustrations. xviii + 313pp. 6⅛ x 9¼.
21445-1 Paperbound $2.00

THE WONDERFUL WIZARD OF OZ, L. Frank Baum. America's finest children's book in facsimile of first edition with all Denslow illustrations in full color. The edition a child should have. Introduction by Martin Gardner. 23 color plates, scores of drawings. iv + 267pp.
20691-2 Paperbound $1.95

THE MARVELOUS LAND OF OZ, L. Frank Baum. The second Oz book, every bit as imaginative as the Wizard. The hero is a boy named Tip, but the Scarecrow and the Tin Woodman are back, as is the Oz magic. 16 color plates, 120 drawings by John R. Neill. 287pp.
20692-0 Paperbound $1.75

THE MAGICAL MONARCH OF MO, L. Frank Baum. Remarkable adventures in a land even stranger than Oz. The best of Baum's books not in the Oz series. 15 color plates and dozens of drawings by Frank Verbeck. xviii + 237pp.
21892-9 Paperbound $2.00

THE BAD CHILD'S BOOK OF BEASTS, MORE BEASTS FOR WORSE CHILDREN, A MORAL ALPHABET, Hilaire Belloc. Three complete humor classics in one volume. Be kind to the frog, and do not call him names . . . and 28 other whimsical animals. Familiar favorites and some not so well known. Illustrated by Basil Blackwell. 156pp.
(USO) 20749-8 Paperbound $1.25

EAST O' THE SUN AND WEST O' THE MOON, George W. Dasent. Considered the best of all translations of these Norwegian folk tales, this collection has been enjoyed by generations of children (and folklorists too). Includes True and Untrue, Why the Sea is Salt, East O' the Sun and West O' the Moon, Why the Bear is Stumpy-Tailed, Boots and the Troll, The Cock and the Hen, Rich Peter the Pedlar, and 52 more. The only edition with all 59 tales. 77 illustrations by Erik Werenskiold and Theodor Kittelsen. xv + 418pp. 22521-6 Paperbound $3.00

GOOPS AND HOW TO BE THEM, Gelett Burgess. Classic of tongue-in-cheek humor, masquerading as etiquette book. 87 verses, twice as many cartoons, show mischievous Goops as they demonstrate to children virtues of table manners, neatness, courtesy, etc. Favorite for generations. viii + 88pp. $6\frac{1}{2}$ x $9\frac{1}{4}$.
22233-0 Paperbound $1.25

ALICE'S ADVENTURES UNDER GROUND, Lewis Carroll. The first version, quite different from the final *Alice in Wonderland*, printed out by Carroll himself with his own illustrations. Complete facsimile of the "million dollar" manuscript Carroll gave to Alice Liddell in 1864. Introduction by Martin Gardner. viii + 96pp. Title and dedication pages in color. 21482-6 Paperbound $1.25

THE BROWNIES, THEIR BOOK, Palmer Cox. Small as mice, cunning as foxes, exuberant and full of mischief, the Brownies go to the zoo, toy shop, seashore, circus, etc., in 24 verse adventures and 266 illustrations. Long a favorite, since their first appearance in St. Nicholas Magazine. xi + 144pp. $6\frac{5}{8}$ x $9\frac{1}{4}$.
21265-3 Paperbound $1.75

SONGS OF CHILDHOOD, Walter De La Mare. Published (under the pseudonym Walter Ramal) when De La Mare was only 29, this charming collection has long been a favorite children's book. A facsimile of the first edition in paper, the 47 poems capture the simplicity of the nursery rhyme and the ballad, including such lyrics as I Met Eve, Tartary, The Silver Penny. vii + 106pp. 21972-0 Paperbound $1.25

THE COMPLETE NONSENSE OF EDWARD LEAR, Edward Lear. The finest 19th-century humorist-cartoonist in full: all nonsense limericks, zany alphabets, Owl and Pussycat, songs, nonsense botany, and more than 500 illustrations by Lear himself. Edited by Holbrook Jackson. xxix + 287pp. (USO) 20167-8 Paperbound $1.75

BILLY WHISKERS: THE AUTOBIOGRAPHY OF A GOAT, Frances Trego Montgomery. A favorite of children since the early 20th century, here are the escapades of that rambunctious, irresistible and mischievous goat—Billy Whiskers. Much in the spirit of *Peck's Bad Boy,* this is a book that children never tire of reading or hearing. All the original familiar illustrations by W. H. Fry are included: 6 color plates, 18 black and white drawings. 159pp. 22345-0 Paperbound $2.00

MOTHER GOOSE MELODIES. Faithful republication of the fabulously rare Munroe and Francis "copyright 1833" Boston edition—the most important Mother Goose collection, usually referred to as the "original." Familiar rhymes plus many rare ones, with wonderful old woodcut illustrations. Edited by E. F. Bleiler. 128pp. $4\frac{1}{2}$ x $6\frac{3}{8}$. 22577-1 Paperbound $1.25

TWO LITTLE SAVAGES; BEING THE ADVENTURES OF TWO BOYS WHO LIVED AS INDIANS AND WHAT THEY LEARNED, Ernest Thompson Seton. Great classic of nature and boyhood provides a vast range of woodlore in most palatable form, a genuinely entertaining story. Two farm boys build a teepee in woods and live in it for a month, working out Indian solutions to living problems, star lore, birds and animals, plants, etc. 293 illustrations. vii + 286pp.

20985-7 Paperbound $2.50

PETER PIPER'S PRACTICAL PRINCIPLES OF PLAIN & PERFECT PRONUNCIATION. Alliterative jingles and tongue-twisters of surprising charm, that made their first appearance in America about 1830. Republished in full with the spirited woodcut illustrations from this earliest American edition. 32pp. 4½ x 6⅜.

22560-7 Paperbound $1.00

SCIENCE EXPERIMENTS AND AMUSEMENTS FOR CHILDREN, Charles Vivian. 73 easy experiments, requiring only materials found at home or easily available, such as candles, coins, steel wool, etc.; illustrate basic phenomena like vacuum, simple chemical reaction, etc. All safe. Modern, well-planned. Formerly *Science Games for Children*. 102 photos, numerous drawings. 96pp. 6⅛ x 9¼.

21856-2 Paperbound $1.25

AN INTRODUCTION TO CHESS MOVES AND TACTICS SIMPLY EXPLAINED, Leonard Barden. Informal intermediate introduction, quite strong in explaining reasons for moves. Covers basic material, tactics, important openings, traps, positional play in middle game, end game. Attempts to isolate patterns and recurrent configurations. Formerly *Chess*. 58 figures. 102pp. (USO) 21210-6 Paperbound $1.25

LASKER'S MANUAL OF CHESS, Dr. Emanuel Lasker. Lasker was not only one of the five great World Champions, he was also one of the ablest expositors, theorists, and analysts. In many ways, his Manual, permeated with his philosophy of battle, filled with keen insights, is one of the greatest works ever written on chess. Filled with analyzed games by the great players. A single-volume library that will profit almost any chess player, beginner or master. 308 diagrams. xli x 349pp.

20640-8 Paperbound $2.50

THE MASTER BOOK OF MATHEMATICAL RECREATIONS, Fred Schuh. In opinion of many the finest work ever prepared on mathematical puzzles, stunts, recreations; exhaustively thorough explanations of mathematics involved, analysis of effects, citation of puzzles and games. Mathematics involved is elementary. Translated by F. Göbel. 194 figures. xxiv + 430pp. 22134-2 Paperbound $3.00

MATHEMATICS, MAGIC AND MYSTERY, Martin Gardner. Puzzle editor for Scientific American explains mathematics behind various mystifying tricks: card tricks, stage "mind reading," coin and match tricks, counting out games, geometric dissections, etc. Probability sets, theory of numbers clearly explained. Also provides more than 400 tricks, guaranteed to work, that you can do. 135 illustrations. xii + 176pp.

20338-2 Paperbound $1.50

MATHEMATICAL PUZZLES FOR BEGINNERS AND ENTHUSIASTS, Geoffrey Mott-Smith. 189 puzzles from easy to difficult—involving arithmetic, logic, algebra, properties of digits, probability, etc.—for enjoyment and mental stimulus. Explanation of mathematical principles behind the puzzles. 135 illustrations. viii + 248pp.
20198-8 Paperbound $1.25

PAPER FOLDING FOR BEGINNERS, William D. Murray and Francis J. Rigney. Easiest book on the market, clearest instructions on making interesting, beautiful origami. Sail boats, cups, roosters, frogs that move legs, bonbon boxes, standing birds, etc. 40 projects; more than 275 diagrams and photographs. 94pp.
20713-7 Paperbound $1.00

TRICKS AND GAMES ON THE POOL TABLE, Fred Herrmann. 79 tricks and games— some solitaires, some for two or more players, some competitive games—to entertain you between formal games. Mystifying shots and throws, unusual caroms, tricks involving such props as cork, coins, a hat, etc. Formerly *Fun on the Pool Table*. 77 figures. 95pp.
21814-7 Paperbound $1.00

HAND SHADOWS TO BE THROWN UPON THE WALL: A SERIES OF NOVEL AND AMUSING FIGURES FORMED BY THE HAND, Henry Bursill. Delightful picturebook from great-grandfather's day shows how to make 18 different hand shadows: a bird that flies, duck that quacks, dog that wags his tail, camel, goose, deer, boy, turtle, etc. Only book of its sort. vi + 33pp. $6\frac{1}{2}$ x $9\frac{1}{4}$. 21779-5 Paperbound $1.00

WHITTLING AND WOODCARVING, E. J. Tangerman. 18th printing of best book on market. "If you can cut a potato you can carve" toys and puzzles, chains, chessmen, caricatures, masks, frames, woodcut blocks, surface patterns, much more. Information on tools, woods, techniques. Also goes into serious wood sculpture from Middle Ages to present, East and West. 464 photos, figures. x + 293pp.
20965-2 Paperbound $2.00

HISTORY OF PHILOSOPHY, Julián Marias. Possibly the clearest, most easily followed, best planned, most useful one-volume history of philosophy on the market; neither skimpy nor overfull. Full details on system of every major philosopher and dozens of less important thinkers from pre-Socratics up to Existentialism and later. Strong on many European figures usually omitted. Has gone through dozens of editions in Europe. 1966 edition, translated by Stanley Appelbaum and Clarence Strowbridge. xviii + 505pp.
21739-6 Paperbound $2.75

YOGA: A SCIENTIFIC EVALUATION, Kovoor T. Behanan. Scientific but non-technical study of physiological results of yoga exercises; done under auspices of Yale U. Relations to Indian thought, to psychoanalysis, etc. 16 photos. xxiii + 270pp.
20505-3 Paperbound $2.50

Prices subject to change without notice.
Available at your book dealer or write for free catalogue to Dept. GI, Dover Publications, Inc., 180 Varick St., N. Y., N. Y. 10014. Dover publishes more than 150 books each year on science, elementary and advanced mathematics, biology, music, art, literary history, social sciences and other areas.